SERVING THE SILENT SERVICE:

THE LEGEND
OF
ELECTRIC BOAT

"*We will continue to build the most capable submarines in the world and crew them with the most capable sailors.*"

USS Springfield (SSN-761) running on the surface.

John H. Dalton
Secretary of the Navy

SERVING THE SILENT SERVICE:

THE LEGEND OF ELECTRIC BOAT

JEFFREY L. RODENGEN

PUBLISHED BY WRITE STUFF SYNDICATE, INC.

For Ryan

Also by Jeff Rodengen:

The Legend of Chris-Craft
Iron Fist: *The Lives of Carl Kiekhaefer*
Evinrude-Johnson and The Legend of OMC
The Legend of Honeywell
The Legend of Dr Pepper/7UP
The Legend of Ingersoll-Rand
The Legend of Briggs & Stratton

WRITE STUFF SYNDICATE

Write Stuff Syndicate, Inc.

433 Seminole Ave.
Ft. Lauderdale, FL 33312
(800) 900-BOOK/(800) 900-2665
(305) 462-6657

Library of Congress Catalog Card Number: 94-60763

ISBN 0-945903-24-3

Completely produced in the United States of America

10 9 8 7 6 5 4 3 2 1

TABLE OF CONTENTS

INTRODUCTION

The sea is everything. It covers seven-tenths of the planet. Its breath is pure and healthful. It's an immense wilderness where a man never feels lonely, because he feels life astir on every side. ... Ah professor, why not live—live in the bosom of the seas! Here alone will you find true independence! Here I recognize no master! Here I'm free!

Jules Verne
Twenty Thousand Leagues under the Sea

The United States Navy's submarine fleet, known as the "Silent Service," is a stealthy force that maintains a constant state of readiness and vigilance, patrolling the seas of the earth and keeping the peace.

Electric Boat has been serving the Silent Service since the company's inception in 1899. The Groton, Connecticut-based company sold the U.S. Navy its first submarine in 1900, and has continued throughout this century to supply it with high quality, high performance submarines.

From the late 1800s, when Irish schoolteacher John P. Holland, father of the modern submarine, put a pencil to drafting paper, to today, as engineers design submarines using computers in virtual reality environments, the world has changed dramatically.

- The world has encountered, fought and survived two global conflicts and scores of regional skirmishes that have had international consequences.
- The defense industry, which once thrived on a growing military budget that was swelled by fear of the perceived Communist threat, is streamlining and diverting more resources to peacetime products.
- The Berlin Wall has fallen, the Soviet Union collapsed, the Middle East has recognized a Palestinian state and the barriers of Africa's apartheid are being dissolved.
- Faced with possible nuclear annihilation, the world's major powers are less willing to take up arms against one another.
- The United States military has beefed up and slimmed down.

In the aftermath of these developments, new threats have emerged. Smaller countries now have the ability to either develop nuclear warheads on their own or purchase them from a burgeoning black market.

The Goliaths may no longer threaten the earth, but today's Davids, armed with nuclear slingshots, are as deadly as their Biblical counterpart.

"The world wars are over, the Cold War has been won," President Bill Clinton told a recent graduating class of Navy officers at Annapolis. "Now it is our job to win peace.

"For the first time in history, we have the chance to expand the reach of democracy and economic progress across the whole of Europe and to the far reaches of the world. The first step on the mission is to keep our own nation secure."[1]

According to retired Vice Admiral Robert "Yogi" Kaufman, a 30-year veteran submariner: "Deterrence is the whole thing. The submarine, as a deterrent, is the key to keeping America secure.[2]"

This observation is reminiscent of John Holland's admonition to Clara Barton—founder of the American Red Cross and the first woman to ride on his submarine, the *Holland*, while it was submerged—who had expressed her revulsion of the lethal, mysterious nature of his invention by calling it a "deadly instrument of war." Holland responded that there would be no war if "all the nations of the world were equipped with submarines."[3]

Today, not only are the world's great navies equipped with advanced submarine designs, but an increasing number of belligent Third World countries are acquiring submarine technology.

Throughout this century, Electric Boat has continued to change with the world around it. This company's extraordinary flexibility, dedication to purpose and craftsmanship has earned Electric Boat and its employees the reputation and wherewithal to withstand recent years' economic and political fluctuations.

Serving the Silent Service: The Legend of Electric Boat is the company's story, encompassing the last 100 years and chronicling the history-making events which have helped to reshape the world.

FOREWORD

By Captain Edward L. Beach, USN (Ret.)
Author of *Run Silent, Run Deep*

I owe a great deal to Electric Boat, and so do all Americans—everyone living in the Western hemisphere, in fact. Our submarines, pioneered by the same people who created Electric Boat, going all the way back to John Philip Holland, our very first submariner of the modern line, brought us through the greatest naval war in history. They literally destroyed Japan's sea power—if one defines sea power as the ability to use the sea for national purposes. Our entire nation will forever remain in debt to the 16,000 or so men who went down to the deep sea in submarines during World War II. That will always be part of the story of Electric Boat.

All that being said, it is probable that I owe a bit more than most American citizens, for I've had the fortune, at two different times, to skipper one of Electric Boat's submarines. In truth, I "built" both of them, had a hand in their christening, rode them down the launching ways, organized and trained their crews, took them on their shakedown cruises, and held total responsibility for them from the day of official "delivery" until my own detachment about three years later.

"Built them," I say. No less, and with no disrespect to Admiral Rickover, who was not involved with the first one anyway. During the latter stages of a new ship's construction period it is customary in our navy to begin assigning to the shipyard important officers, such as Reactor Control Officer, Engineering Officer, and the Captain, along with the senior enlisted crew members each would need in organizing his future responsibilities in the new ship. The procedure continues during the entire pre-commissioning and pre delivery phases, with the objective that there be a well-organized and well-functioning crew, ready to take over and do its job the moment the shipyard lets go. During wartime or peacetime, there is always a small ceremony to mark this change in status, for during the building period the power and prestige of the prospective commanding officer (PCO) undergoes recognizable growth. He is there full time; he sees everything that is done, holds continual informal meetings with the builder's people, from workmen to managers. He attends regular shipyard conferences in which his opinions are carefully given, carefully weighed, and frequently result in changes in procedures and priorities. He has the navy's authority to hold the shipyard's feet to the fire on any part of it that does not, in his judgement, go forward in accordance with the building specifications, for he must submit periodic reports to the Navy Department in Washington on the progress of the construction.

This can sometimes work in reverse, too; I well remember the official letter I labored over to inform the Bureau of Ships that certain portions of the new *Trigger's* specifications, which it had cited and documented at great length, were unrealistic and even dangerous, in particular places entirely illogical; that the high-speed tests connected with some of them should be performed by a crew, like mine, that was fully familiar with high speed three dimensional maneuvering of a submerged submarine, instead of by a contractor's trial crew who, no matter how well they knew the material on which they had been working, had never gone faster than six or eight knots under water. My letter was unanswerable; the "specs" had to be converted to conform to reality, and the tests of maneuverability at high speed had to be changed. Later I was informally told that this letter had become the basis for a wholesale revision of the specifications and testing procedures for the new generation of fast nuclear subs.

Along with all this, the Prospective Commanding Officer had certain prerogatives, too. Bookshelves, lockers, extra bunks, odds and ends of all kinds that he and his crew felt were necessary or desirable, were built and installed to his own specifications. Many of them were so obviously desirable that they were immediately written into the plans or "specs" for future submarines. Location of the control lever for rigging out the bow planes on diving comes to mind: we wanted it moved forward several feet to where the Chief of the Watch could handle it directly from his station as he opened the main vents, rather than leaving it to a harried lookout, encumbered by wet foul-weather clothing. This was, of course, a wartime innovation. Another was our insistence on elimination of the stalactite-like growth from the center of the overhead of the control room: telephones, heavy shock-mountings for the overhead fathometer, light fixtures, pencil sharpeners, all the paraphernalia that almost automatically grew when there was a place where it could be installed. We wiped all this off with a reason stated in writing: the Diving Officer, the Captain, and anyone else in the control room must at all times have unobstructed vision across it.

The PCO, or his representative, was always consulted on the arrangement of instruments on the bridge for surface cruising. They had to be accessible, serviceable, watertight, and out of the way for quick diving. In *Trigger II* we pointed out that the snorkel, raised to run engines submerged or merely to ventilate the boat, should have an antenna on it, and moreover should have a wave-deflector, like the bow of a toy ship, built around its front side so that it could be operated lower in the water and thus be less detectable by enemy radar. We wound up with two antennae and a neat little boat up there.

The list goes on: *Triton,* troubled by insufficient buoyancy forward at high speed, needed a bigger bow buoyancy tank. This was built, and at considerable trouble. The ship's doctor, a proficient surgeon, needed proper operating facilities which we asked to have built into the officer's pantry. This was an ideal solution, though a bit confined in space; his sterilization equipment fit right in, however, with ample outlets for plug-in devices, and there was plenty of drainage. As for bunks in that huge ship, I had already found places for and Electric Boat had installed five more bunks than the original plans called for. But we had two men still without their own individual bunks. Now, I thought, we'd show everybody a thing or two. Our Navy's newest and biggest submarine would go back to the good old days and have hammocks for these two fortunate crew members. EB duly installed pairs of hooks for the hammocks, one forward and one aft, and gave us two, made of nice new canvas. But this became one item where I had to confess failure. The hammocks were always occupied when I made my daily "walk-through" inspections, usually late at night or in the early morning hours, but never otherwise. Finally I realized that my crew, loyal sailors to the core, were enjoying their own game. Someone always got into the hammocks when the grapevine announced I was coming, just to keep me in a contented frame of mind.

So, we did help build our own ship, as have all the other submarine personnel assigned, wherever and whenever their submarine was constructed. This of course holds true for all other types of U.S. Navy ships as well, but nowhere is there a more intimate connection between builder and ship's crew than in a sub-marine building yard. Everybody profits; and in addition, often a very real personal friendship and devotion develops, not only between the individuals but also, as in my own case, directed at the institution, the Electric Boat Company.

I have one other little episode to describe. Having been oriented toward literary endeavor since childhood because of my father, who had published novels about naval life, I became very interested, as PCO of *Trigger II,* in the birth of what became known as the "Submarine Library." Electric Boat had accumulated quite a respectable file of clippings and articles over the previous years of its life, and I discovered an absorbingly interesting extra-curricular activity in helping to promote and develop the creation of a proper library to house all these papers, photographs, artifacts, and models. For a time, the library was maintained in a small house on the edge of the EB property, where it received good notice and considerable attendance. I have my own fond memory of browsing through there one day with my two boys and finding my audience unexpectedly increased by three more children and their mother. Then, with a change of administration, the house had to be given up. But the Naval Submarine School, a few miles upstream, had by this time become interested in an institutional way and gave the Library two large rooms in one of its buildings. Finally came the day when sufficient funds became available to acquire and begin construction of a new and specially designed submarine library and museum at Goss Cove, a spot I had long thought would be ideal for this purpose, just south of the Naval Submarine Base, Groton.

In due course, that museum became a reality, and not many years later added to its luster by becoming the final resting place for the most famous submarine ever built, the first nuclear-powered ship in the world, constructed at Electric Boat, christened USS *Nautilus* by First Lady Mamie Eisenhower when she was launched in 1954. That boat, or more properly that ship, today stands at the midpoint of our submarine story. A whole panorama of submarine history, including the most terrible war ever fought, in which U.S. submarines made a record never to be equalled, was established before anyone had even thought of building a nuclear powered submarine. Another panorama, of almost equal time, has come afterward. *Nautilus* will more and more become known as the marker, for all time to come, for the most significant, most far-reaching, development in the history of man at sea. The day will come when all naval history will be counted from her own simple message in 1955:

Underway on nuclear power.

Everything before was prologue. The same can today be said of Electric Boat, for that is where it began, and where *Nautilus* herself, proof incarnate, lies today, only a mile or so upstream.

ACKNOWLEDGEMENTS

A great many people and institutions assisted in the research, preparation and publication of *Serving the Silent Service: The Legend of Electric Boat*. The development of historical time–lines and a large portion of the principal archival research was accomplished by my research assistant, Steven Marks. His careful investigations into the early years of Electric Boat history have made it possible to publish much new and fascinating information on the origins and evolution of this unique organization.

The research, however, much less the book itself, would have been impossible without the dedicated assistance of Electric Boat executives and employees. Principal among these is Neil Ruenzel, director of communications, whose courteous and affable guidance made it possible for our research team to locate and identify both prominent records and individuals crucial to the Electric Boat legacy. Both Grace deGrooth and Lisa Trolan helped us to understand the maze of rooms and buildings where archives are stored. Also assisting whenever help was needed was Irene Motta, Dorothy "Dottie" Stillman, Craig Haines, Ron Kiely, Barry Black, Dave Tela, Bill Fitzgerald, Lydia Owens, Dan Barrett and Sherry L. Geer, Herbert E. Berry, John J. Socha, John W. Spinner Jr, Edward J. Behney, Jr., among many others. Special thanks are also due to Steven C. Finnigan, curator of the Submarine Force Museum in New London, Conn. and Russell D. Egnor, director of the Navy Office of Information, News Photo Division in Washington, D.C., the National Press Club and the White House office of communications.

The interest and courtesy of the many interview subjects for the book was most gratifying, and I would like to thank James E. Turner, Jr., president of Electric Boat; John K. Welch, division vice president – programs; Vice Admiral B.M. "Bud" Kauderer, USN (Ret); Vice Admiral R.Y. "Yogi" Kaufman, USN (Ret); U.S. Senator Christopher J. Dodd, Conn.; U.S. Representative Ronald K. Machtley, R.I.; Secretary of the Navy John H. Dalton; Jim Burbank; Ken Brown; Henry Nardone; Lee Morse; Marvin Fast; Bob Whitmire; Pamela Arruda; Bob Gillcash; and especially Captain Edward L. Beach, USN (Ret), contributor and author of the classic submarine thriller, *Run Silent, Run Deep*.

Finally, a very special thanks to the dedicated staff at Write Stuff Syndicate, Inc., and key consultants especially my executive assistant and office manager Bonnie Bratton, Karine N. Rodengen, Executive Editor Le A. Hughes, electronic layout artists Beki Levantini, Becky Young and Kyle Newton, and graphic illustrator and cover artist David "Spuds" Rubinson.

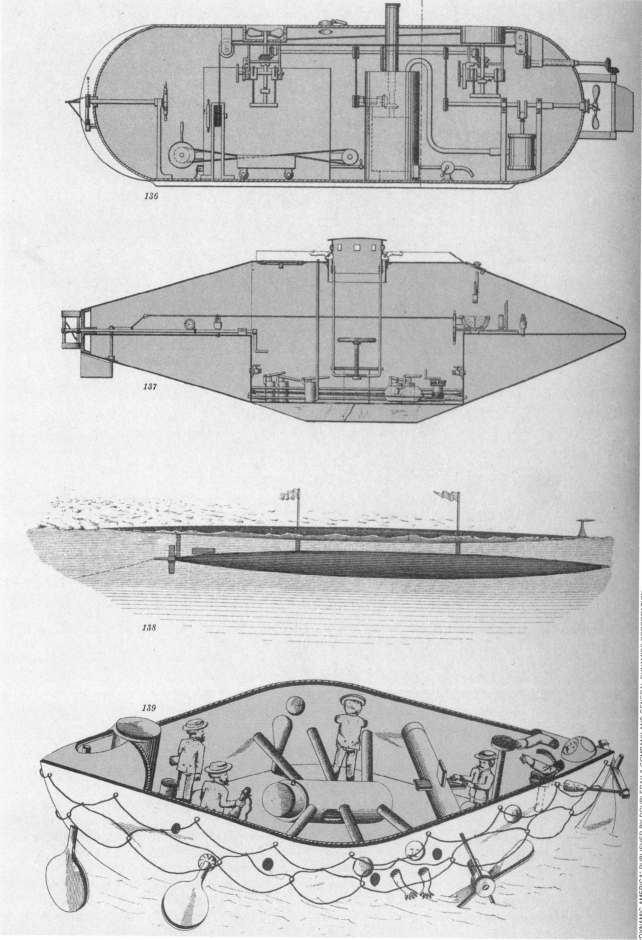

Submarines in the 1800s. Top, one of the many Civil War designs. Second from top, J. Jopling's submarine of 1883. Third from top, Haight and Wood's 1886 design. Bottom, an 1889 submarine that was actually patented.

CHAPTER I

A Brief History of the Submarine

To come upon the most fabled, most mythical being could not have shocked me so much. It is quite simple to believe that prodigious things come from the Creator. But suddenly to find that the impossible had been shaped by human beings: that staggers the mind.

Jules Verne,
Twenty Thousand Leagues under the Sea

Since the dawn of recorded history, mankind has dreamed of living and moving under the seas. The myths evoked images of Neptune and his oceanic kingdom; the ancient Greeks spoke longingly of the fabled lost city of Atlantis and its advanced civilization lost beneath the waves; and contemporary culture sings of exploring the ocean's mysteries in a "Yellow Submarine."

The history of underwater exploration and navigation begins in ancient times with divers, who used air tubes, helmets and diving bells. The Greek historian Herodotus recorded in 480 B.C. that a Greek diver named Scyllias and his daughter, Hydna, used such equipment to cut the anchor cables of Xerxes' invading Persian fleet, which was riding out a storm off the Greek coast. Alexander the Great successfully defended against this same tactic during the siege of Tyre in 332 B.C. Tyrians in diving bells attempting to cut the cables of anchored vessels found iron chains instead of ordinary anchor lines.

Alexander himself was enraptured with life underwater; so much so that he ordered a watertight glass barrel made so that he could descend into the ocean and view its life firsthand. Outfitted with lamps and lowered by chains, the submersible gave the military leader an opportunity to see "many fish that had the form of beasts that live on land and walk on legs ... and many other wonders that were unbelievable. When Alexander had seen enough ... he made signs for those above to raise the iron chains and draw him up."[1]

Tales of undersea adventures, long before the turn of this century, are recorded throughout world history. An Arabian historian of the 12th century, Bohadin, recorded the use of an underwater vessel by a diver attempting to get a message to a city under siege by Crusaders. A 13th century German poem recounts the saga of Morolf, who built a leather-covered diving boat and hid submerged for two weeks, breathing fresh air through a long tube. Inventor-genius Leonardo da Vinci also designed a cylindrical craft for exploring the ocean's mysteries. In

A dramatic print of how the Prussian submarine, Wilhelm Bauer's *Brandtaucher,* put fear into the hearts of the Danish fleet blockading Kiel in 1850. The threat of being attacked unseen was often enough to frighten off both naval and merchant ships.

1538, King Philip I of Spain became interested in experiments with a diving bell conducted at Toledo, Spain.

About this time, the Scandinavians and the pirates of the Barbary Coast were building and operating underwater leather boats. The boats could secretly approach and sink anchored merchant ships by boring holes beneath the waterline. As the victim was abandoned, the pirates boarded their prize and took whatever booty was found. In England in 1580, William Bourne wrote *Inventions,* a book which described the design of a double-hulled plunging apparatus submerged by hand, which included means of trimming the ballast. Bourne never put his theories to the test. In 1609, Buonaito Lorini described an airtight box with glass disks to allow a submariner to observe life under the seas.

Submarines also held a fascination for clergy. In 1634, Fathers Mersenne and Fournier proposed a submarine design with a fish-shaped, metal hull and "two extremities spindle-shaped

to make progress equally easy in both directions." In 1648, John Wilkins, brother-in-law of Oliver Cromwell who was destined to become Bishop of Chester, published *An Ark for Submarine Navigation; the Difficulties and Consequences of Such a Contrivance.* Wilkins described submarines as being private, which he defined as allowing its pilot to go anywhere without being detected—something today's military strategists would call stealth. "A man may thus go to any Coast of the World invisibly without being discovered or prevented in his journey."

Wilkins also described other advantages: Safety from "the Uncertainty of the Tides," "the Violence of the Tempests," "from Pirates and Robbers," and from "Ice and Great Frosts which do so endanger the Passage towards the Poles."

Cornelius Drebbel, a Dutch physician living in England, is considered the "father of submarines," having constructed three submarines, starting in 1624. Preceded by what were really nothing more than diving bells, these were the

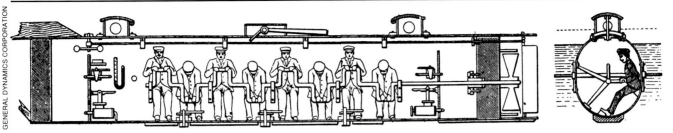

Eight men propelled the Civil War *Hunley* by operating a crankshaft in the manner shown above. The cross-section, right, shows the small space in which the men had to work. The *Hunley's* narrow diameter and disproportionate length of 60 feet made her unstable.

first ships to be propelled and navigated underwater. The largest was made of wood covered with oil-soaked leather and propelled underwater by six oars manned by 12 men. King James I of England was "an enthusiastic patron ... whose scientific and quasi-scientific interests embraced practically everything from explosives to perpetual motion."[2] Unfortunately, there is little surviving data on Drebbel's work, but there are sporadic reports with cryptic references to goat-skin bags that were allowed to fill with water to make the ship submerge and then squeezed out to make it surface, and to liquid air ported in a bottle and administered in dosages of a single drop to the tongue while the craft was submerged.

Much like lighter-than-air craft in later years, submarines over the next 150 years caught the whimsy of an imaginative few. Consider Monsieur de Son, a Frenchman who built a submarine in Rotterdam with dimensions 72 feet long, 12 feet high and 8 feet wide—*that couldn't move.* Or the Venezuelan dentist who created a sub with two hulls: the outside hull designed to spin around the inside one with vanes to propel it.

In 1774, a submarine (of sorts) became the basis for a gambling bet concocted by a Suffolk wheelwright named Day, who talked the famous and wealthy gambler Christopher Blake into backing him. The bet's terms: Day would spend 12 hours at 100 feet in a 50-foot sloop converted into a submarine by adding a waterproof cabin and a bunch of rocks to make it sink. Day had done this previously with a much smaller boat, claiming to have submerged to 30 feet and stayed there for 24 hours. To surface, he simply detached the ballast (rocks). Unfortunately, neither Day nor his convertible submersible were ever seen again. Just how much Blake lost was not historically recorded.[3]

The next serious attempt at submarine development was spawned from one Irishman's intense hatred of the British and their navy. In 1775, the *Turtle* became the very first torpedo boat, and the first underwater craft to employ a screw propeller. David Bushnell built the *Turtle* in Old Saybrook, Connecticut, (about 25 miles from Electric Boat's home in Groton) with the express purpose of blowing up British men-of-war. General George Washington himself, along with Governor Trumbull of Connecticut, supported Bushnell's project. Looking somewhat like two turtle shells glued together, the boat measured approximately 7 feet long, 4 feet wide and 8 feet from keel to conning tower. A hand-operated vertical screw controlled ascent and descent. The operator could look through one of three small windows located just below the hatch. To submerge, the operator would admit water by opening a valve to the boat's ballast tanks; to surface, a small pump expelled the water.

The *Turtle's* only armament was a gunpowder torpedo which could be attached by means of a screw to the hull of the enemy boat. Once attached, a clockwork timer was set, which theoretically would allow the *Turtle* to escape before detonation.

One night in 1776, the diminutive *Turtle* got her opportunity to attack the mighty British fleet, in particular British Admiral Howe's flagship, the HMS *Eagle*, anchored off Governor's Island in New York harbor. Sergeant Ezra Lee, the submarine's operator, successfully maneuvered up to the 64-foot, 50-gun British frigate without being detected, despite an unexpected shift in the tide which originally sent his craft sailing past its target. Once nestled next to the flagship, Lee attempted to attach the torpedo with a drill and screw, but the screw hit metal and refused to remain firmly attached. Finally, frustrated, Lee gave up and attempted to return to shore when a British patrol discovered him. Knowing he could not outrun a row boat, Lee released his mine, narrowly averting capture.

Bushnell then took the *Turtle* up to Fort Lee, where Washington's army was quartered, and made another unsuccessful attempt on a British frigate. No more attempts of this kind were made, although Bushnell went on to design and create sea mines (another unsuccessful venture, how-

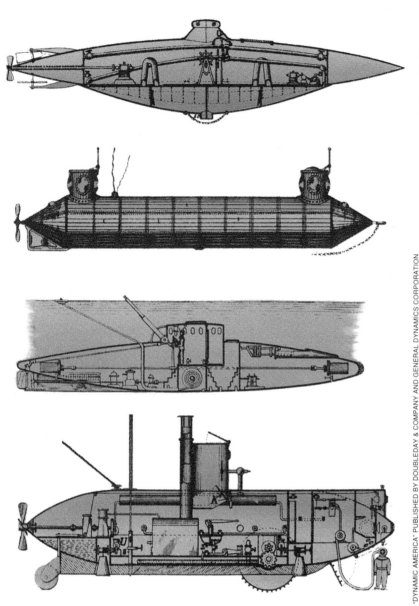

Early submarine designs: Top, an 1892 design. Second from top, a boiler-plated design from 1893. Third from top, design from an 1894 patent. Bottom, Simon Lake's 1896 *Argonaut*.

"DYNAMIC AMERICA" PUBLISHED BY DOUBLEDAY & COMPANY AND GENERAL DYNAMICS CORPORATION

ever). Were it not for the illness of Bushnell and his brother, who were both trained in the boat's operation, perhaps more encouragement and funds might have been forthcoming.

Another American (who coincidentally also hated the British), Robert Fulton, took up where Bushnell left off. Best known for his invention of the steamboat, Fulton submitted plans for a submarine to the French government as early as 1797. In 1800, after two previous rejections by the French and another from the Dutch, Fulton was finally able to interest Emperor Napoleon Bonaparte, who advanced the inventor 10,000 francs for his services. Napoleon, of course, was interested in using the submarine to attack the British fleet.

Fulton's *Nautilus* was 21 feet in length with a 6-foot beam. Constructed of wood and bullet-shaped, the ship carried a hollow iron keel into which water could be pumped for ballast. The *Nautilus* also furthered submarine design by using horizontal rudders to control vertical motion, and employed two means of propulsion—a sail for surface travel and a hand-operated screw propeller for submerged operation. The top speed of the *Nautilus*, either under sail or propeller, was at best 2 knots, which failed to impress Napoleon. Since the *Nautilus* armament consisted of a torpedo towed astern by the submarine and designed to explode on contact with an enemy ship, Napoleon considered the *Nautilus* too slow for operations against the relatively quick British men-of-war. When the Ministry of Marine changed hands again "with icy disdain, Fulton was told that his device was 'fit only for Algerians and pirates.'"[4]

Four years later, Fulton was able to convince British Prime Minister William Pitt to authorize construction of a submarine along the lines of the *Nautilus*. During an inspired demonstration, Fulton's submarine towed two torpedoes on 80-foot tethers astern. When it passed across the cable which held the *Dorothea*, a Danish brig at anchor, the torpedoes, 15 feet below the surface, drifted into the hull and destroyed the ship. The British were impressed with the demonstration—more so with the performance of the underwater mines than that of the submarine, however. The British paid Fulton £100,000 for the rights to the submarine. However, they planned to halt any further development or construction of the ships, fearing that their enemies would be compelled to develop submarines of their own if Britain were doing so. This escalation was seen as a threat to the balance of power, in which Britain held the most favorable position as "Sovereign of the Seas."

In 1806, Fulton returned to the United States and demonstrated his submarine for the U.S. Navy. While the anchored sloop-of-war *Argus* was able to thwart the submarine using nets and spars, it was also trapped. Like the French and British governments before it, the U.S. government lost interest. Fulton turned his full attention to developing the first steamboat, the *Claremont*, which was launched successfully in 1807.

In the ensuing decades, developers in both Europe and the United States continued to experiment with new possibilities for underwater boats, some of which were successful at meeting limited military objectives. It wasn't until the American Civil War that submarines were perceived solely as vessels of war. Often seen as "Davids" combatting the Union's "Goliaths," the Confederate navy submersibles' reputation as deadly weapons was so impressive that Union ships routinely changed anchorage every night to elude Confederate submarine attacks.[5] In reality, these early predecessors of submarines "were basically manned torpedoes for smashing into the sides of their victims." They often ran with their hatches open to provide fresh air to the men below—which meant that they were also swamped by waves or wash from other ships.[6]

The most famous of the Confederate Navy's underwater fleet was the *Hunley*, a true submersible built by Horace L. Hunley, one of a group of private citizens who constructed submarines for the Confederate cause. The *Hunley* was, for all purposes, a converted iron boiler—60 feet long, 3 feet in beam and 5 feet deep. Eight men operating handcranks connected to a propeller shaft propelled the *Hunley* to a top speed of 4 knots. She had two ballast tanks, fore and aft, and two side-mounted planes to control depth. Armament consisted of a lone torpedo which was towed astern.

In 1864, the *Hunley* sank the Union sloop-of-war *Housatonic*, at anchor in Charleston Harbor, with its torpedo. Whether sunk by the blast, swamped by the waves or dragged down by the undertow, the *Hunley* was also lost. The *Housatonic* suffered only minor casualties. When the harbor was cleared after the war, the *Hunley* was found a hundred feet from the *Housatonic*, her crew still inside.[7]

The Union's response to the Confederate submersibles was the *Intelligent Whale*, built by the U.S. Navy in 1864, one year before the end of the war. Like the *Hunley*, the *Intelligent Whale* was hand-propelled and could reach 4 knots, but the vessel was difficult to operate and was finally abandoned in 1872. Thereafter, submarine development proceeded erratically, with largely unsuccessful results. Progress was often made and then halted as developers ran out of capital to further their experiments and governments lost interest.

Mankind's fascination with the undersea world was eloquently depicted in French novelist Jules Verne's *Twenty Thousand Leagues under the Sea*, published in 1870. His skillful narrative is both an adventure story and a revealing treatise on the scientific and technological concepts which governed the operation of the fictional *Nautilus*. Verne based his work on solid facts, creating within its pages a future he thought entirely possible. Verne's own life spanned an interesting period in submarine development: He was born in 1828, 27 years after Robert Fulton launched his own *Nautilus* into the Seine at Paris. When Verne published his classic tale of the *Nautilus* voyages, accounts of submarine use during America's Civil War were publicly known. Verne lived to witness the success of John P. Holland and his submarine, which made U.S. naval history in 1900. Verne died in 1904, on the threshold of astounding development in submarine design and uses, principally led by the Electric Boat Company.

John P. Holland emerges from the hatch of his submarine the *Holland*, April 1898. A hands-on inventor, the Irish-born Holland would operate the submarine's controls himself while running underwater.

CHAPTER II

Early Electric Boat History

A new kind of warship far more radical than either the torpedo boat or the torpedo boat destroyer was soon to be added—the sea-going submarine. ... The first to be commissioned would be the privately built Holland, *purchased in 1900.*

Edwin Bickford Hooper,
United States Naval Power in a Changing World

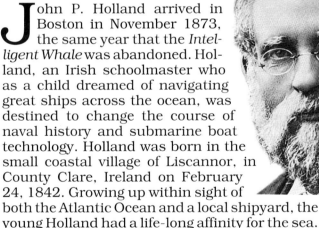

*Isaac Rice,
Electric Boat's
first president*

John P. Holland arrived in Boston in November 1873, the same year that the *Intelligent Whale* was abandoned. Holland, an Irish schoolmaster who as a child dreamed of navigating great ships across the ocean, was destined to change the course of naval history and submarine boat technology. Holland was born in the small coastal village of Liscannor, in County Clare, Ireland on February 24, 1842. Growing up within sight of both the Atlantic Ocean and a local shipyard, the young Holland had a life-long affinity for the sea. At the age of 14, he successfully passed a navigation exam, but his acute nearsightedness quashed all chances of realizing this dream. But Holland's love for seagoing vessels did not die. By 17, he had already drafted plans to build boats that could be operated while submerged. However, there was little that the impoverished young man could do to advance his theories so Holland became a schoolmaster.

Like so many other families, Holland's chose to emigrate to America. He followed the next year, sailing "from Liverpool, as a steerage passenger, with little in his pocket, but amongst the few personal possessions that he carried were the drawings of his first submarine design."[1]

Just days after arriving in Boston, Holland slipped on ice, fell and broke his leg. While lying idle in the hospital, he pondered his submarine designs. He defined several principal problems that arose during submersion that needed to be resolved—creating propulsion power other than human, renewing the air supply, and navigating in horizontal and vertical planes. Holland believed he could overcome these obstacles to undersea operation, but he wouldn't get the opportunity to try until five years later. Meanwhile, Holland taught classes at a parochial school in Paterson, New Jersey.

By 1875, Holland had found investors who were willing to back him—if he secured the U.S. government's endorsement for his innovative submarine plans. He designed plans for a one-man submarine, about 15 feet in length, which he presented to the secretary of the Navy. These were turned over to Captain Edward Simpson, then stationed at the War College in Newport, Rhode Island. Captain Simpson studied the plans and opined that the craft was technically feasible, but he doubted that anyone could be convinced to serve underwater. Holland immediately countered that the Confederate Navy

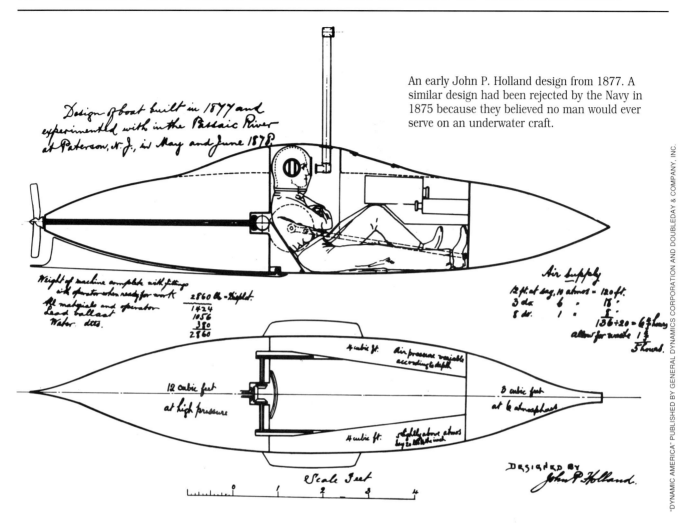

An early John P. Holland design from 1877. A similar design had been rejected by the Navy in 1875 because they believed no man would ever serve on an underwater craft.

had an abundance of volunteers, even though a number of men had drowned in various accidents. The U.S. Navy remained unconvinced; Captain Simpson recommended that Holland abandon his plans. This was only a few years after the *Intelligent Whale* submarine project, started in the waning days of the Civil War, had been abandoned.

Holland was undaunted. Two years later, in 1877, he secured backing from a group of Irish patriots known as the Fenians, who thought Holland's submarine could aid the cause of freeing Ireland from British rule. (Hatred of the British and their navy seemed to be a recurring motivational theme in early submarine development projects.) Holland first built a 30-inch proof-of-concept model propelled by coiled springs which resulted in the construction of a craft almost 15 feet long in the summer of 1877. Although this boat did not perform perfectly—it leaked and the engine repeatedly balked—Holland proved his ideas were sound. The inventor could finally afford to quit teaching and devote himself full-time to submarine development.

In 1879, Holland began constructing the *Fenian Ram,* a craft 30 feet in length, 6 feet in diameter and with a displacement of 17 tons. The boat's design incorporated both vertical and horizontal rudders, a torpedo tube and a 17-horsepower oil internal combustion engine. The *Fenian Ram* took two years to build and cost $13,000. Many people watched the boat's progress during construction, including a U.S. Navy officer, two representatives from the Turkey government and John Ericsson, who had designed the iron-clad *Monitor* of Civil War fame. The *Fenian Ram* performed well in her early trials, although this did not dispel skepticism. She could operate submerged, fire a torpedo and surface safely after reaching a depth of 37 feet. The *Ram's* major problem was retaining sufficient compressed air on board for prolonged underwater activities.

For more than a year, Holland continued testing the *Fenian Ram* and making refinements. In the interim, he began building a smaller one-man submarine, just 16 feet long, which would carry one torpedo. When it seemed to his Irish nationalist supporters that Holland was more interested in his submarine's design than the cause for which it was intended, factions of the Fenians became distraught with the slow

Scale model of the *Holland No. 1* in the Paterson Museum, Paterson, New Jersey. Holland also built a proof of concept model which he tested at Coney Island in 1877.

progress. On a dark night in 1882, a tug pulled stealthily alongside the *Fenian Ram* at her berth in Bayonne, New Jersey. Papers forged with Holland's signature were shown to the lone watchman. Under orders from the Irish, the captain lashed the *Fenian Ram* and Holland's smaller submarine to the tug and pulled away. While underway to New Haven, Connecticut, the smaller submarine went adrift and sank. Once in New Haven, the Fenian rebels were faced with the prospect of operating the *Ram* without knowing how. They brazenly asked Holland to assist them. He refused. "I'll let her rot on their hands."[2] He did not even prosecute the men who had stolen his boats.

Holland, left with little money after the Fenian affair, took a job as a draftsman at the Pneumatic Gun Company where he met U.S. Army Captain Edmund Zalinski, a well-regarded ordnance expert. In 1886, Zalinski organized a company, the Nautilus Submarine Boat Company, for the purpose of building an experimental submarine— the Zalinski boat—based on Holland's designs with two of Zalinski's dynamite guns intended to be fired from a surfaced submarine.

According to one source, Holland's heart didn't seem to be in the ill-fated project. The Zalinski boat had an iron frame covered with wood, measuring 50 feet long and 8 feet in diameter. At its launch on September 4, 1885, under the watchful eye of a young engineer for which Holland reportedly had little respect, the submarine's launchways collapsed, sending her crashing onto a piling and ripping gaping holes in her side and bottom. She was recovered and repaired for a brief time, but soon was discarded as a total failure. It would be years before Holland could recover his reputation and credibility to secure enough backers for what would become the predecessor of modern submarines.[3] First, however, Holland would encounter a series of setbacks that might have destroyed the heart of a lesser man.

In 1888, naval officers convinced President Grover Cleveland's Secretary of the Navy, William C. Whitney, to secure an appropriation from Congress for a submarine. Congress approved $150,000 for the project, and Secretary Whitney invited submarine developers to submit their designs and competitive bids.

Holland and his competitors from the United States and overseas vied for the contract. One was Professor Josiah Tuck, who had experimented with his underwater craft, the *Peacemaker*, in the Hudson River in 1885. The submarine ran on steam generated by caustic soda introduced into a boiler. The boat never made more than several short trips. A more

JOHN P. HOLLAND, PUB. 1966, USNI

The *Fenian Ram* was stolen from Holland one dark night in 1882 by backers who wanted the boat for action against the British.

impressive competitor was Thorsten Nordenfelt of Sweden who, along with his associate the Rev. George William Garrett, had already built boats for Turkey, Russia and Greece. The boats, which more resembled short eels than graceful porpoises (like Holland's craft), were propelled by steam stored in hot water tanks at 150 pounds-per-square-inch of pressure. However, Nordenfelt's boats literally ran out of steam—they could not travel more than 500 yards underwater.

As it turned out, none of the designs submitted during the 1888 competition were selected. The government abruptly cancelled its plans for submarine procurement without any explanation.

In 1889, the U.S. government issued another invitation to bid on the design and production of an experimental submarine. This time, the government went through the selection process, choosing Holland's design. Unfortunately, in the interim, a new president was elected and with him came a new secretary of the Navy who expressed no interest in submarine development and diverted the funds to other projects.

Meanwhile, submarine development overseas, particularly in France and Spain, progressed. As Congress grasped the potential danger emanating from submarine development abroad, it appropriated $200,000 in 1895 for production and design of an experimental sub-

marine. It once again put the submarine contract out to bid and received eight designs from competing submarine developers, among them Holland, Tuck, Nordenfelt, Simon Lake and George C. Baker. Holland's company, the Holland Torpedo Boat Company, was selected to receive the very first contract for a U.S. Navy submarine on a bid of $150,000. Construction commenced at the Columbian Iron Works in Baltimore on the new submarine, to be named *Plunger*. Holland saw his chance to prove his designs to a skeptical world. (Ironically, an earlier ship of the same name, *La Plongeur*, was built and launched in France in 1863. The ship was 140 feet long, had a displacement of 420 tons and was powered by an 80-horsepower compressed air engine. It had a problem maintaining a depth line; observers described its movements as resembling those of a playful dolphin. The crew members didn't take *La Plongeur's* antics so lightly; neither did the French government, who had funded it and *La Plongeur* was dispatched as a failure.[4])

Secretary of the Navy Hilary A. Herbert expressed concern, based on reports of submersible action during the Civil War, that the submariners might be crushed by shock waves from its torpedoes exploding a target. The secretary sanctioned an experiment by the U.S. Navy in which a watertight tank simulated a submarine, crewed by a cat, a rooster, a rabbit and a dove.[5]

The tank and its unusual crew were submerged. At a suitable distance, the experimenters exploded a charge of gun cotton. They repeated the experiment several times, moving the explosion closer to the tank each time. On the final trial, the experimenters exploded the gun cotton only a hundred feet from the tank. The tank was undamaged; the rabbit and the dove did not survive this final trial, but the cat and the rooster were unharmed. According to one account, "The cat fled, highly incensed, with distended tail; the rooster flew out and crowed."[5] The experiment convinced Secretary Herbert that a submarine could withstand the impact of its own torpedoes exploding on an enemy target.

For unknown reasons, the Navy had taken an adversarial position with Holland over the *Plunger's* final design. Its representatives insisted that every item and plan be submitted to its committee of experts for approval or modification. "The building of the *Plunger* consequently proceeded at a snail's pace, subjected to manifold changes devised by naval technicians," according to Captain Frank T. Cable, the *Holland's* first trial captain. "The outcome was a boat that departed far from the ideas over which Holland had labored. It was improved to such an extent that it failed. Holland was ill during much of the time the vessel was on the stocks and his absence gave the naval technicians their opportunity."

The Navy required that the craft reach a maximum speed of 15 knots on the surface and then submerge in less than one minute, causing a critical problem for the *Plunger*. To achieve that speed, the 85-foot submarine needed a powerplant that could generate 1,500 horsepower. There wasn't a gasoline engine made that could provide the necessary power output, so three petroleum-burning steam boilers drove the three propeller shafts.

To complicate matters, the Navy required twin screws; Holland had never designed a multiple-screw ship. He was "convinced that it was necessary to have a propeller at the axis of a submarine." The compromise was three propellers—the two outside propellers driven by 600-horsepower engines and the center propeller by a 300-horsepower engine. The enormous and complex propulsion system was destined for failure, as "the engine room was so completely filled with machinery and piping that it was almost impossible even to crawl through it, and the heat which escaped from the boiler, piping and engines raised the temperature to a point which simply could not be endured."[6]

To meet the Navy's performance requirements after it submerged, the submarine switched to an electric motor powered by heavy storage batteries to drive its center propeller. Cable described the unbearable results:

The *Zalinski* boat as drawn by an artist from *Scientific American*, August 7, 1886. An inventor of military devices, Army Lt. Edward Zalinski hired Holland as a draftsman and was impressed by Holland's submarine designs.

A last view of ill-conceived *Plunger,* just before it was scrapped. Note the triple screws. The *Plunger's* steam propulsion made the boat's interior unbearably hot for the crew when the submarine was sealed for underwater runs.

ELECTRIC BOAT COMPANY

"The limit of time given from the instant her engine-room telegraph was set at 'stop' until her funnel was hauled down, hatches closed and the boat fully submerged, was not to exceed one minute. One could imagine what would happen to a crew of men sealed up in an air-tight case with a boiler that a few seconds before had been developing 1,500 horsepower. The naval experts did not insulate their fire boxes, and, as a result, no human being could stay inside with the hatches closed, so intense was the heat."[7]

Unfortunately, nothing ever resolved the problems of the *Plunger*. Although she was formally launched in 1897, "She never got beyond her dock at the Columbian Iron Works, Baltimore, where she was built, except for her final disposal to the little town of New Suffolk, Long Island," Cable reported. "There her hull lay until the [Second] World War, when she was removed to New London, Connecticut and used for the training of divers by the Navy."[8]

Holland had foreseen the failure of the *Plunger* as early as 1896 and proposed to his company

that he build a submarine according to his designs, solely under his supervision. Company officials realized that they could expect no future contracts if their only model was the *Plunger*, so in 1896 workers laid the keel for the *Holland* at the Crescent Shipyard in Elizabethport, New Jersey. Smaller than the *Plunger*, the *Holland* was 54 feet long and 10 feet in diameter with a displacement of 75 tons submerged. A 50-horsepower Otto gasoline engine propelled her on the surface, while a 50-horsepower electric motor fed by a 60-cell storage battery provided power while submerged. She could attain speeds of 7 knots on the surface and 5 knots submerged.

Eric Ewertz was then in charge of construction at the Crescent Shipyard. At his first meeting of John P. Holland in the office of shipyard owner Lewis Nixon, Ewertz was told that they were going to build a submarine for the inventor. When he asked to see the plans, Holland produced a single 18" x 24" sheet. Ewertz must have stood and stared in disbelief, because Nixon hastened to add that Mr. Holland would be at the

STEEL FISH WITH REVOLVING TAIL THAT WILL PROTECT OUR HARBOR AGAINST ANY FLEET

The Holland Submarine Terror, the Newest Wonder of Naval Science, Which Dives and Swims Under Water and Noiselessly and Unseen Creeps Up Under an Enemy's Side, Hurling Into It Thunderbolts of Dynamite from Its Torpedo Guns.

The *New York Herald* (April 15, 1898) depicts the interior design of the mysterious *Holland* which had been seen cruising the waters off New York. Holland and his backers were most likely pleased that their mystery had been uncovered and publicized.

site to help. "That would be a damn good idea," Ewertz replied.[9]

After so much frustration, Holland felt success could not evade him now—he was building a submarine based on designs he had labored over for years. But, as one historian remarked, "he should have realised that every Irishman has to play against Murphy's law... "[10]

On October 13, 1897, John Holland stood at the dock's edge and peered down into the water where, just the day before, the submarine bearing his name had been berthed. Sunk by a worker's carelessness, the *Holland* laid on the bottom, full of corrosive salt water, for 18 hours. Holland knew that the exposure was corroding the newly installed electrical equipment and machinery, and he may have imagined his dreams being eaten away as quickly.

After she was raised, Holland's company "vainly tried every known method of drying out the motors and generators by applying heat externally."[11] The company's officers even discussed removing all of the machinery damaged by the salt water and replacing it with new, but

The crew of the *Holland* prepare the boat for her trials before the U.S. Navy's Board of Inspection on April 10, 1898. The trials were inconclusive and Commander Charles S. Sperry recommended further tests for the submarine.

JOHN P. HOLLAND, PUB. 1966, USNI

William F. C. Hindemann, an employee of the Holland Torpedo Boat Co., assembles some internal equipment for the dry-docked *Holland* at the Morris Heights shipyard on the Harlem River in New York during the winter of 1898-99.

rejected the idea believing that this would have taken them beyond the deadline they felt they had to demonstrate the ship as being fully operational. Additionally, the *Plunger's* problems had left the struggling Holland Torpedo Boat Company short on funds.

Holland implored the Electro-Dynamic Company, which had supplied the electrical equipment and motors, to send expert help. The Holland Torpedo Boat Company owed Electro-Dynamic a considerable amount so, in part to protect their investment, the latter dispatched its best electrical engineer to the site to effect repairs (and, if possible, collect a little on the account). The company sent Frank T. Cable, a man who would play an integral part in modern submarine development.

Cable confirmed that the field coils and armature windings of the main propulsion motor were saturated with salt water. The young engi-

neer, having little to lose, used a drastic method to dry out the motors and generators: He converted "one end of the double-ended motor armature into a generator and, forcing current into the other end, heat was developed, and this trick did the work. The windings and parts were made dry."[12]

Holland was so pleased with Cable's work that he asked the young engineer if he would like to take a test run in the *Holland*. "Not on your life," replied Cable. "You couldn't pay me to go down in that thing."[13] Even so, Holland hired Cable for more than he was making at the Electro-Dynamic Company. Cable wasn't exactly pirated from Electro-Dynamic, however; the Philadelphia-based company considered Cable to be a debt insurance policy. They even assured Cable that he could return to his old job should Holland's company fail. The informal alliance benefited both companies.

The *Holland* was launched—and made her first successful dive—on St. Patrick's Day, March 17, 1898. When asked in the 1940s when the *Holland* made her first submerged run, Eric Ewertz replied that it was the very day of launching. His responsibility at the time was weights and measurements, and he recalled being asked repeatedly whether the submarine would float. He assured the questioners that he had no doubts that she would. Launched, the *Holland* quickly slid into the water and submerged—so quickly that a worker on her deck had to jump clear and swim to shore. For 20 long seconds, the submarine remained out of sight before "sleekly [surfacing] to float at the prescribed depth."[14]

As engineer in charge of operations with the title of trial captain, Cable immediately set out to make the *Holland* into an underwater craft acceptable to the U.S. Navy and one which could compete with submarines being developed abroad, particularly in France. Among many of the *Holland's* improvements credited

to Cable were placing rudders aft of the propellers to improve steering; dividing the chores of operating the diving and steering rudders between two men (previously, Holland himself had manned both rudders with sometimes clumsy results); and creating a novel method of adjusting the trim of the boat before submerging, eliminating the need for tugs to carry pig iron for ballast.

While the *Holland* moved steadily toward completion, the company continued to have financial problems. Funds were needed to ready the *Holland* for demonstration. A letter dated December 15, 1897 from Holland Boat Company's attorney Norman G. Johnson was a clear solicitation for investors. The three-page letter announced the *Holland* to be nearing completion and that the present stockholders were confident the boat would prove its value to the government. Johnson then generously offered to allow new investors to become stockholders and directors. Johnson wrote that "we are ... desirous of

John P. Holland inspects his underwater invention, after years of hard work during which his ideas were spurned and ridiculed.

ELECTRIC BOAT COMPANY

The *Holland* reflects the sun at the New Suffolk, Long Island plant of the Holland Torpedo Boat Co. The hatch below the superstructure covers the boat's lone torpedo tube.

raising $5,000 or $10,000 to meet the expenses attendant upon our final trials and the placing of our patents and inventions before the powers of Europe and Asia."[15]

Johnson concluded his letter by offering to "make it six months, with interest at 6 percent," or to convert their investment at the end of term for stock "at $25 per share, par value of the shares being $100 each."[16]

Cable, who shared the daunting task of finding capital, turned to Isaac L. Rice, president of the Electric Storage Battery Company of Philadelphia, which supplied the storage batteries used aboard the *Holland*. Rice had made his reputation and fortune in several fields. In 1893, he became involved in the massive reorganization of the railroads; by 1898, he was established as somewhat of the battery king of his time. He was also schooled in law and considered an authority in patent law. This combination of knowledge, organizational skills and capital made

Rice a very welcome potential addition to the struggling submarine company.

By July 4, 1898, Cable had convinced Rice to come aboard for a ride in the *Holland*. Rice was so enthused by the prospects of submarine manufacturing that he decided to form a new company—the Electric Boat Company—and obtained backing from prominent bankers such as the Rothschilds of Great Britain. Upon his first visit in 1899 with Lord Rothschild and the Admiralty, Rice encountered an England sharply divided over the ethics and effectiveness of undersea craft. Early submarine development was spurred by an intense dislike of the British; now, the country's naval officials spoke of the submarine with disdain. Admiral of the Fleet Sir Arthur Wilson called the craft "underhand, unfair and damned un-English ... we cannot stop invention in this direction, but we can avoid doing anything to encourage it." Nonetheless, Rice nearly succeeded in bringing home a £34,000 contract.

However, when the Admiralty realized how unacceptable an American-built submarine would be, the contract was awarded to a British company—which eventually built the boat under license from its American builders.[17]

Birth of Electric Boat

On February 7, 1899, American businessman Isaac Rice incorporated the Electric Boat Company, which absorbed the Holland Torpedo Boat Company and, shortly afterward, purchased the Electro-Dynamic Company and the Electric Launch Company of Bayonne, New Jersey, which built luxury yachts and tenders. At its May 12, 1899 board meeting, the newborn company claimed an impressive list of officers and directors:

President, Isaac L. Rice; vice president, Hoffman Atkinson; secretary-treasurer, William Dulles, Jr.; directors, Robert McA. Lloyd (electrical engineer of the company), Elihu B. Frost (president of the Holland Torpedo Boat Company), J.G. Cham-

berlain (general manager of the Electric Launch Company, later merged with the Electric Boat Company), and John P. Holland.[18]

By the time Electric Boat was established, the *Holland* had already gone through much in the way of sea trials and shakedown cruises. The two years stretching from early 1898 to the *Holland's* acceptance by the U.S. Navy in March 1900 were punctuated by a series of announcements: "The finishing touches are being put on the boat. This week should see her go through further trials." These announcements were followed by weeks or months of making the modifications which the trials showed to be necessary.

The early trials were conducted from a new base of operations in Perth Amboy, New Jersey, to which the *Holland* had been moved so that it could "undergo preliminary dives by way of feeling out her mechanism." Although officially not interested, the U.S. Navy kept a watchful eye on the *Holland's* movements, which was made evident by the following episode.

JOHN P. HOLLAND, PUB. 1966, USNI

The *Holland* just before the trial dive on April 20, 1898.

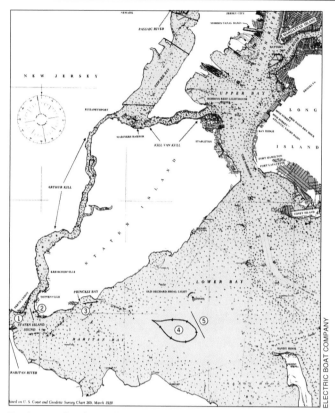

Trial areas for the *Holland* during 1898. (1) Raritan Dry Dock Basin, first dockside submergence, March 11, 1898. (2) First submerged run, March 17, 1898. (3) Testing grounds, April 1898. (4) Trial run, April 20, 1898. (5) Area of official Navy test, November 12, 1898.

War with Spain was imminent in early 1898. The United States sent the USS *Maine* to Havana as a signal of its resolve; Spain countered by ordering the warship *Vizcaya* to boldly anchor in New York's harbor. As tensions escalated, the State Department began to worry that John Holland might brazenly send his submarine into the harbor to sink the *Vizcaya* to prove its merit in wartime. Ironically, the *Holland* was preparing to leave Elizabethport for its new berth in Perth Amboy. Workers placed dummy wood projectiles in the 8-inch gun mounted on her bow which, according to witnesses, looked real from a distance. Several hours after the *Holland* departed, a Navy tug appeared, its captain demanding to know the whereabouts of the *Holland*. Frank Cable reported that "some workmen informed the tug's captain that we were loaded with dynamite shells and had gone down the river."[19] The tug set off in hot pursuit.

Arriving at Perth Amboy, the *Holland* "tied up out of sight in a basin behind an old canal boat." Cable related (with obvious glee) that the tug passed by without spotting the submarine and continued searching for her all day without success. The Navy's crew was so anxious that they telegraphed New York, expecting to learn

that the *Vizcaya* had been sunk. The *Vizcaya* remained safe, however, and the Navy located the *Holland* several days later. It became painfully apparent the fear and anxiety an underwater warcraft could generate.

Soon after, the Navy became officially interested. A March 9, 1898 letter from the company to Commander Charles S. Sperry acknowledged his impending inspection. Roughly two weeks later, a Holland Torpedo Boat Company official expressed some serious doubts about Sperry. In a letter to the company's attorney in Washington, D.C., Frost, as company secretary, wondered whether it wouldn't be better to disregard Sperry and "take the boat down to Washington and put her through trials which fully demonstrate her submarine abilities." Frost went on to describe Sperry as a "dyspeptic" whose impressions would "be largely influenced by his frame of mind at the time."[20] Frost also surmised that Sperry was probably very distracted at the time in view of the hostility with Spain. Most likely as a consequence of these sentiments, Lieutenant Nathan Sargent was ordered to go to Perth Amboy for a trial run on March 27, 1898. Frost was upset that an officer of such low rank was dispatched at the request of Theodore Roosevelt, who was then assistant secretary of the Navy. Sargent spent "half-an-hour examining the drawings and about an hour inside of the boat into everything minutely."[21] The *Holland* then departed with Sargent aboard, accomplishing four or five dives and reaching nearly 11 knots with the conning tower still awash. After the run, Sargent announced that the boat had "fully proved her ability to propel herself, to dive, come up, admit water to her ballast tanks, and to eject it again without difficulty."[22] Soon thereafter, the company sent a letter to the Navy, formally offering to sell the *Holland* for $175,000.

Holland and his colleagues at Electric Boat had regained public confidence. The price of their stock rose with each favorable piece of news from trials. When the price of a share reached $60 on March 29, 1898, Frost reported that 160 new shares were quickly sold. On April 6, Frost solicited bids for construction of submarine boats similar to the *Holland* from Bath Iron Works in Maine. He was confident that a new bill would soon be introduced in Congress to appropriate funds for the boats. He even advised Captain Jacques, then president of the Holland Torpedo Boat Company, to forego foreign marketing initiatives and to concentrate his efforts on the U.S. Congress and U.S. Navy.

The Navy, however, continued to appoint review boards to observe the *Holland*. On April 20, 1898, a board headed by Commander Sperry observed the *Holland* make a 4-mile submerged run in Prince's Bay at Staten Island. During the run, which lasted about two hours, the *Holland* fired a dummy torpedo and a dummy projectile from the dynamite gun. Electric Boat was very uncomfortable with this series of trials, as the review board had not given any guidelines. As a result, the company used the schedule of requirements that was part of its *Plunger* contract. In a letter to Roosevelt later, Frost claimed that the *Holland* had more than met those requirements. Nevertheless, Sperry's board recommended further trials, criticizing the *Holland's* steering. (John P. Holland admitted in a letter to long-time friend, supporter and investor Commander William W. Kimball that the rudder configuration had caused sluggish steering, as Cable had also observed.)

A salvo of letters was fired off to Washington. In a five-page letter to Roosevelt, Frost lamented the Sperry board's lackadaisical attitudes and revealed that a foreign power was also interested in the *Holland*. (The French government had telegraphed the company offering $100,000 for the *Holland*, "just as she stands."[23]) Roosevelt was critical of the trial boards' conduct; he decided there would be no more trials until November 1898. The company used the opportunity to make modifications.

The second set of trials in November 1898 were no more conclusive than the ones in April. The board, now headed by Captain Robley D. Evans, a national hero widely known as "Fighting Bob" and commander of the mighty battleship *Iowa*, again reported an erratic steering problem. The *Holland* fired a Whitehead torpedo, but a part of the boat's structure had to be removed to load the torpedo. Following these trials, Cable made a number of changes. He decided to reposition the propellers forward and the rudders aft, and remove the dynamite gun. Since the boat had a relatively small displacement, allowances had to be made to compensate for loss of weight when a torpedo was fired. Compensation tanks were installed so that the torpedo tube "could be blown or pumped in order to load another torpedo,"[24] allowing the boat to maintain consistent trim while submerged.

According to Cable, these changes were completed by April 1899—yet investors remained anxious over what they perceived to be slow progress. The boat was launched, investors observed, so what was the purpose of these continuous changes? Cable reported that they were instructed to "leave the engineering stuff alone."[25] The company also decided it was unsafe to conduct additional experiments around New York, where shallow water and frequent boat traffic hampered underwater trials. In June 1899, the company moved its operations to Peconic Bay at New Suffolk on Long Island, to which the *Holland* was towed by a steam lighter.

"DYNAMIC AMERICA" PUBLISHED BY GENERAL DYNAMICS CORPORATION AND DOUBLEDAY & COMPANY, INC.

The U.S. flag and the Navy jack of the *Holland* are preserved at the Submarine Library on the Submarine Base at Groton, Conn. An old postcard of the *Holland*, at bottom, attests to the popular interest in the Navy's first submarine.

Engineers and crew put the *Holland* through a number of difficult tests. Between trials, they put on exhibitions for the press, representatives of foreign navies and friends. One of the guests was Clara Barton, founder of the American Red Cross, who was the first woman to take a run on the boat while it was submerged. Barton was reported to have been displeased with the cre-

Laborers, machinists, electricians, pipefitters, and deckhands formed the work force of the Holland Torpedo Boat Co. at its New Suffolk, Long Island plant. The company's main offices were on Broadway in New York City. Standing, left to right: Lawrence Sullivan, laborer; William Wood, machinist; Thomas Delaney, apprentice machinist; Ben Horton, laborer; Harry Morrill, chief electrician; Charles Lewis, laborer; Hugo Momm, machinist; Terrence Magee, apprentice machinist; Herman Noblett, electrician; Leroy Hammond, electrician; John Wilson, supervisory machinist; Patrick Glenn, captain of the tender *Kelpie*; William Deslette, machinist. Sitting: Frank Acker, apprentice machinist; Charles Becktold, pipefitter; Peter Rehill, machinist; Harry Kirby, assistant supervisory machinist; John Sanders, machinist; Charles Berg, deckhand; Conrad Stick, machinist; Karl Kuester, machinist.

ation of a "deadly instrument of war."[26] Holland explained to her there would be no war if "all the nations of the world were equipped with submarines."[27]

In October 1899, as the *Holland* completed another exhibition and was returning to the dock, Cable gave the order to disconnect the engine and engage the motor, since the engine could not reverse. There was no response from the three men below decks. They found the chief engineer had fainted and, as Cable was having him hauled above, the chief machinist exclaimed, "I am going, too!" and fell unconscious. The electrician, left below deck clinging to consciousness, manned the motor. When he did not verbally reply to the stop signal, Cable went below

to check on the crewman and found him unconscious as well.

Fortunately, two men on deck were able to throw a line ashore and make the boat fast. All of the unconscious victims were taken from the *Holland* and placed on the dock, some "nearer dead than alive," according to Cable.[28] Many wondered if this was the end of the *Holland* and whether she would ever find another crew, though all had been revived. (It took four hours to revive one man.) The next day, every member of the crew "reported for duty on time."[29]

The men had fainted because of carbon monoxide fumes escaping from a leaky exhaust pipe. For years, Cable reported, they had tried to determine methods to detect the presence of the deadly gas. At last, he said, they "resorted to the old-fashioned mouse test." A cage of mice went out with the *Holland*. "When the mice died," wrote Cable, "it was time to go home."[30]

Finally, on November 6, 1899, the *Holland* underwent sea trials before a special board of naval officers at New Suffolk, Long Island. The trials were a success from the company's perspective and seemed to have convinced a number of naval officers of the submarine's seaworthiness. Plans were announced to move the *Holland* to Washington, D.C. to undergo demonstrations for Congress and key government officials. On November 9, the *Holland* left New Suffolk on a 39-day trip that took her to the Washington Navy Yard on the Potomac River.

Cable said that the company learned that insurance companies would not cover an open sea voyage after the boat had reached New York. Consequently, the boat traveled an inland route using rivers and canals. Special pontoons were supplied to buoy the *Holland*, which would normally draw 8 feet of water, through the 7–foot-deep Raritan Canal. Along the route, the *Holland* attracted considerable attention from spectators, with some crowds growing to more than 5,000 people.

At a midnight stop in Princeton, the crowd was large and inquisitive. One of the most frequent questions was: "What did the crew do for air when submerged?" Cable reported that one of the crew responded very seriously, saying that each of the crew "carried a small bottle of liquid air." When the air became stale, the crew member said that "he would touch his tongue with a drop of the liquid" and that would sustain him.[31] (This was reminiscent of Dutch physician and inventor Cornelius Drebbel, whose 17th century submarine crew also made references to "liquid air.")

The USS *Holland* after her commissioning on October 12, 1900. Note the funnels aft of the conning tower. They were used for the intake of air and venting of exhaust from the gasoline engine when running on the surface.

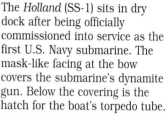

The *Holland* (SS-1) sits in dry dock after being officially commissioned into service as the first U.S. Navy submarine. The mask-like facing at the bow covers the submarine's dynamite gun. Below the covering is the hatch for the boat's torpedo tube.

ELECTRIC BOAT COMPANY

After arriving in Washington D.C., Cable and his crew set about reconditioning the *Holland* after the long journey and laid out courses on the Potomac for the new trials. Amusingly, Cable said that he and others among the crew were surprised to learn that the Potomac froze over during the winter. "We had supposed when we reached Washington," he wrote, "that we would be in a part of the sunny South."[32] With no chance for winter trials, the company turned its attention to gaining the support of Congress and the Navy, and to enticing the interest of foreign governments. In a message to Rice dated January 10, Frost recounted a visit with an old college friend, John Porter, President William McKinley's private secretary. Porter revealed that the president was aware of the *Holland*, and that he would try to convince him to witness the submarine on a

run. Frost reported to Rice on January 31, 1900, that "we are showing the boat every day."[33]

Another letter from Frost to Rice on January 31 detailed a strategy for gaining support in the Senate: The Electric Boat Company would distribute appropriations from the Navy for submarine construction among three shipyards—Bath Iron Works in Maine, Trigg and Company in Richmond, Virginia, and Union Iron Works of San Francisco, California. Frost wrote that "it does not cost the company a cent and we gain a very strong backing in Congress."[34]

Meanwhile, Electric Boat negotiated terms of acceptance for the *Holland* with the Navy's Board of Construction. By January 24, the board agreed that, provided the company satisfactorily settle the *Plunger* contract, they would recommend granting a new contract to build one or two submarines along the designs being developed by Holland. The agreement required Electric Boat to place $90,000 in trust, payable to the Navy should the *Plunger* not be accepted. Frost disclosed details of negotiations with the French government and the presence of a "young Japanese officer here, who has just arrived on a secret mission."[35] Frost said he suspected that the "secret mission" concerned the *Holland*, as "he spends a good part of his time at the office, asks a great many questions, gets all the literature we have, etc."[36]

The company's strategy was to sell the *Holland* as quickly as possible, but not to deliver it to the Navy until all congressional and official exhibitions were completed.

A major exhibition was scheduled for March 14, 1900, which would include Admiral George Dewey, members of the House and Senate, the secretary and assistant secretary of the Navy, and members of the press. Frost worried about a wind shift to the southeast and cloudy skies, but remained confident for a successful demonstration. At eight o'clock the following morning, Admiral Dewey's aide, Lieutenant H.H. Caldwell, reported to Cable aboard the *Holland*. Ten minutes later, the *Holland* headed toward the exhibi-

tion course, followed by the *Sylph* carrying naval officials, the *Josephine* carrying congressmen and senators, and the *Tecumseh* carrying the press. Arriving at the start of the course near Mt. Vernon, spectator yachts jockeyed for position as the *Sylph* sounded the signal of two whistles for the exhibition to begin. The *Holland* responded with a single whistle and, within a few seconds, vanished beneath the waves:

> "Flags on long staffs had been secured to the Holland so that Navy observers could track her position during the ten–minute run, approximately one mile, down the Potomac. At the end of the run the Holland suddenly surfaced, a roiling of bubbly water could be observed at her bow, followed by the wake of a blank torpedo fired as an attack exercise. As spectators watched the torpedo's course, the Holland disappeared once again, reversed course and headed up stream to demonstrate the ability to escape an enemy response to an attack. On the return course, the Holland porpoised several times, briefly surfacing and then quickly diving once again. Admiral Dewey said little more than the Holland had successfully carried out her program, as he intently observed the exhibition from the stern railing of the Sylph. Lieutenant Caldwell, aboard during the run, enthused in his report to Admiral Dewey. "Throughout the performance there was no accident

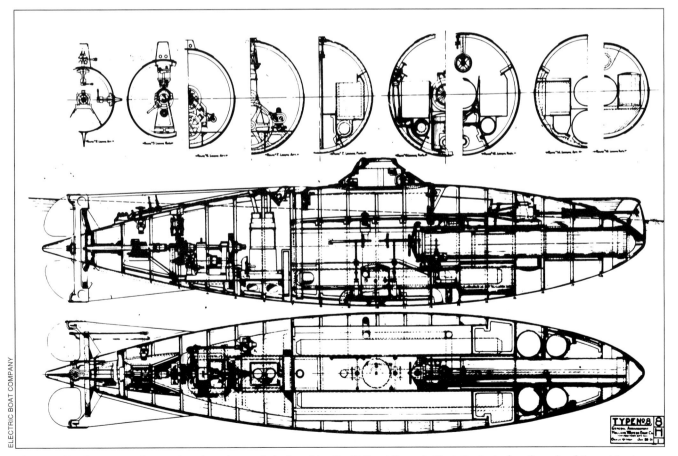

ELECTRIC BOAT COMPANY

The Type No. 8 was one of several underwater craft designed by the Holland Torpedo Boat Co. just after the sale of the original *Holland*. The company used these designs to attract foreign buyers.

or hitch of any sort and the ease with which either part of the mechanism of the boat was manipulated was particularly impressive.

"Each member of the crew had a special station, where he remained during the runs. Although these men were all highly skilled and showed a confidence due to their long service in the boat, I think the duties could easily be performed by the Petty Officers of the Navy after a short trial. The boat did not roll and she only pitched slightly at the time of diving, but righted immediately after attaining the required depth. The torpedo was discharged with the greatest ease. Only a very slight shock occurred to the boat when the torpedo was fired. The Captain gave orders to the Engineer by the ordinary method of bells and to the torpedo men and pump men by word of mouth. When submerged the boat was kept at chosen depth without any difficulty by the means of the horizontal rudder. The evenness of the immersion was well shown by the depth gauges, but must have been apparent from the other vessels from the position of the flags. It is worthy of note from first immersion the water as seen thru the deadlights was entirely opaque and at the maximum depth it looked almost black. During the nearly three hours we were in the boat the air was perfectly pure."[37]

Frost wrote Congressman George E. Foss, chairman of the Committee on Naval Affairs, requesting that the committee question the ad-

miral before he left town. Frost even respectfully submitted six questions for Admiral Dewey to answer, designed to reflect favorably on the results. Dewey's aide, Lieutenant Caldwell, told Frost that he had spent many sleepless nights waiting for the Spanish fleet at Manila, but with a half-dozen *Hollands* at the harbor entrance, "the other fellows would have had the sleepless nights," and offered to so testify before the House Committee.

Though Holland was buoyantly optimistic, he had not forgotten his earlier treatment at the hands of his detractors:

"We are in great shape now; no one laughs any more at the "Holland"; the laughing in fact is down on the other side of their mouths. One dignitary, very high in the Navy Department, was good enough to call us thieves; another was pleased to say our boat was a toy; two others opposed it all they knew how, I believe not through conviction but because they got talked into it. We are now officially informed by John D. Long that his Board is not at all opposed to submarine boats but on the contrary that they favor them. This radical change of opinion was very remarkable and very sudden but I believe very insincere, but it don't amount to a row of pins because they are virtually obliterated by the late appointment by the Secretary of the Navy of a general staff with Admiral Dewey at its head."[38]

The *Holland* underway in 1901. The dapper gentlemen are probably among the hundreds of dignitaries, government officials and potential customers who went out on exhibition runs.

ELECTRIC BOAT COMPANY

The *Fulton*, launched June 12, 1901, at dockside with her crew posing atop the boat. The *Fulton* was a working model for A-class submarines built by the Electric Boat Company.

The *Fulton* underway during a sea trial. Built to demonstrate the Electric Boat Co.'s latest designs and developments, the *Fulton* eventually found its way into the hands of the Russian navy.

As the Navy pondered its decision, the company was granted permission to testify before the House Committee on Naval Affairs, and meanwhile, entertained "some two to three hundred people" at *Holland* exhibitions.[39] Each crew member was issued a share of common stock in the Electric Boat Company. By the end of 1899, the capital stock of Electric Boat was valued at $10 million, divided equally between preferred and common shares.[40]

Despite Admiral Dewey's flattering testimony before the House Naval Committee, the Navy remained reluctant. The board cited the history of the *Plunger*, and the $99,716 already paid to the Holland Company. They resisted purchasing the *Holland* or contracting for more boats until the *Plunger* issues had been settled. Admiral Philip Hichborn disagreed, saying the Navy should actively encourage the development of submarines by purchasing the *Holland* and funding construction of two additional boats of the Holland type.

On April 4, 1900, the company offered the *Holland* to the Navy for $150,000,[41] agreeing to deposit $90,000 in trust pending resolution of the *Plunger* matter, construct additional boats for $170,000 each, and train a Navy crew to operate the *Holland*. (Lieutenant Caldwell later became the first U.S. Navy captain of the *Holland*.) The Navy accepted the offer a week later on April 11 and the *Holland* was delivered to the Navy Department on April 30, 1900.

In her final version, the *Holland* was 53 feet long, 10 feet-3 inches at the widest beam and displaced 74 tons. Her frame was made from circles of steel set about a foot apart that gradually narrowed in diameter to form the bow and stern. The crew used the flat superstructure on top of the hull as a walking platform, but the structure also enclosed exhaust pipes, mooring lines and a small anchor. A turret about 2 feet in diameter and extending about 18 inches above the superstructure served as the boat's only entrance and exit. Underway, the *Holland* could reach a speed of 6 knots on the surface under engine power and 5 knots submerged under electric motor power. The *Holland* had a range of 1,500 miles on the surface, and could travel 40 miles underwater without surfacing. The maximum submerged depth was 100 feet and she could reach 20 feet in just eight seconds. There was sufficient compressed air in the on-board tanks to supply the crew with fresh air for 30 days, if not used for other purposes, such as blowing the ballast tanks.

To dive, the crew opened valves to flood the main ballast tanks. Simultaneously, the diving planes were rotated and forward momentum smoothly drove the boat beneath the sea. Submerged, the *Holland* switched to an electric motor powered by large batteries stored beneath flooring in the forward two-thirds of the vessel, where ballast and gasoline tanks were also located.

For armament, the *Holland* was equipped with one forward torpedo tube, one bow-mounted pneumatic dynamite gun, and three short Whitehead torpedoes. The forward end of the torpedo carried an explosive charge that detonated on contact.

The *Holland* had no periscope (it had not yet been perfected) so the crew looked out of the "deadlights," plate-glass windows at the top of the turret measuring about 1 inch by 3 inches. On the surface, an observer had a 360-degree view if the sea was smooth; while submerged, the ship was navigated solely by compass. A small electric light in the turret provided sufficient illumination to check both heading and depth.

Torpedo attacks employed a "porpoising technique": As the *Holland* approached the target, it would bob to the surface just enough that the turret was awash. The operator would quickly establish the bearing and distance to target; then the boat would submerge to escape detection and retaliation.

With the *Holland* delivered to the Navy, the Electric Boat Company made steady progress in three critical areas—sales of additional boats to the U.S. Navy, refinement of design and cultivation of foreign governments' heightened interest. Eight hundred pamphlets were printed, detailing the testimonies of Admiral Dewey, Rear Admiral Hichborn and Lieutenant Caldwell before the House Committee on Naval Affairs on April 23, 1900 in which they recommended "the purchase of 20 submarine torpedo boats of the 'Holland' type."[42] The Senate passed an amendment the following month for the purchase of five

boats. Frost wrote that once a contract was issued, the company should "push one boat night and day," so that it could be accepted before the next session of Congress decided otherwise."[43] On June 23, Electric Boat asked Secretary of the Navy John D. Long for a sixth contract. Referring to the appropriation of 1896 and 1899 which resulted in the purchase of the *Holland*, the company reminded the secretary that those deliberations called for two boats. By June 27, Frost wrote that a sixth boat had been awarded, with the stipulation that two of the boats be built on the Pacific coast. A subsequent agreement with Union Iron Works of San Francisco required Electric Boat to station one of its engineers at the site to assist with the construction. The "most delicate apparatus," records indicate, were to be constructed in the East and installed there as well.[44] Structural components and smaller assemblies were to be manufactured by the Union Iron Works, and the California shipbuilder would receive $35,800 for each boat. The first West Coast boat was scheduled for completion in eight months, the second to follow a month later.

The *Holland*, meanwhile, had sailed from Washington D.C. to her new home at the Navy Torpedo Station at Newport, Rhode Island, where Electric Boat personnel were to instruct the Navy in her operation. Captain Cable recommended that the crew consist of an electrician, two machinists and two seamen gunners along with the boat's commanding officer. The commander selected was Lieutenant Caldwell, a candidate for whom Electric Boat had lobbied vigorously.

JOHN P. HOLLAND, PUB. 1966, USNI

The USS *Moccasin* (A-4) during her trials in Little Peconic Bay, Long Island in the summer of 1902. The A-class, of which there were seven boats, was the first class of submarines built after the *Holland*.

JOHN P. HOLLAND, PUB. 1966, USNI

The New Suffolk, Long Island basin of the Holland Torpedo Boat Co. in 1902. At left is the USS *Shark* (later A-7) with the tender *Kelpie* just behind the submarine. At right is the USS *Moccasin* (A-4) and the USS *Adder* (A-2). The surface torpedo boat, USS *Craven*, is in the background.

Cable's training program began with surface runs to acquaint the new crew with essential controls and to bolster confidence in the vessel since only Caldwell had ever before been aboard a submarine. Cable then instructed the crew in diving procedures at dockside, prior to attempting submerged runs. Within 90 days, on September 1, 1900, Cable pronounced the Navy crew, "competent to handle her without our assistance."[45] Cable described the transfer of the *Holland* like watching a child go off to college.

> "With some natural misgivings I stayed out of the boat for the first time and watched her operations with her new crew. Had my heart been weak I may not have survived the experience. A submarine navigator when inside the boat, with everything under his control, can confidently confront emergencies, he knows them so well. But looking on outside the boat, where he can do nothing in case of an accident, he is in the helpless position of being unable to exercise his knowledge."[46]

Cable's apprehension was not unfounded. Not much later, a crew member prematurely opened a valve to fill the after ballast tanks. The stern quickly descended about 15 feet, causing the bow to thrust out of the water at a dangerous angle. Cable was mortified that the *Holland* "was going to stand upon her tail like a spar buoy and sink."[47] Fortunately, Lieutenant Caldwell recognized the solution to the problem and immediately ordered the forward tanks filled, returning the *Holland* to rest on an even keel.

Under naval command, the *Holland* then commenced nighttime attack exercises. An "enemy" target tug boat was placed in Narragansett Bay, and the mission of the *Holland* was to close near enough to launch a torpedo strike before being detected. During the first exercise, the "enemy" spotted the *Holland* because the submarine was displaying navigation lights. In subsequent approaches with the lights extinguished, the *Holland* approached unobserved though running with the conning tower awash. Even the cruiser *New York*, also anchored in the bay, was unable to detect the *Holland* until it had gotten to within 150 feet, and then only with the aid of searchlights.

Construction of the six new submarines proceeded at flank speed. By May 11, 1901, Electric Boat had resolved to "work the entire 24 hours from now on" to complete the first boat.[48] The new

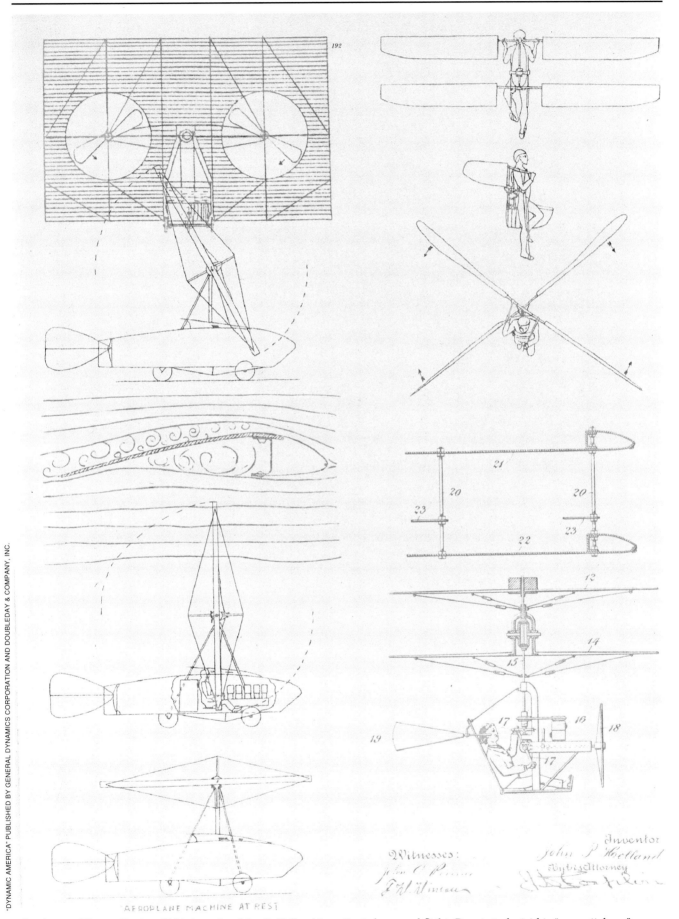

After leaving Electric Boat in 1904, inventor John P. Holland investigated powered flight. Drawings depict his "convertiplane."

A jaunty, young U.S. Navy Lieutenant Lawrence Y. Spear was a witness to the *Fulton*'s record 15-hour submergence in 1901. Spear gave up a promising military career in naval architecture and marine engineering to join the exciting new company of Electric Boat in 1902.

"DYNAMIC AMERICA" PUBLISHED BY GENERAL DYNAMICS CORPORATION AND DOUBLEDAY & COMPANY, INC.

design was known as the A-class submarine, after the *Adder*, the first to be launched at the Crescent Shipyard on July 22, 1901. The A-class was 64 feet long, 11 feet wide and displaced 120 tons. The *Moccasin*, also built at Crescent Shipyard, followed on August 20 of that year. Extensive outfitting and trials followed launching. The Navy finally accepted all six boats in late 1903.

To facilitate construction of these boats, Electric Boat designed and built another experimental boat to evaluate new design features before deployment in the Navy boats. This test bed was named the *Fulton*, and was built at the Crescent Shipyard in the summer of 1901. The *Fulton's* dimensions were identical to those of the A-class boats, but incorporated a larger torpedo tube. Engine and motor horsepower ratings were also increased to 160 horsepower and 70 horsepower respectively. That fall, the *Fulton* was taken to Washington, "in order to stimulate further inter-

est in submarine construction." Cable had the boat "meticulously groomed" for this occasion and all was ready when the *Fulton* met a fate common in early submarine design: During the night of December 1, the *Fulton* sank at the dock after a crane operator lifted the stern of the boat while the main hatch was still open. As the water rushed in, two of the three men struggled out. Discovering that their crew mate had not escaped, one of the men returned below, managing to grab the other crew member and hold his head within an air pocket expressly designed for this type of emergency. When the water stopped flowing through the hatch, both men swam out, through the hatch and up to the surface.

All of the *Fulton's* electrical equipment was ruined and the company was forced to substitute the *Adder* at the demonstrations in Washington.

The *Fulton* was repaired, but was struck with another catastrophe in late April 1902.

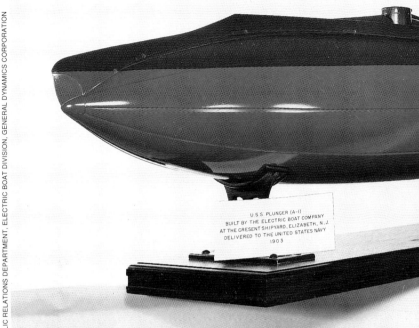

Although the original *Plunger* was scrapped, the name was resurrected for the first of the A-class submarines in 1903. This class had somewhat sleeker lines compared with those of the *Holland.*

While cruising off the Chesapeake capes, the boat was rocked by a powerful explosion triggered by the ignition of volatile gases from the storage batteries. One naval officer was literally blown out of the conning tower, while another man's scalp was badly torn. Though submarine designs were becoming safer, the new, rapidly evolving technology still carried heavy risks as the submarine crews and designers learned through experience.

The development process attracted Lawrence York Spear to the Electric Boat Company. Born in 1870 at Warren, Ohio, Spear entered the Naval Academy at Annapolis when he was only 16 years old. Four years later, he graduated second in his class and the Navy rewarded his efforts by granting him permission to seek a bachelor of science degree in marine engineering and naval architecture at the University of Glasgow in Scotland. Following Spear's return to the United States, he was assigned to various positions in the construction and repair of Navy ships. In 1898, Spear was assigned to teach naval architecture at the postgraduate school in Annapolis. A year later, he returned to supervising ship construction and repair. Part of this

tour of duty brought him to the Crescent Shipyard, where he viewed the *Holland,* the *Fulton* and the A-class submarines in production. Spear became fascinated with the new technology, resigned his naval commission and went to work for Electric Boat, soon becoming a vice president with total responsibility for submarine design and construction.

With Spear becoming head of design, friction soon developed between himself and Holland, who had long held this position. One of the first skirmishes occurred over the use of automatic controls Holland had invented to operate the A-class submarines. Holland envisioned an operator activating buttons and switches to control diving and steering. The experience of both Spear and Cable had led them to conclude that hand-operated equipment was far more reliable. They removed Holland's automatic controls from one of the A-class submarines without his knowledge. According to one account, Holland emerged from his office to see his new equipment strewn all about the dock. He was furious. "You might expect this from a young whippersnapper from the Navy," Holland snorted. "He has ruined my life's work."[49]

The launching of the *Fulton* on June 12, 1901 at Lewis Nixon's shipyard in New Jersey. The *Fulton* had a number of mishaps, including an on-board explosion, before redeeming itself in Navy trials in the summer of 1904.

CHAPTER III

Pre-World War I

They were American submariners ... a breed apart, even within their own Service. Their legacy was the courage of the brave men who went down in the first American submarines when others doubted they would come up.

John H. Dalton, Secretary of the Navy
May 14, 1994

Electric Boat continued to attract the interest of foreign governments. While the *Holland* was berthed at the Washington Navy Yard awaiting fair weather, the company sent a letter to Commander Ketsuro Narita, naval attache to His Imperial Majesty's Legation, offering a tour of the boat. Submarines were offered for $170,000 each for shipment to the Japanese Imperial Navy. Lieutenant Ide, who was central to an eventual contract between Electric Boat and Japan, was aboard for a dive on the *Holland* on April 5, 1900. Earlier that year, Electric Boat had refused to consider the sale of just one boat to the French government. "If we sold to them at all, they would have to order a number," wrote Frost.[1] The French remained interested—if Holland would guarantee a speed of 13 surface knots and at least 9 knots submerged with the new class of boats. At the same time, the company held discussions with Captain Henry R. Lemley of the U.S. Army about the introduction of "Holland submarine boats in some of the South American countries."[2] Following the *Holland's* March 14, 1900 trials for the U.S. Navy, more nations expressed interest: Turkey and Venezuela, followed by inquiries from Mexico, Sweden, Nor-

way, Denmark and Russia. In Great Britain, the House of Commons considered a submarine program and debated the merits of the *Holland*.

Electric Boat Company President Isaac L. Rice preferred selling to foreign governments, travelling to Europe for the express purpose of drumming up international business. Ironically, foreign sales would ultimately keep the company from sinking out of sight before the onset of the First World War.

A letter to Mexico's minister of war, dated July 9, 1900, referred to a meeting between President Diez and Electric Boat's counsel "in reference to building submarine boats for your government." The boats offered were "similar to those now under construction for the United States government." The agreement stipulated the cost to be "four hundred thousand dollars, Mexican," along with Electric Boat's pledge that the boats "have passed the experimental stage." Electric Boat also offered to allow representatives to see "the boats now in course of construction."[3]

This final enticement was a favorite of Isaac Rice, who was a master promoter. Representatives of countries around the world were continuously invited to trials, construction yards, launchings and submerged runs.

Photographs of the *Fulton* during the 1904 Navy trials in Narragansett Bay, Rhode Island. Top left, at rest in light condition, bow on, just before the trials began. Top right, partially trimmed. Middle left, just after firing a torpedo which is making a track toward the trees on the island. Middle right, light condition, full speed, bow view. Bottom left, surfaced condition after full speed submerged run. Bottom right, habitability trial at dockside after 12 hours of submergence.

As Electric Boat received inquiry after inquiry from foreign governments, heady optimism blossomed for a brisk international trade. Company secretary Elihu B. Frost, in a letter to a captain of the Royal Danish navy, said that it was the company's "intention to form sub-companies in every maritime nation in Europe."[4] A further strategy was to employ foreign agents abroad to secure contracts with their governments. Many prominent foreign nationals offered their services in this regard. Frost wrote to Rice in Heidelberg to inform him that they had been contacted "by a friend of yours who had important connections with the Russian Government." This "man of wealth and standing," who wished to remain anonymous (but who was

ELECTRIC BOAT COMPANY

Officials, workmen, dignitaries and guests attend the launching of a Russian submarine in Russia, approximately 1905. The vessel was constructed from an Electric Boat design. Representatives of the company are reportedly in this photograph.

probably the Marquis de Passano), was also a friend of the chief constructor of the Russian navy, as well as the minister of marine and finance. "The arrangement, if you approve," Frost wrote, "and I trust you will—is price $190,000, of which we receive net $170,000, less the discount on the Russian Government gold bonds of 4 percent ... The commission to our friend is to be paid in the same securities as we receive."[5]

The following day, Frost wrote to the financial agent of the Russian government in the United States agreeing to the price and terms for a period of six months. Specifications for the boats were included with the letter, along with the promise to "train a Russian crew in the operation of the boat." The Russians, Frost explained, would pay to transport the submarines to St. Petersburg. In a postscript, he made a final guarantee. "Should less than the guaranteed speed be made by any of the boats there is to be a deduction of $8,000 for each knot per boat."[6]

As early as October 27, 1900, Electric Boat concluded agreements with Vickers Sons and Maxim Ltd., the British shipbuilding company, which was granted a license to manufacture Holland submarines in accordance with Electric Boat patents. This relationship was to be a long one, lasting until 1939. Following the grant of this initial license, Rice authorized licensing and agent relationships with:

Societe Francaise de Sous–Marin (France)
Nevsky Works (Russia)
Emprezia Dimprairo Industrial Portugueza (Portugal)
De Schelde (Holland)
Whitehead Torpedo Company (Austria)
Deutsche Parsons Turbonia (Germany)

Additional arrangements were concluded with Canada, Chile, Denmark, Finland, Italy, Japan, Norway, Peru and Spain.

The Russo-Japanese War of 1904-1905 provided Electric Boat with business from both sides of the conflict. Russia and Japan had held discussions with the company since 1900. A letter dated August 27, 1901 described how Frost had met with the Russian naval attache and provided a demonstration. "They pronounced the *Fulton* a very fine boat and said that after they had seen her dive they would recommend their government to invest some money in Holland boats, and also that they would secure an invitation from the Minister of Marine for Mr. Rice to visit St. Petersburg. Mr. Frost says he has no fears of the result if Mr. Rice should go there."[7]

Rice did not travel to St. Petersburg, but sent a cable to Vickers in London on February 19, 1904 indicating the success of negotiations.

"Confidential, can sell *Fulton* for cash. Agent will not disclose principal. Believe moral effect sale will help us materially to secure larger appropriation this year. Have you any objection. Telegraph reply."[8]

Rice asked Vickers if they had any objection because Vickers and Electric Boat had already jointly entered negotiations with the Nevsky Works to construct boats in Russia. Vickers withdrew. Rice later thanked the British company for thinking "so well of the Russian business. I feel quite certain that when they see the *Fulton* operate, they will be in quite a hurry to get a large number of the boats."[9] On May 14, 1904, Basil Zaharoff, Electric Boat's European director, cabled Rice, informing him that the "*Madame* sold for two hundred and fifty thousand dollars"[10] to the Nevsky Works of Russia. The *Fulton* had been code-named the *Madame* to escape public detection of the transaction. Frank Cable described the succeeding events in an unpublished paper.[11]

"We did not desire public strictures on our action," Captain Cable wrote, "nor did we intend that Russia should be deprived of the boat (which was subject to usual tests) because of the war." He continued, "Our knowledge of American neutrality laws made us dubious of similar success in delivering the *Fulton* overseas as an ordinary shipment."

The company determined that the only way to deliver the *Fulton* to the Russians "was to smuggle her out of the country, and that involved an equal risk of her confiscation as contraband if any naval prowler discovered us." To this end, they chartered a steamer and a derrick craft to rendezvous somewhere off the tip of Long Island on the night of June 28, 1904. Under cover of darkness, a tugboat pulled alongside the *Fulton*, which was berthed at the New Suffolk proving station. The two crews secured the submarine to the tug and slowly made their way to the rendezvous in Gardiners Bay.

Some time after midnight, they sighted the steamer and derrick craft, and began the long and difficult process of slinging the *Fulton* in order to hoist her aboard the steamer. All work was accomplished in darkness, except for "an occasional lantern, used when absolutely necessary." At one point, the men sighted the "flame erupting from the funnels of a destroyer ... evidently heading in our direction."

"We feared our lantern had exposed our nefarious operations," Cable wrote, "and instantly came visions of heavy fines and imprisonment. But we had eluded naval sleuths before, and we did so now. The destroyer disappeared and welcome darkness shielded us again."

By 3:30 a.m., the *Fulton* was ready to be hoisted. It took 10 minutes to lift the 80-ton submarine onto its cradles aboard the steamer. "There," said Cable, "she was fastened down and swathed in canvas to guard against discovery from prying eyes ..." When all was secure, the

A Russian submarine being transported on a flatcar. The submarine is probably a "Type 8," a slightly more advanced design than the original *Holland.*

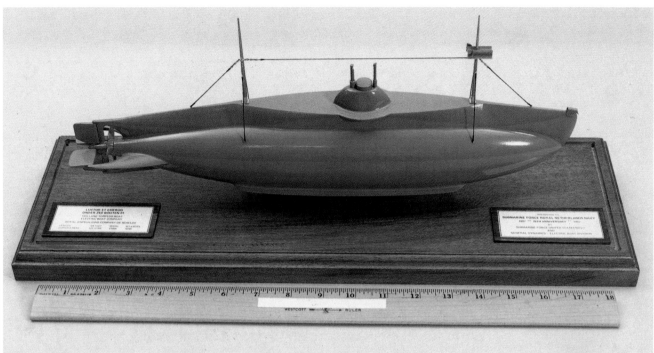

A model of the Dutch submarine *Luctor et Emergo*. The actual submarine was built by the Dutch shipbuilder, De Schelde. Electric Boat had a number of licensing agreements with companies around the world, principally in Europe.

steamer headed for the three-mile limit and the safety of the open seas. Cable returned to New Suffolk and later sailed to Russia with a special crew aboard a passenger steamer, but was careful not to place his name on the passenger manifest.

Once in Russia, Cable and his crew prepared the *Madame* (as the *Fulton* was renamed in Russia) for service in the Russian navy. Cable departed Petrograd on October 24, 1904, after meeting the tsar and declining an offer to accompany the *Madame* to Vladivostok, where it would join the war against Japan. Cable concluded "that New York City was safer."

There is no record that the *Madame* ever sank any Japanese ships, but upon returning to harbor one day, "she was mistaken for a Japanese torpedo boat by the fort gunners, who opened fire on her." Cable wrote that she was not hit, and that she "immediately submerged, staying on the bottom until night, and entered under the cover of darkness."

Captain Cable wasn't home for very long. In 1905, he supervised the assembly of five Holland-type submarines for the Japanese navy at the Yokosuka Dockyard. Serious negotiations with the Japanese were underway while the *Fulton* was being sold to Russia. Only 11 days following the sale of the *Fulton* (*Madame*) to Russia, a contract was negotiated with Japan, payment for which was determined to be:

"One-third (1/3) on the signing of the contract;
One-third (1/3) on shipment, against bill of lading;
One-third (1/3) after trials."[12]

The contract for construction was awarded to the Fore River Ship and Engine Company of Quincy, Massachusetts. Electric Boat was anxious to complete the work as soon as possible. Fore River was authorized to "work night and day, Sundays and holidays"[13] to meet the schedule which specified no more than 120 days, and preferably less than a hundred.

Vickers Sons and Maxim Ltd.

The Vickers company of Great Britain held an exceptional status in Electric Boat's foreign relationships. The agreement, undertaken in October 1900 between the two companies, required a term of 25 years and granted Vickers the right to license other companies or governments throughout all of Europe.[14] In return, Electric Boat received two-thirds of all profits so generated for a period of time and one-half thereafter. Great Britain became the largest customer of Vickers under this relationship. Five Holland-class submarines were built by Vickers between 1901 and 1903, 13 A-class boats between 1902 and 1905, 11 B-class boats between 1904 and 1906 and 32 C-class boats by 1910.[15] During the period while the U.S. Congress and U.S. Navy were indecisive about submarine development and crucial appropriations, the income from Vickers decided the difference between success and foreclosure.

As early as 1901, Electric Boat depended on payments from Vickers to meet growing obligations.[16] A year later, Rice wrote to Sigmund Loewe, a member of the Vickers board, describing the company's "unsettled" business as wholly dependent on uncertain government appropriations.[17] He also suggested to Loewe that he purchase 200 shares of Electric Boat stock at market price. The directors of Vickers had been purchasing Electric Boat stock for some time and held "a considerable minority holding."[18] The growing investment by Vickers led to disagreement, and by 1903, Vickers would debate Rice's own salary and deferred compensation.[19] On the eve of 1904, Rice wrote a seven–page explanation of why the £70,000 so far procured from Vickers would not be enough to ensure the survival of Electric Boat. The financial viability of Electric Boat remained in doubt throughout 1904 and 1905, and on December 6, 1905, Rice asked the Vickers Company for £10,000 to pay the company's January dividend.[20]

Electric Boat was still in weakened condition when the financial panic of 1907 erupted. Rice applied a considerable sum in personal funds to cover mounting debts, but still needed assistance from Vickers.[21] On January 7, 1907, Rice reported to Vickers that "we are extremely short of funds." He estimated that another £10,000 would allow them to operate through July, by which time he hoped the government would appropriate $1 million to purchase additional submarines. Rice noted that Vickers had just "received a new order for five boats," and requested that Electric Boat be allowed an advance on these boats. To underscore the urgency of his request, Rice concluded by saying he "should consider it a special favor if you would cable me your permission."[22]

Assistance from Vickers arrived promptly then and on several more occasions over the next several years. The constant need for funds would eventually cause friction between the two companies. On November 30, 1909, Rice received a curious cablegram from the Vickers Company regarding the membership of the Electric Boat board of directors:

> "London.Nov.30 – Have dummies retired and responsible directors been named in their place? Vickers.

To which Rice replied:

> "New York.Nov.30 – Cable incomprehensible. Name alleged dummies. Rice." [23]

Vickers must have realized that their cable had upset Rice, and sought to explain in another cable that by "dummies" they meant directors who held a position on the board but had no "serious financial interest of their own." Rice assured Vickers that all of Electric Boat's directors had serious financial interest and were committed to the company.[24]

Fulton vs. the *Protector*

In early June 1904, just prior to the clandestine shipping of the *Fulton* to Russia, Navy trials were conducted off Newport, Rhode Island demonstrating that the new design performed exceptionally well. Rice was enthusiastic on June 23, 1904 when he wrote that the report of the naval board was "very favorable" and that they recommended a "contract for three boats 75 feet, one boat 100 feet, 850,000 dollars in all."[25] Meanwhile, the Lake Company, led by Simon Lake, Electric Boat's principal competitor, had sold a submarine, the *Protector*, to Russia and had secured a contract to build five more for the tsar.[26] Electric Boat had learned a great deal about the Lake Company's Russian contract through Simon Lake's chief engineer, who was an informant. Within days of transferring the information, the engineer applied for a position at Electric Boat.

Rice was openly contemptuous of Simon Lake's method of business.

> "You will readily perceive that a responsible company cannot compete with an irresponsible one that will make all sorts of extravagant claims and guarantees in order to obtain the first payment. That this has been the policy of the Lake Company I have, on good authority. Mr. Lake, himself, I am told, has said to someone of his own people who were questioning his method of guaranteeing impossible things, that he thought it good business to get 50% down— never mind what happened afterwards."[27]

The Peace-making Terror of the Seas

The October 1904 issue of *Women's Home Companion* contained an animated description of the *Fulton* undergoing trials earlier in June. The *Fulton*'s challenges included remaining submerged for 12 hours at dockside:

> "Another test was of habitability. With cards, cigars, food, and such comforts, nine men locked themselves in the steel hull, and sank her in twenty feet of water alongside a Newport dock, where she remained over twelve hours, and only during the last hour was it found necessary to replenish the vitiated air."[28]

Tough men they must have been to survive 12 hours of cigar smoke in very cramped quarters.

The ever-intrepid President Theodore Roosevelt goes on a three-hour dive below the surface in August 1905. The drawing depicts the president making inspections and trying his hand at steering.

The article included a firsthand account of an attack run at a target. Running only 12 feet below the surface, the *Fulton* was able to keep an eye on the surface world through a new innovation known as a periscope. The captain ordered a further dive to 20 feet, rendering the periscope useless. A compass became the sole navigation tool.

> "Twenty minutes go by, and the commander motions to his aide at the diving-gear. The boat approaches the surface, lifts the lens of the periscope out of the water, and resumes the horizontal, while the captain searches the periscope. Nothing but haze, and a dim line of horizon on which are a few sails and columns of smoke—nothing of that doomed battleship. Again the boat sinks, and goes on for another twenty minutes, and again she rises for a peep, to no results—she has gone but half the distance, and it is too soon to expect them. Thirty minutes later she rises again, and nothing shows; but another peep ten minutes later discloses an anchored boat flying a flag, and soon the other is seen.
>
> "Now the torpedo tube in the bow is manned, and the disturbance of trim must be counteracted by the inclination of the diving-rudder. The torpedo carried in the tube is always ready; all that is required to discharge it is to open the bow port and to eject compressed air into the breech. The torpedo does the rest."[29]

Rice described "a most satisfactory audience with the President of the United States" in January 1904. His impression was that President Theodore Roosevelt was "favorable to submarine boats."[30] On August 26, 1905, President Roosevelt demonstrated both his interest and courage by taking a three–hour dive in the new *Plunger*, named after its predecessor of 1895. The president was not the first of his family to make such a dive. His daughter, Alice Roosevelt, had taken a submarine run in September 1903.[31] Electric Boat successfully used publicity from both dives to further their cause both at home and abroad.

John P. Holland Leaves Electric Boat

As the designs and technology of Electric Boat submarines advanced, John Holland became isolated from the company he had founded. The arrival of talented engineers and designers such as Captain Cable and Lawrence Spear steadily moved Holland further away from the mainstream of Electric Boat activity. Holland was unaware, for example, of Electric Boat's negotiations with the Vickers Company until some time near agreement.

Holland and Rice clashed repeatedly over issues they considered to be fundamental. Holland wanted to perfect his invention and Rice wanted to sell boats to customers. Rice said that

no person, not even Holland, could build a submarine by himself.[32] Faced with the fact that the business had moved out of his hands and into those of engineers and managers, Holland left the company in 1904 following the expiration of his five-year contract.[33]

Tensions between the two men continued after Holland's departure. In late 1904, Rice wrote Holland to say that he had not told one of the company captains that he was paying Holland "$10,000 per year for the use of your name, inasmuch as the statement itself is an absurd one." As a reminder, Rice continued, "As you are well aware, we long ago acquired the legal right to the exclusive use of your name."[34] Rice quickly scuttled John Holland's later attempts to design and build submarines claiming possible patent infringement.

U.S. Navy Orders Four Submarines

On the strength of the *Fulton's* performance in her 1904 trials, the government Board of Inspection and Survey recommended that Electric Boat be granted the year's entire appropria-

The *Cuttlefish* under construction at the Fore River shipyard. Electric Boat did not build a submarine at its own shipyard for the U.S. Navy until 1934. Coincidentally, that submarine was named the *Cuttlefish* as well.

Launching of the *Cuttlefish* (B-2) at the Fore River shipyard in Quincy, Mass. on September 1, 1906. The *Cuttlefish* was one of a group of four submarines built for Electric Boat at Fore River and delivered to the Navy in 1907.

ELECTRIC BOAT COMPANY

tion of $850,000, an increase from the $500,000 appropriated in 1903. Electric Boat was awarded contracts to construct four submarines.[35] It is not universally known that Electric Boat did not build a submarine for the United States at its own yards until 1934. Many of the boats in these early years were built at the Fore River Ship and Engine Company in Quincy, Massachusetts, the same yard which produced the five submarines shipped to Japan during the Russo-Japanese War of 1904-1905. The four new submarines, all built at Fore River, were named *Octopus, Cuttlefish, Viper* and *Tarantula*. They were delivered to the Navy in 1907.

1906 was quite favorable for the Electric Launch Company (or ELCO), an affiliate (along with Electro-Dynamic) of the Electric Boat Company. ELCO received a contract for six self-bailing, self-righting, 34-foot motor-driven boats for the Life Saving Service (which eventually became part of the U.S. Coast Guard). ELCO would ultimately build 120 of these rescue boats for the U.S. government.[36]

The *Lake* versus the *Octopus*

Among the submarines built at the Fore River Ship and Engine Company yard under the 1905 contract was the *Octopus*. Known as a C-class boat, the *Octopus* was larger and faster than the original Holland class and the previous three B-class submarines built at Fore River. Like the *Fulton*, the *Octopus* was originally built as a prototype to demonstrate superior design and performance. The customer that Electric Boat most wanted to impress was the U.S. Navy, that was preparing to award submarine contracts from an appropriation of $3 million approved by Congress. The new C-class design was 105 feet long, with a 14-foot beam, and displacement of 270 tons. On the surface the *Octopus* could attain a speed of 10 1/2 knots from twin propellers, each driven by a gasoline engine capable of producing 250 horsepower. Two 150-horsepower electric motors propelled the boat while it was submerged with a top speed of 9 knots. The *Octopus* was equipped with two 18–

The Electric Boat Co. draftsman gather for a group photograph shot in 1912. Electric Boat's design force was, and still is, a unique assemblage of talent and experience.

inch torpedo tubes and met the Navy's performance goal of being able to dive and cruise to 200 feet.[37]

The Lake Company was equally hopeful of obtaining the Navy contracts and built the *Lake* to showcase their latest design. The *Octopus* and the *Lake* were pitted one against the other in a 10-day series of rigorous Navy trials in May 1907 off Newport, Rhode Island. Among the tests was the requirement for a submarine with a full crew to remain submerged for 24 hours. The *Octopus'* performance was impressive. The Navy board's opinion was unanimous that "the *Octopus* is the superior boat presented for tests; and furthermore, that she is equal to the best boat now owned by the United States and under contract."[38]

The large payments were eagerly anticipated by Electric Boat to shore up their troubled finances. Anonymous sources—some of whom were suspected to be Lake supporters—spread rumors that Electric Boat had bribed members of Congress, journalists and naval officers in 1907 to get the contracts. The charges were similar to accusations which had surfaced in 1903. Both investigations completely cleared Electric Boat of any wrongdoing. Rice suggested a sinister motive

behind the rumors, claiming that Simon Lake was behind the "great muss, undoubtedly in the hope that by making himself so obnoxious we shall eventually have to buy him out."[39]

While the Lake Company did receive an order for one submarine, Rice rather gleefully noted nearly two years later that the Simon Lake boat was "only 28 percent completed," whereas Electric Boat had completed seven submarines in the same time period,[40] all of which were built at Fore River.

Three of the boats in this wave of construction were even larger and more sophisticated than the *Octopus*, part of a group known as the D-class. These submarines were 135 feet long and displaced 337 tons. Two 300-horsepower engines propelled the boats on the surface at 13 knots; while submerged, the new designs could make 9 1/2 knots from two 165-horsepower motors.[41]

The Diesel Engine and NELSECO

Finding suitable engines was a constant challenge during the early years of submarine development. After the disastrous attempt to harness steam power in the old *Plunger*, the company developed its own gasoline engine. Gasoline fumes and engine exhaust, however, caused "much discomfort and hardship."[42]

> *"Many a man was led out from his station at the throttle, or from some other engineer's station, to a place where he could be revived with smelling salts and fresh air. Sometimes a man would collapse where he stood, completely unconscious. And gas intoxication generally left the victim with a splitting headache lasting for hours. The first year of this experience was not so bad, but eventually the strongest men would 'soften up,' and then submarine duty for electricians and engineers became exceedingly tough."*[43]

The author of this description, who served on submarines as early as 1921 and was familiar with even earlier classes, wrote that the "early gasoline engine was a creature of great contrariness and unreliability." The engines were so loud that they were often referred to as "rock crushers."[44]

By 1909, the diesel engine, invented by Rudolph Diesel in 1892, was starting to appear in Europe for marine use. The combination of higher efficiency and reduced vapor volatility was very attractive and Electric Boat immediately saw its potential for submarines. Through Vickers, Electric Boat secured a license to manufacture diesel engines and prepared to build 12 of them at the Fore River yard.[45]

It soon became apparent that the Fore River facility would be unable to complete the work, so Electric Boat decided to build a plant to manufacture the engines along with other technical machinery such as air compressors, pumps and torpedo tubes. Not all company directors supported the decision.[46] Money was so tight that Captain Cable and other employees of the technical department had to raise money of their own to start construction of the new plant.[47] Cable became general manager of the new subsidiary, the New London Ship and Engine Company, or NELSECO, and Spear was named president. The 12 diesel engines which were started at Fore River were completed at the NELSECO plant in Groton, Connecticut, on the site which would later become home to Electric Boat's own shipyard as well. The first two engines were installed on the *E-1* and *E-2*, but "were a far cry from the perfection dreamed of by a long list of American submarine engineers."[48] New crankshafts had to be designed and manufactured to replace the original design, which was too small. NELSECO searched for better engines and obtained a license to manufacture the German MAN (*Maschinefabrik Augsburg Nuremberg*) diesel engine.[49] This engine proved to be far superior. These were installed aboard the *Seawolf* and *Nautilus* in 1913, designated as *H-1* and *H-2*.

Submarine Development from 1900 to 1914

Submarines were being taken more seriously by governments and navies around the world because of the extraordinary technical progress made in such a short time. In a 1906 paper delivered to the Society of Naval Architects and Marine Engineers, Lawrence Spear predicted that in two years "boats of over 500 tons displacement will certainly be completed, and in three or four years a displacement from 700 to 800 tons is probable." He also said that submarines would achieve a "surface speed of 15 knots, with a radius of 2,000 [nautical miles] knots at that speed" and a "submerged speed of from 9 to 10 knots."[50] Nine years later before the same society, Spear contrasted the designs for 1900 and 1914.[51]

	1900	1914
Length	53'10"	230'6"
Beam	10'3"	21'6"
Surface displacement, tons	67	633
Submerged displacement, tons	75	912
Horsepower, surface	50	2,000

	1900	1914
Surface speed, knots	6	17
Horsepower, submerged	50	980
Submerged speed, knots	5.5	10.75
Radius of action–surface, NM	200	3,000
Torpedo tubes	1	8

In the same paper, Spear presented the following comparison of improvement in propulsion power:[52]

	1900	1914
Horsepower, main engines	50	2,000
Pounds per horsepower	78	48
Fuel consumption, pounds per horsepower	0.74	0.50
Horsepower, electric motors	50	980
Pounds per horsepower	57	48
Pounds per hp of storage battery	909	216

Submarine design through this period of rapid improvement was a combination of design engineering and trial and error by builders and submariners. By 1912, however, most submarine developers would agree to the following qualities, which were included in a report assumed to be written by Spear:

> *"In the design of a submarine boat, there are many qualities to be considered. It all depends upon how much importance is attached to certain qualities, in order to determine the resulting design or type. The most important of these qualities are*

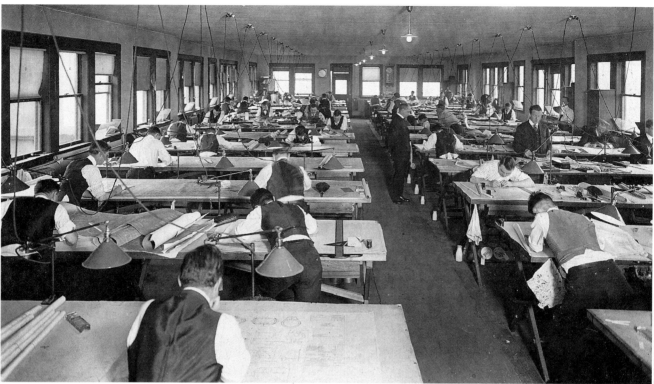

The engine drawing room at Electric Boat during World War I. Today's design force uses the latest CAD (computer-aided design) tools and is at the forefront of using virtual reality as an advanced design tool.

submerged speed and radius of action, surface speed and radius of action, armament, considerations of strength of hull and safety, and means of control. If undue importance is attached to any one of these qualities, the others must suffer in a proportionate degree."[53]

Besides the substitution of diesel power for gasoline-powered surface operation, Electric Boat made improvements to each new class of submarines. D-class boats were designed with four torpedo tubes, a practice which continued for boats built during World War I. D-class boats also benefited from bulkheads constructed in the hull for greater rigidity and safety, and the addition of a second periscope. E-class boats introduced the use of horizontal bow rudders, which helped to maintain stability during dives and underwater navigation.[54] Spear designed a partial double hull as early as 1913, a concept that would provide more reserve buoyancy, greater surface speed and a more comfortable environment for crews.

Advertisements which appeared in *Fred T. Jane's Fighting Ships* attest to the growth of Electric Boat during the period. A 1912 advertisement noted that Electric Boat had built or was building 152 submarines.[55] In 1914, another advertisement raised the number to 300 submarines, crossing out the number 250 which had appeared in an earlier issue.[56] These proclamations further boasted that Electric Boat or its

licensees had built over half of all the world's submarine vessels. The 1912 edition of *Jane's Fighting Ships* contained a section on submarines built by Electric Boat which concluded with a promise of greater things to come:

> *"It may also be mentioned that the Electric Boat Company has under way a design of even greater size and speed than the foregoing. It is reported that the displacement approaches 1200 tons submerged, and the speed 20 knots on the surface."*[57]

Early Submarine Operations

The U.S. Navy acquired 25 submarines between 1900 and 1914, with 16 delivered between 1908-1914. Though not a large fleet, the presence of the American submarine fleet was beginning to be felt around the world. The A- and B-class boats—some of Electric Boat's earliest— saw service in the Philippine Islands. The boats were transported there on colliers (coal ships) and launched overboard in Manila Bay. In 1913, five C-class boats were ordered to the Panama Canal for active patrol duty. Boats from the F, H and K classes saw service on the Pacific Coast, with some of the F-class boats stationed in Honolulu.[58]

Coastal defense of the continental United States and its island possessions became increasingly important in the early years of the

20th century. In 1906, Lawrence Spear wrote an 18-page booklet titled *"The Submarine: An Economical Coast Defense"* which argued the case for submarines in United States military strategy. The booklet also contained a 12-page appendix representing the official report of Vice Admiral Fournier of the French navy, detailing the highly successful deployment of submarines in French naval maneuvers conducted in 1906.

Among Spear's conclusions were criticisms of defense spending practices and a revealing look at how relatively modest the American military might have appeared in 1906:

> *"[These] are actual facts taken from official documents with no intermixture of theory or guess work, and they show (First) that at the present moment we have, after the expenditure of one hundred and nineteen millions of dollars very incomplete protection. (Second) That to complete the material parts of the fixed defenses alone considered necessary by the responsible and competent experts who have carefully investigated the subject, will require an additional expenditure of at least $75,580,916.*
>
> *"(Third) That in order to render these defenses effective an army of 57,388 officers and men must be maintained for this sole purpose at an actual annual charge to the country of about $68,000,000. (Fourth) That even assuming the willingness of Congress and the country to sanction the increased expenditure, it will be a matter of many years before the projects are completed and the fortifications manned, and that in the interval the country is practically in a helpless condition. The fortifications at present are really worse than useless, since they serve to give a false sense of security which is in no way justified."[59]*

Spear pointed out that 150 torpedo boats were ordered while submarine boats were still considered experimental. "Since that time," Spear continued, "the submarine boat has been developed into a pronounced and practical success and is now accepted everywhere as a superior weapon to the surface boat."[60] Spear contended:

1) *They are mobile and "can be easily and quickly moved from place to place to meet changing conditions."*
2) *They cost less to build and less to maintain.*
3) *A sufficient submarine force could be built in one-fifth the time it would take to complete the present fixed coast defenses.*
4) *Fortifications "require 17 times as many officers and men" to protect the coast.[61]*

In conclusion, Spear's arguments were seductive:

> *"The plain question then is, are we to spend $75,000,000 more on our coast defenses and to accept an annual charge of the sum of $69,000,000 manning and maintaining them, getting for all this*

incomplete protection, when another course is open to us which offers complete protection at an expenditure of not more than $35,000,000 with an annual charge for manning and maintenance of less than $7,000,000?...

> *"France, with a small coastline to defend, has about 100 submarines built and building, as against 12 for the United States with an enormous coastline to say nothing of its island possessions and the Panama Canal."[62]*

Submarine Service at the Panama Canal 1913–1914

In 1913, relations between the United States and Japan became sufficiently strained that the U.S. Navy began "to take definite steps to guard against any untoward action by Japan."[63] The Panama Canal was nearly complete, and strategies for protection from attack became one of America's highest military priorities. The Navy elected to deploy its modest and largely untried submarine force for the defensive action. Submarine Division One, which consisted of the *C-1* (the *Octopus*), *C-2*, *C-3*, *C-4* and *C-5*, departed from Norfolk, Virginia under sealed orders. The submarine force was accompanied by the tender *Castine* and the coaling collier *Mars*, both of which towed the submarines into the Atlantic. Most of the officers and men realized that a significant mission was planned since the force carried provisions for six months.

Once in the open seas, the orders were unsealed and read by Lieutenant (junior grade) Richard S. Edwards, who commanded the expedition:[64]

> *"To proceed to Colon, Panama, without stopping at any port en route, there to remove the engines and batteries from the submarines, the hulls hauled up on the beach, the engines, batteries, and hulls placed on flat cars, transported across the Isthmus by rail to Balboa, there to be reassembled for services in the Pacific in waters adjacent to the Panama Canal—for the purpose of repelling possible attacks by the Japanese Navy."[65]*

A few days later, these orders were changed as tensions subsided between Japan and the United States, and the submarines were diverted to Guantanamo Bay, Cuba. Eventually, they were ordered to the Canal Zone on December 7, 1913 to "stand guard on the Atlantic side of the Isthmus of Panama." Most notable was the fact that all five submarines completed the 600-mile journey under their own power.[66] Although they saw no combat action, their presence and ability to perform was in itself a bold statement of American resolve.

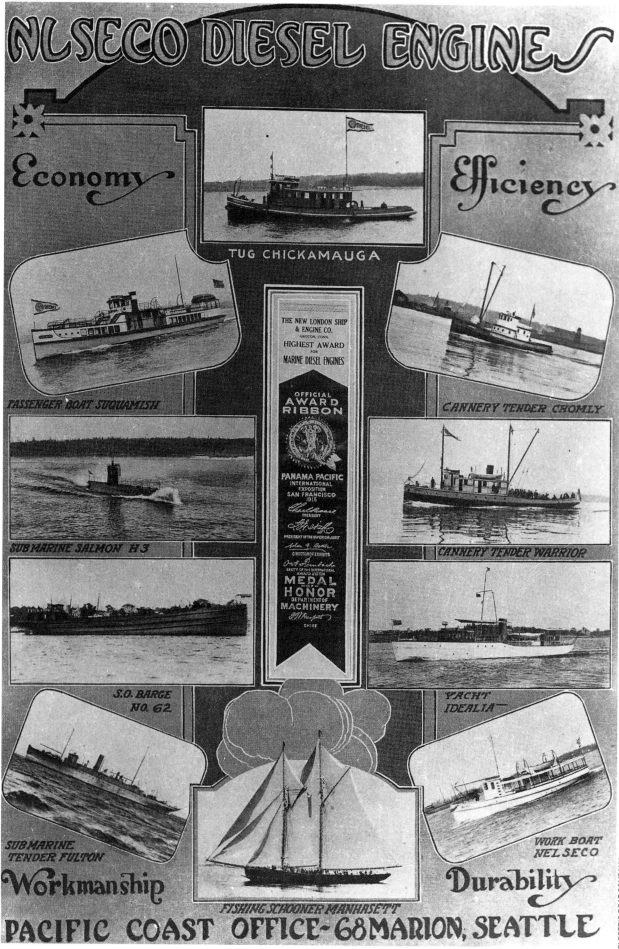

An advertisement (ca. 1915) for NLSECO (sic) diesel engines shows their versatility. NELSECO was formed by Electric Boat employees and later absorbed by the company.

CHAPTER IV

World War I

*A*n intense spirit of great rush pervaded us, body and soul. It was a race
against death and the submarine.[1]

British Officer at ELCO Plant, 1915

It was August of 1914. The uneasy peace of Europe had been shattered and her nations had begun to assemble and deploy modern weapons of war—the airplane, the tank, the armored car and the submarine. Even before the lethal Western Front had been established, the German submarine *U-9* was out on patrol. While surfacing to recharge her batteries, her crew sighted three British cruisers. The *U-9* immediately submerged and maneuvered into position to attack the nearest cruiser, the HMS *Aboukir*.

> "From within 500 yards of this target, she let go one torpedo. To escape the concussion of the explosion, her skipper dove deeper and then came up to take a look. The Aboukir was sinking fast!
>
> "While the other cruisers stood by for rescue work, the skipper of the U-boat turned to the HMS Hogue and from less than 300 yards hit her with two torpedoes. According to an eyewitness, the victim 'seemed to give one jump right out of the water and go straight down.' Like fate met the HMS Cressy which blew up and sank slowly after a strike from the undersea boat's last torpedo."[2]

Within a single hour, the *Aboukir*, the *Hogue* and the *Cressy* lie on the ocean floor claiming 1,370 lives, all victims of torpedo attacks by the deadly German U-boat.[3] Great Britain, an island nation relying heavily on shipping and, thus, freedom of the sea lanes for her survival, was in a panic. Submarine warfare had become a reality.

Lost in the tumult following the onset of war was the death of John P. Holland only two weeks after the start of hostilities. Although some historians maintain that among his principal motivations in designing submarines was to help free Ireland from British rule, Holland repeatedly stated that he viewed his invention as a peacemaker. He believed that, realizing how deadly and effective this instrument of modern war could be, nations would stop fighting each other. Unfortunately, very few people prior to World War I were convinced of the submarine's effectiveness.

Germany had 27 submarines at the beginning of World War I. Only 20 of these boats were active with just 16 additional boats authorized or under construction—an insufficient fleet to be used as a primary strategy.[4] By the end of 1914, the British and French had halted the Germans' advance along the Western Front, where four years of warfare characterized by a high attrition rate would be waged over mere yards of territory. Almost concurrently, Britain had succeeded in blockading Germany's northern coast, effectively cutting off the country's sea lanes to the rest of the world.[5] However, German military strategists realized that, despite Britain's naval superiority, her navy and merchant fleets were vulnerable to attacks by stealthy German U-boats. By autumn of 1914, Germany had already sunk about 100,000 tons of merchant shipping, and had constructed submarine bases at Ostend and Zeebrugge on the coast of Flanders. The British retaliated by mining and patrolling the English Channel, and by deploying a series of nets designed to impede U-boat traffic.[6]

Germany's Strategy Changes— Submarines Used to Strangle Britain

In the early months of the war, Germany's primary strategy was to attack warships. In February 1915, Germany declared all waters surrounding Britain and Ireland, including the English Channel, to be a "war zone." The German navy "announced that they would sink without warning all British merchant-men encountered."[7] Within four months, German U-boats destroyed 500,000 tons of merchant shipping. In the following six months, they sank almost 1 million tons and another 700,000 tons during the first four months of 1916. By 1917, the tonnage lost would reach 9 million. American and British shipyards working together were able to replace only 2 million tons.[8]

Britain was desperate. Germany's strategy to starve Britain out of the war before the United States could enter had begun to show signs of succeeding. Britain rushed to acquire submarines for her own defense. Two boats that Electric Boat had been assembling for Chile at a Seattle shipyard were transferred to Britain, spirited over the Canadian border just three hours before Britain declared war.[9] The United States remained officially neutral. As late as January 1917, President Woodrow Wilson proclaimed, "There will be no war. This country does not intend to become involved in a war."[10] When Britain ordered 20 submarines from the company, Electric Boat shipped parts for 10 to the Vickers shipyard in Montreal and built 10 others at the Fore River shipyard in Quincy, Massachusetts. The 10 Fore River-built boats were not delivered until the United States' declaration of war on April 6, 1917.

Vickers assembled its 10 submarines in a record six months.[11] During this same period, Electric Boat built eight submarines for the Italian navy and 12 for the Russian navy. The Russian boats were also "shipped knocked-down" for final assembly in Russia.[12] These boats saw action in both the Baltic and Adriatic seas.[13]

The 10 boats assembled by Vickers for Great Britain were deployed by the British navy in the Baltic and Mediterranean seas, making the Atlantic crossing under their own power.[14] The first U.S. Navy submarine to cross the Atlantic under its own power was the *E-1 Skipjack* in 1917.[15]

The British submarines saw considerable action in Allied campaigns on the Gallipoli Peninsula in April 1915 to recapture Constantinople. The British submarine *H-1* successfully evaded the coastal defenses around Constantinople. On a mission similar to that of today's U.S. Navy SEALs, the *H-1's* commander swam toward the famous Galata Bridge, towing an explosive charge behind him. Unfortunately, his efforts were for naught; although he was able to secure the charge to the bridge, it did not explode. Making the best of an otherwise failed mission, the *H-1* destroyed a troop train within range of its shellfire on its return trip.[16]

ELCO Joins the Fight Against German U-boats

Soon after Germany had declared the waters around Britain a "war zone," Henry R. Sutphen, a vice president of Electric Boat and involved in the direction of ELCO, proposed building gasoline motorboats as submarine chasers equipped with a 13-pound rapid-fire gun and depth charges. Sutphen advanced two proposals—a 50-foot model capable of 25 knots, or an 80-foot design capable of 19 knots.[17] When asked by the British how many he could build in a year, Sutphen replied 50. The representative from Britain said that his government would consider the offer. ELCO had never built more than six boats of those dimensions in a year. "Well, I had to think things over myself," Sutphen wrote, " and pretty carefully, too."[18]

Within days of the ELCO proposal, the British government was prepared to award a contract if a way could be found to circumvent American neutrality laws. ELCO repeated the Electric Boat strategy by locating shipyards in Quebec and Montreal where the boats could be assembled from components shipped from ELCO's yard in Bayonne, New Jersey. On April 9, 1915, the contract was signed and work began. A British naval lieutenant, at the ELCO yard when work began, later wrote a booklet about the new subchasers, *Hounding the Hun from the Seas...* . Work on the subchasers moved swiftly and smoothly. The lieutenant reported that "by the first of May we had the 'master' or pattern boat in frame."[19]

One week later, a German U-boat, the *U-20* commanded by *Kapitänleutnent* Walther Schweiger, torpedoed and sank the Cunard passenger liner *Lusitania*, killing 1,198 passengers and crew, of which 124 were Americans.[20] Coincidentally, Sutphen was dining at Delmonico's in New York City with a British official when news of the sinking spread through the popular restaurant. The official urgently queried Sutphen on how many more subchasers ELCO could build. "I told him that I would guarantee to build a boat a day for so long a period as the Admiralty might care to name," Sutphen said.[21]

The killing of what were perceived to be innocents horrified people worldwide. America gasped at the enormity of the catastrophe; Germany held her breath that this attack would bring the U.S. into the fray; and Britain rioted at the thought that the unthinkable had been perpetrated against their citizens on one of their luxury passenger liners. Headlines were unanimous as to the disaster's monstrous impact:

- *LUSITANIA TORPEDOED AND SUNK: WORLD AGHAST AT GERMANY'S BIGGEST CRIME*
- *LUSITANIA'S ENORMOUS DEATH TOLL: HUNS MOST COWARDLY CRIME*
- *LUSITANIA SUNK WITHOUT WARNING: 1,300 DIE AS LINER GOES TO THE BOTTOM*[22]

Within days of the *Lusitania* disaster—as the bodies of the victims were being laid to rest in mass graves at Queenstown—the British ordered 500 additional subchasers to be built by November 15, 1916, putting Sutphen's claim to the test. After signing the new contract on July 9, 1915, ELCO had been given 501 days to complete what many thought to be the impossible. (The accompanying list of materials provides some perspective as to the magnitude of the undertaking.)

Sutphen was reasonably confident in his company. ELCO had been experimenting with standardized construction of boats for a number

---

List of Materials Used in the Patrol Boats

LUMBER

Oak (Keels, Frames, etc.) feet, B.M.	1,960,720
Yellow Pine (Planking, etc.) feet, B.M.	2,225,830
Ash, Pine, etc. (Joiner Work) feet, B.M.	3,849,500
Total Lumber Used, feet, B.M.	8,036,050

METALS, PIPING, ETC.

Gal. Iron Forgings, pounds	1,272,875
Bronze Castings, pounds	560,200
Steel Bulkheads, pounds	578,600
Lead Pipe, pounds	28,500
Galv. Pipe, feet	56,450
Brass, Pipe, feet	109,450
Copper Tubing, feet	14,850
Sea Cocks	4,950
Valves	10,450
Rail Fittings	66,000

ELECTRICAL FITTINGS

Conduit, feet	100,650
Wire, feet	535,150
Electric Lamps	25,850
Searchlights	550
Storage Batteries	22,000

BOAT EQUIPMENT

Fresh Water Tanks, 1100 gallons' capacity	110,000
Gasoline Tanks, 2200 gallons' capacity	1,351,900
Linoleum, yards	11,550
Canvas, yards	32,300
Manila Rope, etc., feet	611,050
Bronze Wire Rope, feet	15,000
Galv. Wire Rope, feet	310,000
Ventilators	11,550
Deck Pumps	550
Portlights	16,500
Refrigerators	550

Iron Ladders	1,650
Sinks and Wash Basins	1,650
Toilets	1,100
Engine Telegraphs	550
Pipe Berths	2,200
Name Plates	7,150
Life Preservers	6,600
Brass Deck Plates	4,950
Gasoline Stoves	550
Life Boats	550
Sailing Lights	2,200
Oil Lamps	3,850
Canvas Covers	13,200
Cushions and Mattresses	6,050
Fire Extinguishers	2,200

PAINT, VARNISH, ETC.

White Lead, pounds	102,700
Putty, pounds	83,035
Marine Glue, pounds	34,000
Caulking Cotton, pounds	27,634
Paints and Varnish, gallons	47,475

FASTENINGS, ETC.

Brass Escutcheon Pins, pounds	1,527
Galv. Iron Rod, pounds	24,200
Galv. Nails, pounds	104,190
Copper Nails and Burrs, pounds	250,996
Galv. Washers and Clinch Rings, pounds	401,401
Galv. Screws, gross	12,266
Brass Screws, gross	23,606
Iron Bolts and Nuts	979,504
Wood Plugs	3,705,429
Brass Bolts and Nuts	24,944

FREIGHT IN CARS AND TONNAGE

Arrived in Bayonne	797 cars, pounds 27,434,200
Shipped to Canada	1,144 cars, pounds 40,632,000
Total	1,941 cars, pounds 68,066,200

---

of years. Trainloads of material were sent to the two Canadian shipyards for assembly. The British naval lieutenant assigned to the drafting room in Bayonne found himself organizing operations in Levis, Quebec among a group of French-speaking workers.[23] He described the process of designing and prototyping fabrication in Bayonne what was to be assembled in Quebec:

"Each separate and individual part, from the keel to the little truck at the masthead, was designed, tried out, changed and changed again, until it fitted perfectly. It was then detailed and given a symbol, indicating where, and in what particular boat, it was to go.

"Our Canadian workmen were divided into small groups, each group assigned to a definite operation. The boat parts would come up to use labeled, so that assembling them was much like the working out of a jig-saw puzzle. A 'master key' or chart was kept at Bayonne, with each step of our progress constantly checked up. In that way our work was completely standardized.

"An intense spirit of great rush pervaded us, body and soul. It was a race against death and the submarine."[24]

History repeats itself, even in business. The lessons of organization ELCO's management learned during the fevered rush to build hundreds of submarine chasers in World War I would prove useful again in building PT boats to serve in World War II.

The finished submarine chasers—or motor launches (MLs) as they came to be known—were loaded on railroad cars and shipped by sea from Halifax for the journey to England. Thirteen days before the deadline in November 1916, ELCO completed its 550th submarine chaser. The company then began production of subchasers for the French and Italian navies. ELCO was re-

D-class submarines built and delivered to the U.S. Navy in 1909-10.

Interior shot of World War I submarine showing the air manifold.

The master control station and periscope of a World War I submarine.

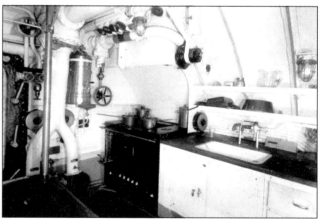

The galley with stove, sink and cooking utensils.

Engine room, looking aft.

Forward end of the engine room on starboard side.

Hand steering gear on left with gyro compass just below.

Officers quarters aboard World War I era submarine.

Electric Boat rescue tank surfaces after engaging submerged submarine.

Torpedo room, looking forward. Berths line both sides.

U.S. submarines *L-1* to *L-4* in left foreground and British submarines *H-11* to *H-17*.

sponsible for launching a grand total of 722 MLs during World War I.

Electric Boat Achieves Financial Success

ELCO's $20 million contract with Great Britain spurred considerable interest on Wall Street in ELCO's parent company, Electric Boat. The shipbuilders projected profits of nearly $15 million and Electric Boat's stock began to rise after many difficult years even before the war.[25] In 1910, the company suspended payment of dividends, a dangerous signal to investors, and it was widely known that both Rice and Frost had loaned considerable sums of their own money to the struggling company.[26] The U.S. Navy had not placed sufficient orders to bring security to the organization, while royalties from such foreign interests as Vickers barely kept the company afloat. The beginning of hostilities quickly ended those years of struggle.

A *Wall Street Journal* article of May 19, 1915 reported that Electric Boat's "common and preferred stock have experienced a steady advance ever since the attention of the public was called by the war to the securities of submarine manufacturing companies."[27] The following table illustrates the keen interest that developed:

	Common Stock	Preferred Stock
Bid 12/17/14	$24	$40
Bid 05/17/15	$73	$98

The article also reported that the company "is now practically without floating debt," and that dividends were expected to resume. Though the U.S. Navy had not yet placed any new orders for submarines, it was expected that "any increase in difficulties with European countries will be followed quickly by the placing of contracts." Investors anticipated that Electric Boat, identified as "the largest submarine manufacturing concern in this country," would be awarded more contracts from the Allied powers.

When the contract granted by Great Britain for ELCO subchasers was signed in July 1915, Electric Boat stock soared to $186 a share.[28] Isaac Rice, Electric Boat's first president, was in failing health and sold 16,000 of his shares at that price for more than $1 million. (Sales of his stock throughout this period were estimated to have secured profits of between $1.5 million and $2.5 million for the aging investor.[29])

In August 1915, Rice resigned as president of Electric Boat, dying that November. Henry R. Carse, a one-time vice president of the Hanover National Bank, succeeded Rice as president. Carse had been named a director of Electric Boat in 1904 and a financial advisor to the company. Ironically, Carse had resigned as a director in 1913, confiding to fellow director Frost that "this company can't pull through."[30] After becoming president in 1915, Carse would lead Electric Boat for 27 eventful years.

Submarine Boat Corporation Formed

The rapid rise in Electric Boat's stock during 1915 prompted company directors to organize a holding company to stabilize and protect its stock. The board of the submarine manufacturer became fearful that an increasing number of shares, and thus votes, would end up in the hands of foreign investors from the Central Powers (the coalition of the German Empire, Austria–Hungary, Ottoman Empire and Bulgaria) or that new stockholders would replace the present management.[31] The resulting Submarine Boat Corporation was initially a closed voting trust.

Sutphen was named a vice president of the Submarine Boat Corporation. Backed by a great deal of experience in building prefabricated boats, Sutphen suggested a plan to the general manager of the Emergency Fleet Corporation, a semipublic corporation, to produce 150 steel cargo vessels of 5,350 dead-weight tons apiece with a running speed of 10 knots. These vessels were the famous Liberty ships, designed to be built with lightning quickness to deliver badly needed war materials and supplies to Europe. The Submarine Boat Corporation acted as an agent in a land purchase at Port Newark, New Jersey, which was soon transformed into a bustling shipyard with 28 construction ways. When completed, the 138-acre site was covered with 20 miles of railroad track and staffed by 15,000 workers.[32]

Components for the ships arrived from 56 different shops around the country—bridge builders, tank fabricators, propulsion fabricators along with boiler and steam turbine manufacturers.[33] In addition, 27 steel mills supplied steel plates.[34] Sutphen once again rose to the task; production reached a peak of one ship every three days and 118 Liberty ships were completed by the time the armistice was signed in November 1918.[35] The Submarine Boat Corporation arranged to purchase the Port Newark facilities and material for the remaining 32 ships, planning to complete the vessels for commercial use.

Expansion of Submarine Building

As of January 1, 1916, Electric Boat had $25 million in backlog orders with net earnings of $5,622,544 in 1915.[36] Henry Carse's report to stockholders resounded with optimism:

ELECTRIC BOAT COMPANY

The *Skipjack (E-1)* was the first U.S. submarine to cross the Atlantic Ocean under its own power in 1917. Electric Boat submarines built in Montreal for Great Britain had made the crossing several months earlier.

"The submarine boat has demonstrated during the past year its inestimable value as a military instrument, and the events which have happened have brought very vividly to the minds of the people the absolute necessity of submarines for defense and offense and there is every expectation that large numbers of submarine boats will be constructed in the future by all nations of the world."[37]

In addition to submarines for England, Italy and Russia, Electric Boat received orders to build 88 submarines for the U.S. Navy as a result of wartime contracts. Expansion had already begun in the yards of Electric Boat subcontractors even before the United States entered the war. Among the many models built, there were seven H-class, eight K-class, seven L-class, one M-class, three N-class, eight O-class, 20 R-class, 31 S-class, and three T-class boats. The Fore River shipyard in Quincy constructed 53 of the boats, while Union Iron Works in San Francisco built 24 of them. Also on the West coast, the Moran Company built two boats and its successor, the Seattle Construction and Drydock Company built three. The six remaining boats were constructed at the Puget Sound Navy Yard.[38] Some of the R-class boats and all of the S and T

classes were built after the war ended in 1918. The NELSECO plant in Groton, Connecticut was expanded to supply diesel engines for the submarines, as well as high-pressure air compressors, torpedo tubes, conning towers, periscopes and other components.[39]

Evolution of the Military Use of Submarines

American submarines did not actually experience a great deal of combat during World War I beyond the critical tasks of patrolling and seeking out enemy submarines. Nevertheless, Lawrence Spear and others continued to anticipate the changing role of submarines in warfare. In a 1915 paper given at a meeting of the Society of Naval Architects and Marine Engineers, Spear delivered a succinct statement on the evolution of submarine development.

"In the early days, the problem of the submarine designer was the production of a practicable boat suitable for harbor defense, a role which did not require high speed, long radius, or great sea-keeping qualities, and hence did not involve large displacement. The submarine, however, did not escape the general law governing the displacement

Highly trained machinists with years of experience fashion the crankshaft of a large NELSECO diesel engine as an inspector in the background supervises their work.

of all naval types, and to meet the demand for increased speed, radius, seaworthiness and armament, it has been necessary to progressively increase the displacement. When the capabilities of the type had sufficiently increased, it ceased to be considered suitable for harbor defense only and it was assigned to the larger role of coast defense, and with further development it has come to be considered as an aid to the high seas fleet, as well as a useful weapon for independent offensive action in enemy waters."[40]

One contemporary account of military strategy for submarines cited five principal factors in their wartime use:

"(1) in the actual sinking of warships;
(2) as a threat against men-of-war, causing them to operate at high speeds and to remain in port over longer periods of time;
(3) as convoys for capital ships and merchant ships;
(4) in provoking an enemy to expend vast efforts in time and money in organizing huge patrol defenses and laying mine-sweeping apparatus, diverting these resources from other effective employment;
(5) as a general threat against all enemy shipping activity, necessitating the use of burdensome auxiliary forces."[41]

Unfortunately, there were many influential people, including Secretary of the Navy Josephus Daniels, who did not see the submarine as a vital component of U.S. naval strategy. In a statement to the House of Representatives, Daniels responded to a request by Congress for a report on building warships "based on the knowledge gained from the prevailing war in Europe" as well as "the values and uses in naval warfare of aeroplanes, dirigibles, balloons, and submarines."[42] Daniels was heavily in favor of traditional warships and devoted only the final three short paragraphs of his five-page draft to submarines. He noted the success in attacking enemy naval forces, conducting reconnaissance and rendering "more difficult and dangerous the overseas transport of troops and supplies." However, he added that "the strength in modern capital ships of no one of the belligerents have been seriously impaired by the operations or attack of submarines."[43]

James L. Slayden, a congressman from Texas, saw the "knowledge gained from the prevailing war in Europe" in a much different light. In a remarkable speech delivered on January 29, 1915, Slayden addressed the arguments of those who supported the building of large, heavily armed warships, or dreadnoughts. He opened his own argument with a report explaining why a British commander allowed defeated German battleships to return to their homeports after losing a naval fight in the North Sea. Reading from a newspaper editorial, Slayden quoted British Admiral Beatty who said that "the presence of the enemy's submarine subsequently necessitated the action being broken off."[44] Slayden continued to read from the editorial which demonstrated that "the mere presence of underwater boats compelled the sudden ending of a victorious fleet action by the most powerful battle cruisers yet produced." Admiral Beatty, who had already successfully dodged an enemy submarine, said he did not believe that a ship running at full speed was a "sufficient defense" against submarine attack.

Slayden strongly opposed the Navy's heavy reliance on large battleships that was reflected in the proposed appropriation bill:

> "Let me state that position in a sentence. I believe that the committee has advised the appropriation of too much money for obsolete weapons and too little for the greatest ever devised by the wit of man. Recent and current events sustain that view. Battleships are helpless in the presence of submarines and in terror if their presence is suspected. They are secure only when locked up in well-protected harbors. That is not merely my opinion; it is the logic of events. The committee and the bureaus seem not to have been impressed by facts of recent occurrence. Why are these two bodies so conservative, so ultra-conservative, one may say?"[45]

Slayden presented a statute from 1792, effective until 1903, that "required by law that every militiaman should be constantly provided with a good musket or firelock of a bore sufficient for balls of the eighteenth part of a pound, two spare flints, a pouch, and a powder horn."[46] as evidence of their antiquated logic. The advent of the submarine, Slayden went on, has "not only brought terror to the commanders of great battleships but it has also disturbed swivel-chair sailors who sit in administration buildings and see danger ahead for their pet project of majestic and expensive dreadnoughts."[47]

Slayden proposed that money be appropriated for submarines in the interest of saving tax dollars. He delivered his final argument to the applause of the congressional assembly:

> "With an adequate supply of submarines, 30 or 40 of which can be built for the cost of one battleship, the United States could not be successfully attacked by any power or possible combination of powers, and millions a year could be saved to the taxpayers."[48]

Military Deployment of Submarines in World War I

By the time the United States entered the war, the German fleet was at port and enemy shipping was at a minimum. Twenty U.S. Navy submarines, however, did sail across the Atlantic to report for duty, principally in the Irish Sea and around the Azores. These 20 subs were the *E-1, K-1, K-2, K-5, K-6, L-1, L-2, L-3, L-4, L-9, L-10, L-11, O-3, O-4, O-5, O-6, O-7, O-8, O-9,* and *O-10.* The O-class submarines never had the opportunity to see action since they left Newport, Rhode Island on November 2, 1918 and didn't reach the Azores until after the armistice had been signed.[49] The *O–6* came under accidental fire, however, even before departure to the Azores. The boat was hit six times by fire in the conning tower and forward ventilator before submerging, but was unable to remain down long as she was taking on so much water. When she surfaced again, an American destroyer fired on her before the *O–6* could identify herself.[50]

A German version of friendly fire, one L-class boat came under attack by two German submarines. One of the German U-boats fired a torpedo, missed the American submarine and sank the other U-boat.[51] American submarines had their own mishaps as well while attacking German U-boats. The *L-4* came upon a U-boat dead in the water and quickly fired a torpedo at the enemy. Apparently, the U-boat commander suspected the *L-4's* presence because the German boat started its motors just as the torpedo was fired, letting the underwater projectile pass harmlessly off its stern.[52]

The *L-10,* literally came under "friendly" fire from an American destroyer while submerged in British waters. The attack forced the *L-10* to the surface where she was able to identify herself, whereupon the skipper of the submarine discovered that his attacker was commanded by his roommate at Annapolis.[53]

Even torpedoes became the victims of friendly fire. When the *L-11* came upon a surfaced U-boat, her crew fired two torpedoes within five seconds of each other at the enemy craft. The second torpedo overran and struck the first torpedo, exploding both just before they hit their target.[54]

In another instance, one German submarine commander's plan of attack may have misfired, sinking his own vessel. On the evening of July 10, 1918, the American *L-2* was returning from patrol off the southern coast of Ireland when the German *UB-65* attempted to torpedo her. A nearby explosion alerted the *L-2* to the attack. The officer-of-the-deck reportedly "observed a large column of water rise out of the ocean about 25 feet off the starboard quarter. After its subsidence, he further observed six feet of periscope in the middle of the disturbed and foaming water."[55] Lieutenant Scott Umsted immediately gave the signal to dive.

The *L-2's* strategy was to dive, circle back around and attempt to ram the *UB-65.* The *L-2* missed in her attempt, but "passed so close that the enemy's churning propellers could be distinctly heard through the thick hull."[56] Using hydrophones, the *L-2* gave chase but eventually had to call it off because the sounds became less and less audible. Night had fallen, forcing the *L-2* to curtail its surface pursuit.

Based on monitored radio messages, it was determined that the *UB-65* was never heard from by German forces again after seven o'clock that evening.[57] In dry dock, workers noticed that the starboard quarter of the *L-2* was "marked and slightly 'dished in.'"[58] Investigators at the time determined that "the best and most likely theory is that the *UB-65*, in making the attack, miscalculated the distance during the approach and struck the American with her bow, causing the torpedo she intended to fire to detonate prematurely within the torpedo tube."[59]

An accident aboard the American *L-4* nearly buried the submersible and her crew in the depths of the English Channel. While on submerged patrol, the boat was running heavy prompting the officer-of-the-watch to give the order to blow 1,000 pounds of water out of the tank used for trim and ballast corrections. An inexperienced sailor opened a sea valve to an auxiliary tank instead, which rapidly began to fill with water. Already heavy, the added weight caused the *L-4* to sink. The crew set the dive rudders to rise position and motors to proceed at flank speed, but it was too late. The *L-4* imbedded itself in mud on the channel's floor—nearly 300 feet below the surface.[60]

> "The pumps could not be used against the high sea pressure. There remained but one method to bring the submarine up. By repeated filling of the adjusting tank from the auxiliary tank and blowing the adjusting tank, positive buoyancy was regained. Then by moving all hands, except those needed at the diving stations, as far aft in the vessel as possible, the main motors were started and air pressure applied to the bow ballast tank. This procedure brought results. The bow commenced to rise slowly until it reached an angle of six degrees up by the bow. Then, pausing momentarily, the submarine suddenly broke away from the muddy bottom and rose rapidly to the surface at an angle of 50 degrees."[61]

What must have been particularly harrowing for the men aboard was knowing that the boat was designed to withstand pressure only to a depth of 200 feet. The *L-4* lay on the bottom for an hour and 10 minutes while the crew struggled to rise to the surface.[62] Despite her brush with disaster, the boat suffered no serious damage— a strong testimony to the quality of Electric Boat design and construction.

Besides British and American submarines, boats from other nations were also involved in undersea operations during the war. Russia deployed her boats in the Baltic, Arctic and Black Seas. Italian submarines patrolled the Mediterranean. France dispatched submarines to assist in the blockade of the Dardanelles and Australia deployed submarines at Gallipoli.[63] Germany, however, far outdistanced all others in constructing and implementing submarines during the conflict. The country built 360 submarines during World War I and had nearly as many under construction when the war ended.[64]

Development of Submarine Seaworthiness

From the typical submarine of 1914 to the T-class ordered for the U.S. in World War I, the submarine had grown from 230 feet to 270 feet, while submerged displacement had increased from 912 tons to 1,484 tons. Engine power had doubled to 4,000 horsepower and electric motor power had increased from 980 horsepower to 1,500 horsepower. Surface speed had reached 21 knots and submerged speed 11 1/2 knots from 17 knots and 10 3/4 knots. Cruising range had dramatically increased to 12,000 miles from 3,000 miles, while the *Holland*, only 20 years earlier, had a mere cruising radius of only 200 miles.[65]

In seaworthiness, the submarine advanced steadily from the *Holland*, which featured a reserve buoyancy of only 12 percent surface displacement. This was largely unsuitable for most sea and wave conditions. Reserve buoyancy increased to 13 percent, 14 percent and 19 percent for the D, E and F classes, respectively. Boats of the Holland type experienced other difficulties which affected their seaworthiness. Because propellers and diving planes were close to the water line, they would often rise above the water in rough weather while cruising near the surface. The stern diving planes would occasionally snap off from constantly slapping against the surface. Although the seaworthiness of boats after the F-class improved as they became larger, none were considered as seaworthy as those whose design incorporated a double hull.[66]

Double and partial-double hull designs were constructed to increase reserve buoyancy. The *M-1*, built in 1913, was Electric Boat's first attempt to construct a partial double hull. This gave the *M-1* a reserve buoyancy of 27 percent, nearly double the 15 1/2 percent of the L-class boats. The new design was not without compromise—the boat was more crowded and less habitable—but increased seaworthiness more than offset these disadvantages. Following the S-class, partial double hulls and double hulls became preferred designs.[67]

The conning tower, or surface bridge, was another important design feature. Before 1917, the bridge consisted of a piece of canvas wrapped around a metal frame. Beginning with the N-class, the bridge became an open metal chariot. This permanent fixture improved seaworthiness by giving the boat's crew a much safer position from which to direct surface operations.[68]

Advances in Armament

During this period, submarine armament was also being improved. The torpedo deployed by the *Holland* was 18 inches in diameter and 11 feet, 6 inches long. The length increased by slightly more than a foot in the B-class and the diameter widened to 21 inches in the R-class boats. Another torpedo tube was added to the B and C classes for a total of two. In 1907, this was increased to four torpedoes on D-class boats.

The firing of torpedoes required even more design changes. A cap on the bow which pivoted on the centerline would rotate until its two openings lined up with both tubes, and a torpedo could then be fired through the opening. Unfortunately, the other tubes could not be readied during firing since all tubes had to be flooded at once. This problem was solved in the L-class by incorporating hinged doors on each tube that could be operated independently.[69]

Except for the pneumatic gun installed on the *Holland*, no submarine carried a gun until the L-class, as designers wanted to minimize drag while submerged. The L-class was armed with a 3-inch, 23 caliber gun that could be retracted into a watertight compartment so that only about half the length of its barrel protruded above the deck. The success of guns on German U-boats led to larger guns with reduced emphasis on sleeker submerged forms. The R-class was armed with a 3-inch, 50 caliber wet gun, a deck gun not retracted into the hull when the ship submerged. The S-class carried a 4-inch, 50 caliber wet gun.[70]

Propulsion

From the beginning of submarine development, the U.S. Navy placed great emphasis on both surface and submerged speed. Designers naturally attempted to squeeze as much power into a submarine as possible. By installing engines which were disproportionately large for the volume of the submarine hulls, the boats could reach between 13 and 14 knots on the surface. In addition to the engines, engine rooms were crammed with air starting and reversing gear, and pumps for circulating lubricating oil and water powered by the propulsion unit. Cramped space around the engines made it difficult, if not impossible, to properly maintain the powerplants. Typically, engines were difficult to keep fully operational for more than a few hours.

In 1915, the policy of packing the submarine with more power was changed. Engine horsepower dropped from between 800 to 1200 horsepower to only 480 horsepower in the N-class. Auxiliary units and pumps were also removed from the engines resulting in a loss of approximately 1 knot, but making the boats far more reliable.[71] Though Electric Boat experimented with various types of two-cycle and four-cycle engines, single-acting and double-acting, the company eventually determined that four-cycle,

single-acting diesel engines were best suited for submarines.[72]

Habitability

Submariners from the early days through World War I, referred to their craft as "pig boats." A World War I submarine carried three officers and a crew of 30 enlisted men. They worked, slept, washed, ate and performed necessary bodily functions in a cramped metal tube about 150 feet long. Air pressure was used to flush waste, which worked reasonably well as long as the outside pressure was less than the inside pressure. When the outside pressure was greater, the flushing operation could unfortunately work in reverse—with a disgusting result colorfully known as "getting your own back."[73]

In very early submarines which never remained at sea more than a few days, lockers were provided for personal effects. Sleeping arrangements improved from folding cots to narrow berths, which could accommodate from a third to half of the crew at any one time. Consequently, submariners had to sleep in shifts and share berths. This practice is still known as "hot bunking." In 1918 with the introduction of the O-class, sailors had both a berth and a locker of their own. The berth, however, was only wide enough if a man lay perfectly straight; the locker was between 1 and 2 cubic feet, excluding the numerous pipes which ran through it.[74]

Maneuverability

Stern diving planes were a standard feature of submarines from the beginning. When the boats were required merely to run on the surface or to dive and run submerged, these planes were all that were necessary. When periscopes were introduced, it became desirable to run at a depth which would allow the periscope to protrude above the water's surface at a constant height. Maintaining depth to within 1 or 2 feet at slow speeds (making handling difficult) was not an easy task. Beginning with the E-class, bow diving planes were added to improve depth control and to keep the boat from broaching (or veering) after a torpedo was fired. During this developmental period, arguments of the "even-keel" versus "diving" method of submerging were ultimately decided in favor of diving. Other designers had erroneously concluded that pushing the bow downward while submerging was dangerous. The Lake submarines of the period deployed hydroplanes near the midsection which were tilted while the boats submerged or rose to the surface, but were proven unwieldy and less precise than the diving method. After the Lake R-class and the *S-2*, the even-keel method was no longer used.[75]

Launching of the *Cuttlefish* on November 21, 1933, the first submarine built for the U.S. Navy at Electric Boat's Groton shipyard.

CHAPTER V

Between the Wars

A submarine is a demanding command in peace or war ... In peacetime there are still the hazards of the malevolent sea—ever ready, with its sequence of inevitable consequences, to pounce mercilessly upon momentary disregard for its laws.

Edward L. Beach,
Run Silent, Run Deep

As World War I—optimistically called the "War to End All Wars"—came to an end in November 1918, people on both sides of the Atlantic celebrated in an age of prosperity and gaiety which became known as the "roaring twenties."

The celebration at Electric Boat was muted with considerations of the future. The company had clearly established itself during the war as the principal builder of submarines in the United States. Though American submarines were not exposed to combat to the same degree as the German U-boats, Electric Boat submarines and their crews performed important patrolling duties with honor and courage. Of the 88 submarines under contract during World War I, 47 were completed following the armistice. This last group included 13 R-class, 31 S-class and three T-class boats.[1]

Electric Boat had reason to be happy with the U.S. Navy's decision to complete the build-up of its submarine fleet, although there was still apprehension about the years ahead. A company advertisement from 1919 is considerably more subdued than the display advertisements which had appeared in *Jane's Fighting Ships* in 1912 and 1914. Earlier advertisements boasted the number of boats Electric Boat had built and declared the company as the production leader of the world. The 1919 advertisement reflects a self-assured company in calmer times. It makes no boasts or claims—it simply depicts a single submarine at rest in placid waters. The advertisement was a premonition of the days to come.[2] However, unlike other military services, the U.S. Navy did not cancel its wartime contracts once peace was declared. Widespread public opinion held that the U.S. had secure borders and shorelines. Indeed, the only fleets capable of attacking us were our own wartime allies—Britain, France and Japan—which fueled debate over maintaining a strong navy.[3]

Liberty Ships Completed

Though originally formed as a voting trust to protect the company's stock, the Submarine Boat Corporation became quite active during World War I. After constructing 188 Liberty ships for wartime transport and cargo in record time, the Government's hastily formed Emer-

The NELSECO shipyard at Groton, Conn., showing a diesel ferry boat and two submarines, probably the Peruvian *R-1* and *R-2* (1924), under construction.

gency Fleet Corporation was expected to cancel contracts for an additional 32 ships. However, sensing an opportunity for peacetime profits, the corporation negotiated contracts to purchase the Port Newark yard, ships under construction and all of the prefabricated materials already on order to complete all remaining ships.

While negotiating for the Liberty ship facilities and materials, the Submarine Boat Corporation also negotiated with the Italian government for the purchase of 18 ships and possibly 10 more. Regrettably, the Italians withdrew soon after the Submarine Boat Corporation had purchased all of the shipbuilding assets from the Emergency Fleet Corporation.[4]

The market for shipbuilding, though, appeared favorable in the first few years following World War I. The Submarine Boat Corporation elected to proceed to build the 32 ships, even in the absence of firm orders. A complex financing arrangement was forged, in which both cash and promissory notes linked to submarine contracts with the U.S. Navy were borrowed from Electric Boat. Cash amounted to $2 million, notes were signed for an additional $2 million, while another $1 million was borrowed from Chase National Bank of New York. The Submarine Boat Corporation and Electric Boat (sharing the same board of directors) were confident that their

expertise in shipbuilding would pay off with international sales. By 1922, all 32 ships had been completed just as the bottom fell out of the shipbuilding business. A worldwide postwar shipping depression left the corporation floundering with a sizable fleet of ships without a market.[5]

As an emergency measure, the corporation formed the Transmarine Corporation to operate the ships. Cargo was shipped throughout the West Coast and between Port Newark, Cuba and South America, but there was little chance of circumventing the growing worldwide shipping depression. The company attempted to operate some ships on the New York State Barge Canal as barges, but this profit avenue was closed as well. Ultimately, the decision was made to cut losses as soon as possible. The Liberty ships ultimately were sold for a fraction of their cost to commercial shipping lines. A similar fate befell the Port Newark facilities.[6]

U.S. Navy Designs and Builds Own Submarines

During World War I, the U.S. Navy became concerned about the quality of the submarines it was purchasing. Its officials expressed fears that its submarines were inferior to "those built abroad, particularly by the Germans."[7] The U.S. Navy also believed that the system of buying ships designed by private companies and built in private shipyards did not provide adequate control and supervision. In fact, in the early years of World War I, the Navy had purchased six H-class boats from Electric Boat in "knocked-down" condition and assembled the submarines itself at the Puget Sound Navy Yard.[8] Soon after, the Navy "decided to establish a design agency under its own complete control. As the first step in familiarizing its personnel with submarines and their designs, an order was placed for the building of the *L-8*, to the design of the Lake Torpedo Boat Company, at the Navy Yard, Portsmouth, New Hampshire. Two years later, the *O-1* of the Holland type was built at Portsmouth to the design of the Electric Boat Company."[9] By late 1916, the Navy was confident that they could develop their own design and working plans for a submarine. This first boat designed by the Navy, the *S-3*, was built at Portsmouth as well.

While the *S-3* was under construction, the Navy also placed orders for the *S-1* to be built by Electric Boat and the *S-2* to be built by the Lake Torpedo Boat Company. Despite all three boats being of the S-class and possessing similar capabilities, the three submarines differed in design to a large degree. About a year after these orders were made, the Navy concluded that its own design was superior to the Lake design and discontinued using Lake's designs. Beginning in 1917, submarine contracts awarded to Lake's company were based on the U.S. Navy's designs.[10] Electric Boat, on the other hand, continued to build submarines based on its own designs and working plans. Work on Navy submarines ended, however, when the last S-class boat ordered during World War I was completed. From 1918 to 1931, Electric Boat experienced a long 13-year drought of government work, as the Navy did not award a single contract to any private submarine builder. In the early 1920s, the Navy began to build its V-class, the first boat of which was accepted by the Navy in 1924. This was the same year that the Lake Torpedo Boat Company went out of business. The last of the eight Navy V-class boats was nearing completion as work on the *V-9*, the first boat contracted to an outside builder in 13 years, began at Electric Boat's shipyard in Groton, Connecticut.

Electric Boat Overhauls S-class Submarines

Electric Boat had survived, primarily from a U.S. Navy contract to refurbish 30 S-class submarines. The work, which was for boats *S-18* through *S-47*, principally entailed rebuilding the engines.[11] To this point in the company's history, all work had been performed at other shipyards under the supervision of company engineers and management. For the overhaul contract, the company expanded its own facilities in Groton where NELSECO was already established. As part of gearing up, the company erected a 25-ton, stiff-leg derrick crane on a dock, installed power shears for iron working, built a temporary warehouse for receiving material, constructed a small tool house and placed a machine shop upon an old Army barge bought from the Submarine Boat Corporation. The company office in Groton consisted of a small building formerly used as a ticket office for the company ferry, which transported workers across the Thames River (separating Groton and New London) to the NELSECO plant.[12]

Work on the submarines began in March 1922, with the arrival of the *S-20*. Electric Boat completed work on four boats in 1922 and added a night shift in 1923 to speed up the rest. The final boat, the *S-47*, was overhauled and returned to the Navy in 1925. Eighteen of the submarines arrived under their own power from their berths at Quincy, Massachusetts. The remaining 12 boats were berthed at San Francisco. Six of these cruised to Groton under their own power by way of the Panama Canal. The company outfitted and overhauled the other six boats by shipping engines and equipment to the West Coast, where Electric Boat engineers supervised the work.[13]

NELSECO's Business Expands

While Electric Boat expanded operations at the Groton facility, NELSECO expanded as well. Both companies worked very closely on the construction of a submarine tender, or mothership, which would carry supplies for submarines, recharge their batteries and effect small repairs. NELSECO developed plans for the floating submarine base and commissioned the Thames River Shipbuilding Company of New London to construct the vessel. The tender, christened the *Isaac L. Rice* after Electric Boat's first president, was launched in 1917. The unique vessel was fitted with a pair of 240-horsepower NELSECO engines which generated power for General Electric direct current generators, designed to recharge submarine batteries and to supply power to auxiliary machinery. The tender, shaped much like a barge, was 130 feet long and 38 feet wide.[14] A contemporary trade journal generously described the interior of the vessel:

> *"Spacious living quarters, consisting of staterooms, lavatories, messrooms, etc..., are arranged for the accommodation of submarine officers and crews. Similar quarters are given over to the vessel's crew and representatives of the Electric Boat Company."*[15]

The mammoth 3,680-horsepower engine built at the NELSECO plant in Groton, Conn. for the USS *Wilscox*. During a 30-day continuous test run, the rumble from the engine could be heard across the Thames River in New London.

NELSECO engines had gained a well-deserved reputation for reliability. The *NELSECO II*, the ferry owned by the company to transport workers across the Thames River, was also used as a passenger ferry between Norwich, Connecticut (12 miles up the Thames River from New London) and Block Island (about 30 miles off New London at the entrance of Long Island Sound). A journalist from *Motorship*, described the heavy duty-cycles for the engines:

> *"For two months of the summer the round trip of about ninety–five miles is made seven days a week. During the season of 1922, the only interruption was a stop of four minutes, occasioned by a leaky valve, which was removed and replaced by a new one in this time. The summer of 1923 passed without incident, except for delays of eleven minutes, also caused by a valve, but in this instance the material was at fault."[16]*

In 1925, NELSECO diesel engines demonstrated that their reliability matched their enormous size. An era photograph displays a diesel engine with a man in the foreground, showing that the powerplant is more than four times the height of the man. The huge engine could generate 3,680 horsepower. To test the engine, NELSECO ran it "continuously for 30 days and 30 nights. The machine's rumble could be heard in New London with no difficulty, while some residents of Groton claim they not only heard, but felt the engine as well."[17] The engine was later installed on the USS *Wilscox*. On January 1, 1929, NELSECO came under direct operation of Electric Boat in a reorganization of the two companies. Henry Carse remained president; Lawrence Spear became vice president and general manager; and Captain Frank T. Cable was named the business manager.[18]

Electric Boat Looks for More Business

With expansion of the Groton shipyard to accommodate overhaul activities, came the building of a new marine railway in 1922. Cleaning, painting and other hull underside work had previously been let to nearby Thames Shipyard, which proved costly and inconvenient.[19] Work on a marine railway, capable of handling up to 2,400 tons and boats with an overall length of 320 feet and a draft of up to 18 feet, was completed in March 1923. The first boat to be hauled that month was the submarine *S–24*, which was 220 feet long and displaced 850 tons.[20] In addition to submarine work, the shipyard worked on a great variety of other boats, including yachts. Sir Thomas Lipton's America's Cup defender, *Shamrock V*, was hauled for work by Electric Boat, including stepping the aluminum mast and painting the bottom.[21] In March 1928, the facility overhauled the Coast Guard destroyer *Shaw*. Word of the excellence of Electric Boat craftsmanship spread rapidly, as overhaul and reconditioning work increased.[22]

New ship construction also continued to grow during this period, with many of the new ships utilizing NELSECO diesel engines. Among the more notable boats built at the Groton shipyard was the *Puritan*, an all-welded two-masted schooner, designed by John Alden of Boston and a beautiful sight to behold under sail.[23] The stylish yacht was 102 feet, 9 inches in length overall, 74 feet, 8 inches at the waterline, had a beam of 22 feet, 10 inches, and a draft of 9 feet,

8 inches. Her mainsail alone required 1,996 square feet of canvas; she carried a total 4,297 square feet of working sails. Another welded boat fabricated at Electric Boat was the *Weldera*, designed by Ed Wheeler the shipyard manager. A 28-foot sloop, the *Weldera* was "built of two plates on each side, with a buckle at the turn of the bilge,"[24] whereas the *Puritan* had welded butts along with lapped and riveted seams. These two projects were particularly significant because these new welding skills were later applied to the first partially welded submarine in 1931, the *Cuttlefish*, which was the first U.S. Navy submarine to be contracted to Electric Boat since 1918.

As Electric Boat scrambled for additional business, management drew a 60-mile radius on a map around the shipyard, instructing executives to go out and talk to every business within that circle that might have a use for the company's services. An eclectic array of local opportunities were discovered, including "the manufacturing

JIM BURBANK

The 102-foot *Puritan*, built at the Groton Shipyard, was one of the first all-welded ships. Designed by John Alden, it was a swift, two-masted schooner carrying a total of 4,297 square feet of working sails.

Hull No.	Name	Ways No.	Contract Date	Keel Laid	Launched	Delivered	Remarks
	VESSELS BUILT AT GROTON						
1	Peruvian Sub - R-1	2	Apr-11-24	Feb-25-25	July-12-26	Oct-4-26	Launched from Ways #3
2	" " R-2	3	.	Feb-25-25	Apr-29-26	July-26-26	
3	Ferry - Elmer Jones	1	Nov-18-25	Jan-12-26	Mar-27-26	May-26	
4	Tug - B.M.Thomas	1	Jan-23-26	May-13-26	Oct-14-26	Dec-26	
5	Ferry - John J.Collins	1	Jan-19-26	Mar-16-26	Aug-21-26	Sept-17-26	
6	Peruvian Sub. R-3	3	Oct-13-26	Mar-7-27	Apr-21-28	July-7-28	
7	" " R-4	2	.	Mar-12-27	May-10-28	July-1-28	
8	Tug - Celtic	1	Dec-3-27	Feb-3-28	Feb-27-29		Built for Stock Sold to Busby 1934
9	Trawler - Cormorant		June-2-28			Jan-8-29	Not Built at Groton
10	Ferry - Wards Island	3	Dec-18-28	Feb-18-29	Sept-25-29	Oct-14-29	
11	" Tenkamas	3		Feb-18-29	Oct-17-29	Nov-11-29	
12	L.H.Tender - Althea	1	Dec-1-28	May-19-29	Feb-24-30	Apr-30-30	
13							Not Used
14	Barge - Steel Weld	North Yard	Mar-13-29	May-24-29	Oct-26-29	Nov-9-29	
15	L.H.Tender - Poinciana	1	June-17-29	Oct-22-29	June-7-30	July-8-30	
16	Sch. Yacht - Puritan	2	July-1-29	Nov-10-29	Apr-25-31	July-31	
17	U.S.Sub - Cuttlefish	3	June-29-31	Oct-7-31	Nov-21-33	June-8-34	1st Launching after Rebuilding of Ways - Sept-33
18	Yacht - Weldera	1	Mar-9-32	Mar-9-32	July-8-32	July-32	
19	U.S.Sub - Shark		Aug-9-33	Oct-24-33	May-21-35	Jan-25-36	1st Launching after rebuilding of New Ways-33
20	" Tarpon	3	"	Dec-22-33	Sept-4-35	Mar-12-36	
21	Peruvian - Amazonas	North Yard	Oct-9-33	Nov-20-33	Apr-5-34	May-34	
22	" Loreto	North Yard	"	Nov-20-33	Apr-12-34	May-34	
23	U.S.Sub - Perch	4	Aug-22-34	Feb-25-35	May-9-36	Nov-19-36	1st Launching on New Ways - Built Oct-1935
24	" Pickerel	5	"	Mar-25-35	July-7-36	Jan-26-37	1st Launching on New Ways-Built Oct-1935
25	" Permit	1	"	June-6-35	Oct-5-36	Mar-17-37	
26	" Salmon	3	Sept-19-35	Apr-15-36	June-12-37	Mar-15-38	
27	" Seal	4	"	May-25-36	Aug-25-37	Apr-30-38	
28	" Skipjack	5	"	July-22-36	Oct-23-37	June-30-38	

ELECTRIC BOAT COMPANY

Sales of submarines to foreign countries and licensing agreements with companies in other nations formed a large part of Electric Boat's business in its early years. Only four of the submarines above were actually built at the Groton shipyard. They were the *R-1*, *R-2*, *R-3* and *R-4* for Peru.

of printing presses, textile machinery, paper-folding and fish-skinning machines, and machines for stamping out novelties and bobby pins. Indeed, the company that had helped to make the world safe for democracy was happy to repair hair curlers for a beauty parlor."[25]

Others attempted to interest Electric Boat to invest in novel enterprises. H.E. Page, of Page Engineering Company (sole manufacturers of patented "Bulldog" products) attempted to interest Electric Boat to build hat-blocking machines:

> "This machine has proven of keen interest to the trade and even though the price is in keeping with the times there is a nice margin of profit. I have no means of knowing conditions at your plant but I know that you were interested in new developments in the past and I thought that this machine, together with other developments of a different nature I have under way, might be of interest to you, either as a means of utilizing your present facilities or for expansion of your business."[26]

Electric Boat politely responded that the company would consider manufacturing the hat-blocker—if Page had money to invest.[27]

Alexander Stefanidi, a sponge packer from Tarpon Springs, Florida, offered the company another unique opportunity: Stefanidi wanted Electric Boat to sponsor the construction of a 45-foot long submarine to pick sponges from depths inaccessible to divers. In a letter to Lawrence Spear, Stefanidi explained, "this is not a wildcat proposition, and neither treasure hunting,"[28] and hoped that the two could "get together in the construction of this outfit, and that we will mutually benefit by it very extensively."[29] Electric Boat declined the unusual offer, but would "not condemn entirely as impracticable the idea of employing submarines to gather sponges in fairly deep water."[30]

Submarines for Peru Built in Groton

In 1924, the Peruvian government awarded a contract to Electric Boat for the construction of two submarines, the first ever to be built at the Groton shipyard. The company had to assist the Peruvian government with financing in order to conclude the deal.[31] In preparation for the work, Electric Boat expanded its facilities by erecting a new fabricating shop and furnace building, a new plate yard and three new ways equipped with overhead ship cranes.[32]

The contract specified two submarines of the 707-D design, 24 torpedoes, and "buildings, fittings, equipment, etc. for one submarine base in accordance with specifications to be hereafter submitted by the Contractor." The submarines cost $1,218,000 each, the torpedoes and accessory items totalled another $264,000, while the submarine base was valued at $400,000 for a total contract of $3.1 million.[33] Keels for the two boats, the *R-1* and the *R-2*, were laid on February 25, 1925. The *R-2* was launched on April 29, 1926. In that same year, Peru ordered two more submarines from Electric Boat.

In 1927, Electric Boat entered negotiations with the Japanese government for the purchase of submarines. Sir Trevor Dawson of Vickers wrote to Lawrence Spear that he had read in the *Public Ledger & North American—Philadelphia* that Electric Boat had been awarded an $85 million contract by the Japanese. "If the Japanese were placing such contracts for submarines, it certainly would be of great interest to our people over here, who would probably be inclined to take it into account in fixing their programme and estimates for the new year," Dawson suggested.[34] In a cautiously worded reply, Spear referred to "an order for submarines from a certain foreign power which we are seeking to close."[35] He informed Dawson that he would keep Vickers and the British Admiralty advised of negotiations. Spear also indicated that the United States government will authorize building 32 submarines, and "since, for preliminary purposes only, they put the average cost down at $5 million per boat, you will readily see that they are contemplating fairly large units."[36]

In the early 1930s, Electric Boat was approached by Paul Koster, who had acted at various times since 1912 as an agent for the company, about selling submarines to the Russian government. Spear told Electric Boat President Henry Carse that, unlike President Herbert Hoover's administration, the new administration of President Franklin Delano Roosevelt might allow the company to build boats for the Russians.[37] Carse replied that perhaps Koster contacted Electric Boat because no one else would negotiate for the Russians, who had become notoriously bad credit risks.[38] The following day, Spear wrote company Vice President Sterling Joyner, advancing an argument to convince the Roosevelt administration to authorize building submarines for Russia:

"A good many of our naval officers feel that we ought to have a type developed of about 800 tons displacement which could be put into rapid production in time of war, and if we do this job for the Russians, that object would be accomplished as there would be a complete set of plans available and the engines and other machinery would all be fully developed."[39]

	Class-B Cruisers U–138 – 141	Class-A Torpedo Boats U–93 – 98
Length overall	301' 10"	234' 9"
Displacement, surface	1930 tons	800 tons
Total B.H.P. Engines	3500	2400
Surface speed	15.8 knots	16 knots
Maximum cruising radius, nautical miles	20,000	5,500
Maximum submerged speed	7.6 knots	8.6 knots
Depth test	246 feet	– – –
No. of torpedo tubes	6	6
No. and size of torpedoes	19 – 50 cm.	10 – 50 cm.
Guns	2 – 15 cm. 1 – 8.8 cm.	1 – 10.5 cm.

L.Y. Spear compares an older class of German submarines (torpedo boats) with a newer class (cruisers) in this table from a 1927 paper he wrote on submarine development.

When Joyner raised the issue of submarines for Russia to an official in the State Department, he received a cool reception:

"He was not at all cordial to the idea; nothing like the attitude he held on the last occasion when we requested the reaction of the Department to any negotiations with Russia for the construction of vessels of any type that might be used for war purposes."[40]

The United States still maintained cordial relations with Russia, although Lenin and his Bolsheviks had established a communist government following the October Revolution of 1917. After Russia was officially recognized and granted a credit of $200 million by the U.S. government, Spear observed that "it seems likely that the new political atmosphere created by the recognition (and the credit if made) can be made to have a considerable influence in our favor on the submarine business."[41] He pointed out in a letter that he thought granting the credit was "foolish" on the part of the U.S. government. Though Spear remained optimistic, the company's chief engineer, E. Nibbs, pointed out that Russia had been requesting a catalog a month and that they had made "no specific inquiries." He added that "apparently the Russians simply want catalogs as a source for new ideas," and concluded by stating that his department now had a "policy of simply ignoring all such correspondence from the Soviet Republic."[42]

Submarine Design and Development

In a paper he delivered to The Society of Naval Architects and Marine Engineers in 1927, Lawrence Spear analyzed the classes and characteristics of the world's submarine fleets. He defined three principal types of submarines: submarines whose primary role was to attack warships, submarine cruisers whose primary role was to attack commerce and to scout, and mine-laying submarines.[43] He also presented a succinct argument against attempting to eliminate by treaty submarines used for other than defensive purposes. All submarines of sufficient displacement are capable of extending their military role of harbor defense, Spear explained. "It should be obvious that any submarine capable of operating in enemy waters is an 'offensive' submarine," he said.[44] To illustrate his point, Spear cited Electric Boat's H-class submarines that were delivered to Great Britain during World War I. By 1927 standards, they were boats of modest displacement; yet, they were able to cross the Atlantic under their own power and then proceed to action in the North Sea and the eastern end of the Mediterranean. A boat which might be classified solely as defensive, has "a radius of action of 3,000 to 4,000 nautical miles, and could be ordered into an offensive posture in most of the seas of the world."[45]

Spear continued with a thorough classification and analysis of submarines during this era, illustrating the wide range of design and displacement of the world's submarines designed for attacking warships. Interestingly, Spear concluded that smaller submarines are often preferable to larger ones. He believed that "once battle contact with the enemy is established, a distinct advantage lies with the smaller vessel on account of its superior maneuvering qualities and the smaller depth of water required for operation."[46]

ELECTRIC BOAT COMPANY

Launching of the *R-1* for Peru on July 12, 1926, the first sub built by Electric Boat at the Groton shipyard.

With respect to submarine cruisers whose primary task was to attack commerce and to scout, Spear felt that although 40 were proposed by the Germans in World War I, only three were completed and commissioned. The table on the preceding page compares the Class "B" cruisers with the smaller Class "A" German submarine. The larger displacements of the Class "B" boats allowed them to accommodate a much larger store of ammunition, torpedoes and fuel for longer patrols and range.[47] The U.S. Navy at the time was developing designs of this new class, Spear noted. These were reported to displace 2800 tons to 2900 tons, achieve a surface speed of 16 knots to 18 knots, and deploy six torpedo tubes and two 6–inch guns.[48] Spear also disclosed that Great Britain was working on a cruise submarine, the X–1 or so-called "mystery submarine."

Mine-laying, or Class "C" submarines, were also introduced by the Germans in World War I. There are two principal types of Class "C" sub-marines: those that employ "wet" systems and those that employ "dry" systems. In the "wet" system, mines are stored in exterior tubes or tanks which are inaccessible to the crew and "subject to the action of sea water."[49] "Dry" systems store mines in the interior of the boat "where they are always accessible for inspection and free from the action of sea water."[50]

Spear concluded his unique insight into the evolution of submarines with a brief description of two final types of submarines. The first was the "Monitor" type, of British design. Boats of this type were armed with a 12-inch gun which was "provided mainly for the purpose of attacking high speed unarmored vessels; such, for instance, as light cruisers and destroyers which might well be totally disabled, if not sunk, by a single hit with a 12-inch shell."[51]

The last type was the anti-submarine submarine, also of British design. Before World War I, it was assumed that submarines could not attack other submarines. Spear noted that action during the war "demonstrated that this was a complete fallacy. As a matter of fact, the Allied submarines proved to be the most efficient of all types of craft including aircraft which were employed by the Allies in the campaign against the German submarine."[52] The best example of this type was the British R-class.

A Tour of an American S-class Submarine

In 1927, 49 of the 51 S-class submarines built for the U.S. Navy during World War I and the early 1920s were still in service. The S–5 and S–51 were lost at sea in accidents. Many of these surviving S-class submarines saw action in World War II. Although there was a great deal of variation in this class, the average specifications of this type was "231 feet long, 21 feet wide amidships, 1092 tons submerged, four torpedo tubes, two 1000-hp (horsepower) diesel engines, two 1200-hp main motors, and manned by four officers and 39 men."[53] The hull itself was cigar-shaped, with a deck superstructure supporting a conning tower with a bridge and periscopes. Each submarine included five major areas (listed from forward to aft): the torpedo room, battery room, control room, engine room and motor room.[54]

The torpedo room is where weapons are stored, repaired, maintained and fired. It is also the area where the torpedo crew berths, often above the explosive devices themselves. Aft of the torpedo room is the battery room which doubled as quarters for both enlisted men and officers. Secured below the deck of this area were 120 lead-acid storage cells with a total weight of 160 tons, slightly more than a ton for each cell. Below and outboard of the batteries were ballast tanks along with storage tanks for both fuel and oil.[55]

Amidships is the control room which is divided into four smaller areas: the galley, radio room, refrigerator space and wardroom.

"The control room contains the air manifolds for blowing tanks; chart and plotting desk; controls for the main motors; controls for the vent valves for the ballast tanks; kingstons for the main ballast tanks; gyro compass; main and auxiliary switchboards; periscopes; trim pump for the fore and aft trim; and other less important equipment."[56]

The control room was the nerve-center of the boat, the place where most submerged functions of the submarine were coordinated. Aft of the control room was the engine room, which contained two diesel engines. The final compartment, the motor room, contained the two electric motors powered by the batteries for submerged propulsion.[57]

The S-class proved to be a durable and reliable design. In August 1924, nine boats (S–21 through S–29) departed New London for the Panama Canal under the command of Admiral M.M. Taylor. After participating in fleet maneuvers at the Pacific entrance of the canal, the boats continued on their journey to San Francisco where they were joined by five more submarines (S–30, S–31, S–32, S–34, S–35). The flotilla of 14 boats then made its way to the Hawaiian Islands where it was part of the attacking force in maneuvers to test the islands' defenses. During the war exercises, the submarines remained submerged for all daylight hours and were used in mock actions against boats of the Electric Boat R-class. While on active patrol, which lasted for several days, the boats never made port for rest or maintenance. Once maneuvers were complete, five of the boats were dispatched for duty off China, six were ordered to San Francisco, and three boats (S–21, S–22, S–23) returned to New London via the Panama Canal. On their voyage home, this small flotilla was joined by the S–18 and S–20 during a six–day layover at the canal, the only stop the original three submarines made on the entire trip home. In fact, the three boats had travelled a total of 15,000 nautical miles. Upon arrival, "material and personnel were both in excellent condition and ready for active service, requiring only to take on fresh supplies of fuel and stores."[58]

The *Cuttlefish*

Though Electric Boat was not immune to the effects of the Great Depression—losing $1 million in both 1930 and 1931[59]—more prosperous days were soon to come. After designing and building eight V-class submarines in their own yards, the U.S. Navy decided to invite bids from private yards for a ninth boat. Two companies submitted bids; Electric Boat was awarded the contract for the *Cuttlefish* on June 29, 1931. The keel was laid on October 7, 1931, the new submarine was launched on November 21, 1933 and delivered to the Navy on June 8, 1934.

The *Cuttlefish* was built according to the Navy's design for the V-class, although Electric Boat had permission to improve some elements of the design. Whereas the Navy-built boats ranged in length up to 385 feet, the *Cuttlefish* was the smallest of the V-class at 274 feet long. The unique boat had a surface displacement of 1,120 tons and a "clipper ship" bow that enhanced surface operations.[60] In many respects, it was the forerunner of the Fleet type attack submarines which became famous in World War II. The *Cuttlefish* would see action during World War II on three patrols, sinking a Japanese ship during one of them.[61]

ELECTRIC BOAT COMPANY

The *S-47*, built after the end of World War I, was commissioned in 1925. The ship remained active until it was decommissioned in 1945, after seeing action in World War II.

In building the *Cuttlefish*, Electric Boat was able to draw on the pioneering expertise gathered over the years in shipyard welding. Designed for full double hull construction, the *Cuttlefish*, was "about 40 percent welded and 60 percent riveted,"[62] representing a compromise between all-riveted and all-welded Navy vessels. Pleased with Electric Boat's work, the Navy awarded the company two more contracts in September 1933 for the *Shark* and the *Tarpon*, both of which would be launched in 1935. Additional contracts were awarded by August 1934, providing the impetus for Electric Boat to construct new building ways at the Groton shipyard. These new ways were built next to the existing ones in what had come to be known as the North Yard.[63] By 1936, the company had regained sufficient financial stability to start paying dividends once again.[64] From 1936 to 1939, Electric Boat built about three submarines a year.[65] By 1939, submarine orders accounted for nearly 95 percent of the company's sales.[66]

The Nye Committee Investigations of the Munitions Industry

There was pervasive belief in some branches of government that the munitions industry had collected windfall profits during World War I, and even that some manufacturers had conspired with other countries and Wall Street to instigate the war.[67] As the first step in drafting laws which would limit future profiteering and bolster neutrality laws, the Senate formed a committee under Senator Gerald P. Nye of North Dakota to investigate the industry. Electric Boat, as a company with considerable international associations, was thrust into the spotlight. Electric Boat president Carse and vice presidents Spear and Sutphen testified at the Nye Committee hearings for three days in September 1934. The committee transcriptions of their appearance is 458 pages long with "an appendix containing 200 tabulations, letters, reports, and other exhibits from the company's files."[68]

The questioning focused on Electric Boat's foreign business, foreign patents and licensing agreements. The committee carefully scrutinized company profits, tax records, salaries, commissions, expense allowances and activities of the company's Washington representatives.[69] Discussion also raised "talk of patent monopoly, of fomenting an arms race between Chile and Peru, and of irresponsible business practices."[70] Electric Boat executives argued that their dealings with foreign countries allowed this country to keep abreast of international submarine development. In February 1936, 18 months following the Electric Boat testimony, the Nye Committee issued their report.

The committee agreed that "it is essential that the worst of these practices be stopped if it is possible to stop them, and the nature of the foreign practices of American munitions companies and their profits on contracts for the military services of the United States should be strictly limited and controlled."[71] Furthermore, a majority of the committee agreed that "the national defense will be greatly aided by the estoppel of the practice of selling American military inventions abroad."[72] The committee recommended government takeover of the manufacturing facilities of the arms industry, while a vocal minority stated that the nation's welfare would be "better served by rigid and conclusive munitions control than by nationalization."[73]

For Electric Boat, the hearings effectively placed their overall business under tighter governmental control. Designs for the boats being built in the late 1930s were prepared by both the U.S. Navy and Electric Boat. The Navy, however, coordinated the design effort and combined the best features of both sets of designs. As it turned out, this was soon to be in the best interest of the country. Many, among them Captain A.I. McKee of the Navy (later the design director and assistant general manager of Electric Boat), felt that this arrangement "led to more rapid development of the submarine than would have been accomplished by either of these agencies alone."[74]

That "rapid development" would become essential to the United States just a few short years later.

The Strike of 1937

On February 23, 1937, Local 6 of the Industrial Union of Marine and Shipbuilding Workers of America (IUMSWA), initiated a sit-down strike at the Groton shipyard. The principal reason: The company's refusal to allow the IUMSWA to have "a vote to test the strength of the union against that of the Employees' Association, recognized by the company as the collective bargaining agency."[75] The Employees' Association had protested that 200 to 250 members were not involved in production or maintenance, but in clerical, drafting or administrative duties. As

such, they should be barred from voting, the association said.[76]

The vote itself soon became irrelevant. Union officials declared that 800 men had stopped working during the action and that 500 more would participate at the change of shift. Management disputed the numbers, claiming that only 100 strikers were involved. The union demanded a "$1 an hour minimum for skilled mechanics, rerating of employees, the continuance of a 36-hour week and equal pay for equal work."[77]

Initially, Electric Boat refused to negotiate, maintaining that they had already negotiated with their own union, the Employees' Association, which had been authorized in June 1933 under Section 7 of the National Recovery Administration.[78] In a statement to the press, Vice President Lawrence Spear said that the company was not opposed to labor organizations:

> "[Electric Boat] is now operating and has for some years past been operating under agreements arrived at by collective bargaining with such a labor organization, viz.: the Employees' Association of the Electric Boat Co., Groton Conn., Inc, to which a very large majority of its employees belong."[79]

By May, the National Labor Relations Board prepared for hearings to investigate complaints charging the Employees' Association was "sponsored, dominated, controlled and financed by the management of the Electric Boat Co. in violation of the Wagner labor relations act."[80] Following days of testimony, the board mandated on June 2, 1938 that Electric Boat reinstate 125 sit-down strikers who had been discharged the previous year. The board also determined that the Employees' Association was company-dominated "and ordered the company to disestablish it as a bargaining agency."[81] In August, Electric Boat recognized the Marine and Shipbuilders as the sole collective bargaining agency. The company notified the union that it had received a petition with 1,705 signatures, or 90 percent of the employees eligible to join the union.[82]

With the strike behind them, Electric Boat was able to concentrate on preparing the company for the crisis which was developing in Europe. Within a year, Hitler would invade Poland, plunging the world once again into global conflict.

SPEED TO COOK DER FÜHRER'S GOOSE
AND *TIGHTEN* HIROHITO'S NOOSE

MAKE EVERY MINUTE COUNT
Electric Boat Company

Electric Boat created many imaginative posters during its World War II efforts to unify workers and boost morale.

CHAPTER VI

World War II

In 124 days, U-515 traveled 20,383 nautical miles, sank 10 Allied merchant ships totalling nearly 58,500 tons, and endured 9 depth-chargings, one air attack, and 43 crash dives to avoid enemy aircraft.

Timothy P. Mulligan,
Lone Wolf: The Life and Death of U-Boat Ace Werner Henke

By September 1939, Electric Boat had built 17 new submarines for the U.S. Navy in a construction program that began with the *Cuttlefish* in 1931. While Electric Boat had struggled in 1931 "to find enough odd jobs to hold together a nucleus of some 200 trained men at Groton," by January 1939 employment had grown to 2,300.[1] As Hitler's Panzer divisions surged across the Polish border, Electric Boat was already expanding. The news from Europe only served to hasten the process, as the government began a program to shore up the country's defenses.

In January 1940, the company began to develop plans to expand the North Yard by constructing four additional ways, bringing the total at the Groton plant to nine. By the time of President Franklin Delano Roosevelt's visit to the shipyard in August 1940, the annual production rate at the yard had doubled from three submarines to six and the president surprised the press with a staggering prediction:

"Twice as many submarines as before are being constructed there now, and soon they will be turning them out at the rate of one a month."[2]

A month after Roosevelt's visit, further expansion plans were announced. Work commenced in the South Yard on three additional ship ways, increasing the total to 12. On March 1, 1941, the keel was laid for the *Grunion* in the new North Yard. Employment had swelled to 4,783, more than double the number in early 1939. There were 5,513 workers employed at Electric Boat by the time the first keel was laid in the new South Yard, on June 7, 1941 for the *Barb*.[3]

The government had subsidized Electric Boat's South Yard expansion.[4] Following the Japanese attack on Pearl Harbor in December 1941, the government purchased the Groton Iron Works plant just to the south of Electric Boat, and construction quickly began on 10 more shipping ways. The government invested $9.5 million in building the new yard, described as "a huge undertaking, with much of the yard being blasted out of solid rock."[5] This newest yard, known as the Victory Yard, was officially opened on July 22, 1942, as the keel for the *Dace* was being laid. Employment continued to skyrocket at Electric Boat, reaching 10,249, nearly double that of the previous year.

President Franklin Delano Roosevelt (right rear in car) inspects the Electric Boat-built *Tautog* in 1940.

Personnel Shortages, Recruitment and Training

The rapid expansion of Electric Boat produced two additional challenges: recruiting and training. Submarine construction is considered by many to be the most difficult of shipbuilding jobs. "Submarine space and weight requirements dictated an almost unimaginable complexity of pumps, valves, electrical circuits and mazes of piping."[6] To quickly train new workers, Electric Boat established a unique orientation, similar to an apprenticeship program. Groups of six to eight new hires were sent into the North and South yards to observe and learn from trained mechanics and other personnel. By the time the Victory Yard was completed, they were able to begin working there immediately. "This foresight of the company," said one source, "in hiring learners and enabling them to master the fundamentals of submarine construction made it possible to meet the huge submarine building schedule which was requested later on."[7]

The company also established official apprentice schools in April 1942 in New London and Norwich with the assistance of Connecticut Congressman William J. Fitzgerald and the State Department of Education. Their mission was crucial:

> "At these schools, applicants were taught welding, after which they were assigned to production work. Other new employees were trained at private schools under company direction. Supervisors conferences were set up for foreman training. These were followed by 'Training Within Industry' courses after the War Manpower Commission was established. The 'Training Within Industry' program set up by the Electric Boat Company was the first complete program of its kind in the nation."[8]

Electric Boat also developed an extensive recruiting program to supply manpower at all levels. Before the establishment of the War Manpower Commission, the company worked closely with the U.S. Employment Service throughout Eastern Connecticut. Eventually, the demand for interviewees was so urgent, the agency established an office at the Groton plant to increase the rate of hiring.[9]

Soon however, the pool of talent in the region had been tapped dry. Electric Boat began to look toward other New England states in 1942, and further into New York, West Virginia, Washington D.C., Minnesota and as far away as Puerto Rico. By January 1943, it became necessary to obtain permission from the State Department of Labor to hire 16- and 17-year-old workers. In February 1943, Electric Boat began to hire women to perform construction work and welding tasks which had been performed exclusively by men.[10]

The demands of this enormous growth caused Electric Boat to organize car pools and provide bus service for workers living outside of the area. Housing for new employees and families was also a major challenge. The company implemented questionnaires to determine housing needs and canvassed regional landlords to match employees with homes.[11] On June 26, 1944, employment at the Groton plant peaked at 12,466.

The Construction Record

In 1942, Electric Boat launched 16 submarines, 10 more than in the previous year. President Roosevelt's prediction of one submarine a month had come true, and even higher production rates would follow. In 1943, the company launched 25 boats and in 1944, it launched 23 more, for a rate of nearly one submarine every two weeks at the peak of production. By 1945, as an end could be seen to the war, production levels were cut back to 11 submarines. Electric Boat had delivered a total of 74 submarines to the Navy from the Groton shipyard—more than any other yard in the country. At the peak of production in 1944, women made up 16 percent of the total plant work force.[12] "Production in 1944 by Electric Boat amounted to over $90,000,000," a company official disclosed, "or an approximate rate of $250,000 a day. Ninety–nine percent of output was for direct war purposes, possibly a record for American industry of comparable volume."[13]

This impressive volume of production required an intense level of teamwork. Employees

Pride of the Fleet, a World War II submarine built by Electric Boat, fires two torpedoes at periscope depth.

Nicknamed "giant-killers," ELCO PT boats are depicted here attacking a Japanese cruiser at night.

participated in War Production Committees which convened to find "ways to speed production," and also to consider "suggestions for keeping up morale through the study of worker problems."[14] Labor and management worked in close harmony during the war years, under the supervision of the War Production Board.

Approximately 5,500 men and women employed at Electric Boat were called for service in the military.[15] Even so, the company maintained one of the lowest employee turnover rates of any shipyard in the country, training a total of 7,431 men, women and youths from 1943 through 1945.[16]

The quality and efficiency of construction at Electric Boat was so impressive, that it was awarded the Navy "E" pennant with four stars for "its outstanding performance in the design, construction, and delivery of Submarines for the United States Navy."[17]

"The Navy has seen fit to recognize our efforts and the results we have achieved during the past months. It is now up to us to continue these efforts towards increased production in the future in order that the Navy "E" may be kept flying from our flag staff. In other words, all hands must and will "KEEP 'EM SLIDING."[18]

In 1942, in the midst of the war effort, Electric Boat President Henry R. Carse died. He had been president since the death of Isaac L. Rice 27 years before. Lawrence Y. Spear, who had been serving as vice president and who had joined the company in 1902 was selected to succeed Carse. Henry R. Sutphen was elected executive vice president of the company.

Submarine Construction at Manitowoc

Along with managing its own shipyards, Electric Boat also supervised the construction of 28 submarines at the Manitowoc Shipbuilding Company on Lake Michigan. Eric Ewertz was sent out to Wisconsin to establish the operation. Ewertz, at Electric Boat since its founding, had supervised construction of the *Holland* at the Crescent Shipyard in 1896, and was the individual who remarked that it would be "a damn good idea" if the inventor, John Holland, was present during construction. In June 1941, the first keel was laid at the Manitowoc shipyard.[19]

Unlike the slide launchings at the Groton plant, Manitowoc submarines were launched sideways into Lake Michigan. Because of depth limitations, the subs were shipped on floating docks, which drew only six feet of water, along the Chicago Sanitary & Ship Canal from Lake Michigan to the Illinois River, to the Mississippi River to New Orleans. After arriving at the Gulf of Mexico, the boats got underway on their own power to sail to Groton for sea trials.[20]

Other War Production

Besides submarines, Electric Boat and its divisions were responsible for a wide range of other wartime production. Among these strategic products were:

6	Large special compartmented marine caissons (for invasion landing facilities).
7,667	Electric motors for submarine, fire control, and other uses (Electro-Dynamic Division).
33,738	Smoke pots for surface and air combat screen (ELCO).
113	Quadruple 20 millimeter gun turrets.
133	Pieces of naval ordnance, such as torpedo tubes, gunmount and depth charge racks.
15,000	Mortar traversing gears.
210	Detonating devices.
857	Breech blocks and mortar yokes.[21]

ELCO PT Boat Construction

ELCO got into PT construction after the Secretary of the Navy asked the company to submit designs. Sutphen and Irwin Chase, ELCO's chief designer, went to England and secured the design, blueprints and rights to build a fast, 70-foot boat designed by Hubert Scott-Paine. The deal cost ELCO $300,000. A prototype, built in Bayonne, along with a complete set of plans, was delivered to New London just three days after war broke out in Europe in September 1939. The boat was put through rigorous trials, then delivered to the Navy, which commissioned it as the PT 9. This first ELCO PT boat had four 18-inch torpedoes carried in four bow tubes, was powered by three Rolls-Royce engines and could sustain speeds of 50 knots in smooth water.[22]

Following the U.S. Navy's acceptance of the PT 9, ELCO manufactured 10 boats of similar design, powered by three 1,200-horsepower Packard engines. These boats were eventually transferred to the British under the lend-lease program. ELCO then began work on a larger 77-foot boat displacing 50 tons, which was armed

with four, 21-inch torpedoes. By July 1941, the company had delivered 28 of these new boats to the U.S. Navy.[23]

Other shipbuilders, anxious for wartime naval orders, had also submitted designs for this PT class of boats. The Navy elected to hold competitive trials, later nicknamed the "First Plywood Darby." Three ELCO PT boats entered the competition. The trio took the first three places, averaging 38 knots over the 160-mile course. In the "Second Plywood Darby," ELCO PT boats again finished first.[24]

The final ELCO PT boat design, on which the majority of the 399 boats delivered to the Navy would be based, was slightly larger at 80 feet long, with a 21-foot beam and a 5-foot draft. Fully loaded, the boat could still top 40 knots. The boats could be armed with either four torpedo tubes or two tubes and eight depth charges, or four mine racks along with machine guns, anti–aircraft guns and smokescreen generators. The boats carried a complement of 11 men, including two officers.[25] Among the most famous of these officers was Lieutenant (junior grade) John F. Kennedy, who commanded the ELCO-built PT 109 and was destined to become the 35th president of the United States. In 1943, Kennedy's boat was cut in half by a Japanese destroyer in the South Pacific. Kennedy was declared a hero for swimming three-and-a-half miles to a nearby island while towing an injured member of his crew; he was discharged in 1945 with the Purple Heart and the Navy and Marine Corps medal.

Electric Boat Submarines in World War II

The overwhelming majority of American submarine combat action during World War II was found in the Pacific theatre. For a short time during the early months of the war, the U.S. Navy had a submarine squadron based in Scotland. America's European allies had decided to conduct Atlantic submarine operations following the Axis invasion of North Africa. The Scotland-based squadron managed to score a few kills but those numbers were insignificant in comparison with submarine warfare in the Pacific.[26]

Following Pearl Harbor, when a significant portion of America's Pacific fleet was destroyed, submarines were considered "the thin gray line of defense,"[27] the only "naval forces that could penetrate enemy controlled waters and operate offensively against Japanese sea-power."[28] Although the submarine service accounted for only 1.6 percent of the Navy's total personnel, submariners accounted for an incredible 63 percent of all Japanese merchant ships sunk and destroyed a record 276 combat vessels. In sum, American submarines dispatched 2,637 ships totalling 10,689,800 tons.[29] Submarines built by Electric Boat, "accounted for 39 percent of the total tonnage of Japanese ships sunk unassisted by all U.S. submarines during World War II. ... The Electric Boat submarine sinking the greatest tonnage was the *Flasher*, with 100,231 tons to her credit. Another Electric Boat submarine, the *Tautog*, holds the record for the largest number of Japanese ships sent to the bottom, with a total of 26 enemy vessels sunk."[30]

An inventory of enemy vessels sunk, includes the following categories:

Merchant ships	2,422
Small warships	121
Submarines	28
Destroyers	42
Cruisers	15
Carriers	8
Battleships	1[31]

American submarine forces paid dearly for these prizes in action. Fifty-two submarines were lost during the conflict, resulting in the deaths of more than 3,500 submariners.[32]

Submarines aided the war effort in other important ways. They "carried supplies to beleaguered Corregidor, supplied and reinforced guerillas in the Philippines, were of inestimable value in reconnaissance, and succeeded in rescuing 504 Allied aviators from enemy-controlled waters."[33] A Navy pilot named George Bush was among the naval aviators rescued at sea by America's submarine force, picked up by *Finback* after being shot down by the Japanese. This same George Bush later became America's 41st president.

The Japanese considered the courageous exploits of American Navy submarines extremely effective. "One of the decisive factors in our defeat was the activity of American submarines which cut off the supplies from that source entirely,"[34] said Shun Namura, who was in charge of Mitsui Oil industry during the war, regarding obtaining crucial oil supplies from Japan's principal source in the Dutch East Indies.

Features of World War II Submarines

The typical World War II submarine was 311 feet in length, had a beam of 27 feet and displaced 1,527 tons. It carried one deck gun and two anti-aircraft guns. Its major threat came from the 24 torpedoes the boat carried which were fired from six bow tubes and four stern tubes. The boat was powered by a full diesel-electric drive which generated 5,400 horsepower and propelled the boat to 20 knots on the surface and 9 knots submerged. Operating all this power and armament was a crew of 65, which increased to about 80 during the war.[35]

A great many improvements were made from the submarines of the First World War. Among the principal design changes was the use of a partial double hull, which was first implemented in the construction of the *Cuttlefish*. The main hull, which housed the crew and equipment, remained circular in its cross section. An outer hull was constructed around portions of the main hull, the space between forming the main ballast tanks. Designers placed a superstructure over the full length of the boat atop both hulls.

The full diesel-electric drive was the latest step in powerplant evolution which attempted to solve the dilemma of how to get high power out of a compact size. Initially, designers doubled the number of engines from two to four, setting the engines up in tandem on each propeller shaft. However, this arrangement did not prove satisfactory. Next, a partial diesel-electric drive was implemented in which two large engines each turned a propeller shaft while an electric motor added its "output to that of the main engines thereby boosting the total propulsion power accordingly."

The next phase saw a new breed of high-speed diesel engines which were smaller, lighter, more reliable and less subject to vibration. The result was almost a 3-knot increase in speed, but the high-speed engines could not be coupled directly to the propeller shafts. At first high-speed motors were connected to the propeller shafts with reduction gears to handle the output of the high-speed diesel engines. Eventually, both motors were reduced in speed sufficiently to eliminate the need for reduction gears.

Torpedoes also went through an evolution from slow, erratic projectiles to new designs capable of speeds of more than 40 knots. The first torpedoes of World War II were driven by compressed air. These were soon succeeded by larger, faster steam-driven models. Steam-driven torpedoes were propelled by igniting "a combustible mixture of compressed air, a liquid fuel and water." Stability was improved by adopting the use "of two oppositely rotating propellers, one directly back of the other."

Submarines continued to go through an evolution of their own. Radar and a 20 percent increase in fuel capacity enhanced submarine efficiency. A new valve design on the main ballast tanks shortened diving time by one-third. By the end of the war, the ships' interior noise levels were reduced to a mere one percent of what they were at its beginning.

These developments, and others, extended the range of submarines to several thousand miles. Maintaining crew comfort was vital to maximizing crew efficiency on patrols lasting many weeks. Thus motivated, designers set out to improve living accommodations. To the bare

The posters shown here were part of an effort by Electric Boat to boost morale, improve safety, maintain security and encourage participation in war bond drives.

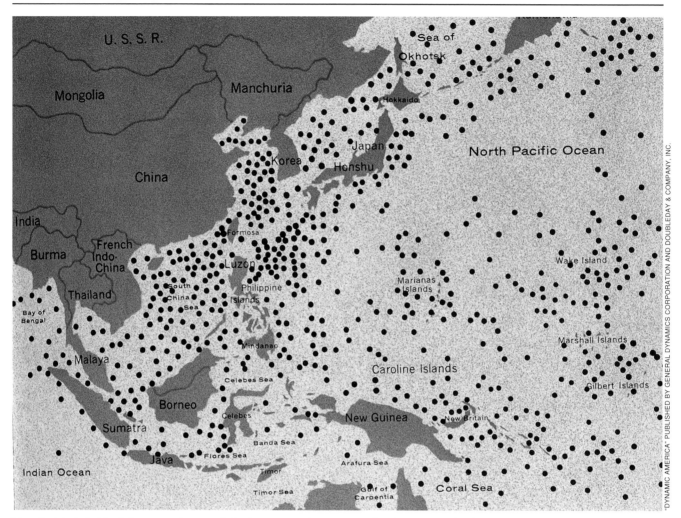

Map depicts individual Japanese ships sunk by American submarines in the Western Pacific during World War II.

necessities of folding cots, an electric stove and a water closet, were added berths and lockers for crew members and staterooms for officers. As early as 1920, submarines used forced air ventilation and air conditioning. Refrigeration and freezer storage soon followed, making it possible to store fresh vegetables and meat for more than a month. Fresh water was supplied by evaporators which purified sea water.

Submarines in Action

Within days of the bombing of Pearl Harbor, the U.S. submarine *Swordfish* sank a 9,000-ton Japanese freighter named the *Atsutusan Maru*. Soon, submarines were making five to six kills a month that "climbed steadily to a heady 69 in one month of 1944." By the end of the war, more than 14,500 torpedoes were fired.[36] Japanese shipping, which numbered 2,337 merchant ships at the beginning of the war, had been winnowed to 231—less than a tenth of the original fleet size.[37] U.S. submarines had ventured close enough to Japan to

hear the voice of Tokyo Rose who "at first boasted that American submarines were of little consequence—mere playthings, as it were—and that they soon would be annihilated by Japanese men-of-war. But later she changed her tune. As Jap ship after Jap ship went down, she began referring to Yankee undersea craft as 'The Black Panthers of the Pacific.'"[38]

On September 8, 1939, these submarines were in active commission:

R-2, R-4, R-10, R-11, R-13, R-14, S-18, S-20 through S-30, S-34 through S-47, Argonaut, Nautilus, Narwhal, Dolphin, Cachalot, Cuttlefish, Porpoise, Pike, Shark, Tarpon, Perch, Pickerel, Permit, Plunger, Pollack, Pompano, Salmon, Seal, Skipjack, Snapper, Stingray, Sturgeon and Sargo.[39]

The Battle of Midway "marked a turning-point in two respects," according to historian Richard Garrett. "It put an end to the Japanese advance across the long and empty expanse of the Pacific. It also signified the coming of age of American submarines. The days of defective torpedoes and apprenticeship in tactics were over. They knew what they had to do and did it very well. ...It may have been a defensive action, but it was carried out in an offensive manner. This was something that submariners understood. There was no question of hoping that the intended victims would come to them. They went out and found them."

Nine American submarines stationed at Midway were ordered to intercept the incoming Japanese naval force. Two of these—ships built by Electric Boat—became famous for their roles in the offensive. The *Cuttlefish* was the first ship to alert the American armada of the Japanese navy's approach while the enemy was still 700 miles away. The *Tambor* inadvertently caused two Japanese heavy cruisers to collide while pursuing her, consequently aborting their mission to bombard Midway.[40]

The company's 1945 annual report gave accounts of Electric Boat submarine conquests and the bravery of their crews in action.

"... The USS *Greenling* departed Midway on 22 September, 1942, for the waters off Honshu. During 41 days at sea, four ships were sunk by torpedo fire, one sampan by gunfire, and a 22,000-ton converted carrier was damaged by two torpedoes ... "

"Another E.B.Co sub, the USS *Sealion* ... sank the 30,000-ton *Kongo*, a Japanese battleship, with wakeless torpedoes. It was the first time in history that a lone Navy vessel of any type had sunk a Jap battleship unassisted ... In addition, the *Sealion* rescued 54 Australian and British prisoners of war, survivors of the Jap prison ship, *Rykuyu Maru*, sunk by the *Sealion* during her second war patrol... "

"... The *Barb* braved the perils of a tropical typhoon to rescue fourteen British and Australian prisoners of war who had survived the torpedoing and sinking of a hostile transport ship enroute from Singapore to the Japanese Empire ... "

"...The USS *Salmon*, on one of her many war patrols, contacted a large hostile tanker, boldly approached in defiance of four vigilant escort ships cruising within 1,000 yards of the target and launched her torpedoes to score direct and damaging hits. Damaged by terrific depth charging, the *Salmon* battle-surfaced to effect emergency repairs and fight it out. Firing only when accurate hits were assured, and confusing the enemy by her evasive tactics, in a brilliant surprise attack she charged her opponent with all available speed and opened fire with every gun aboard, destroying most of Jap topsides. Still

Thousands of women eagerly answered Electric Boat's wartime personnel shortage and helped to "Keep 'em Sliding" for America's defense.

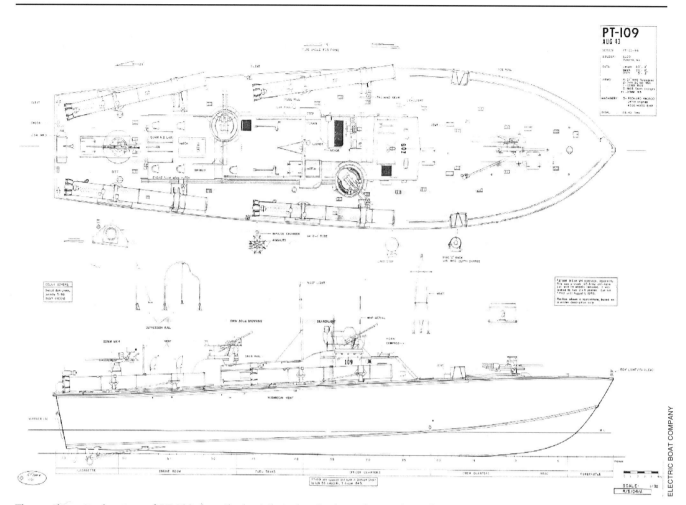

These schematic drawings of *PT 109* show the boat that played a key role in military history and a presidential legacy.

maintaining her fire, she escaped into a rain squall ... "

> "The story of the USS Darter and USS Dace, two E.B.Co submarines, provides a dramatic example of wolf pack tactics used with great success. When Japan was deploying her naval forces for her desperate attempt to save the Philippines, our subs Dace and Darter sank two heavy cruisers, the Ataggo and Maya, and so badly damaged a third that it was inoperative to the end of the war... It was the laying of the keel for the Dace, on July 22, 1942, incidentally, that marked the opening of the Electric Boat Company Victory Yard, which attained an outstanding record for speed in submarine production and thus materially hastened the successful ending of the war in the Pacific." [41]

Electric Boat was quite proud of its service in building battle-worthy vessels which proved more than capable under the most severe battle conditions. The company's 1945 annual report boasted that Electric Boat submarines and their crews received 777 citations: 10 Presidential Unit Citations, 8 Navy Unit Commendations, 2 Medals of Honor, 97 Navy Crosses, 16 Legion of Merit awards, 254 Navy Silver Stars, 81 Navy and Marine Corps Medals, and 309 Bronze Stars.[42]

The Record of the *Tautog*

The *Tautog* was launched as part of the Tambor class which included 12 submarines, six of which were built at Electric Boat. The *Tautog* had an operational design depth of 250 feet and a range of approximately 10,000 miles at 10 knots surfaced, a maximum surface speed of 20 knots and a submerged speed of just over 8 knots. Among her armaments were 10 torpedo tubes, six at her bow and four astern. The *Tautog's* battle career began on the day Pearl Harbor was bombed—when she made her first kill. It was not another submarine or sea-going vessel of any type but an airplane which was shot down with her deck guns as it swooped down on the submarine.[43]

Early in the war, the *Tautog* made her way to the Marshall Islands. During the voyage, her crew spotted a Japanese submarine's periscope in a position indicating that the enemy vessel had just fired a torpedo. The *Tautog* made a hard left rudder, brought her stern tubes into position and fired a single torpedo. An explosion confirmed it found its mark. The pilot of the patrol plane called in to inspect the area reported debris in the water. The 1,000-ton *RO-30* became one of a rapidly mounting number of Japanese vessels successfully targeted by U.S. submarines.

The *Tautog* was also involved in laying mine fields along the coast of Indochina and off Balikpapan in the Makassar Strait. According to Clay Blair Jr., author of *Silent Victory*, one of these mines sunk the Japanese destroyer *Amagiri*, the vessel which had earlier in the war cut LTJG John Kennedy's *PT-109* in half. The *Tautog* carried both mines and torpedoes on many of her missions.

The *Tautog's* officers and men were very proud of their submarine. Her last commander, Thomas Baskett, said, "We prided ourselves in still being around at the end of the war; we were one of the oldest fleet subs left."

The submarine was decommissioned in 1945 and used as a training vessel until 1959. She was then sold to a former World War II submariner who tried to establish her as a national shrine. Eventually, he was forced to scrap her, but he sent the *Tautog's* periscope, torpedo door, sonar and helm wheel to the Milwaukee Public Museum in Wisconsin. Eventually, the parts were transferred back to the Navy in the 1970s.

The conning tower of the *Flasher*, the submarine which held the record for most tonnage sunk during the war, is now on display in a memorial park in Groton, less than a mile from where she was built.

Postwar Planning

Electric Boat was determined not to find itself in the same position after World War II that it found itself in after World War I. There was a general cutback in arms production beginning in mid-1944. Electric Boat had its final launching, the *Corporal*, in the Victory Yard on June 10, 1945. It was the last of 11 launchings for the year.

Electric Boat was confident that resources already committed would not be lost when wartime contracts were cancelled. The company had only to review the lean years just after World War I to remind themselves that postwar planning was crucial. As early as 1943, Electric Boat reported the establishment of postwar reserves.

> *"Your Board is mindful of the contingencies which in all likelihood may face the Company in the transformation from war to post-war conditions and, as a result, during the three years ended December 31, 1943, the sum of $4,120,226 has been accumulated out of net earnings, after all*

> *taxes, in reserves to meet contingent post-war and other unascertained expenses." [44]*

Beyond financial planning, Electric Boat also began a system for exploring postwar opportunities:

> *"This subject is being given constant consideration both by the management and the Directors, who have recently appointed a special committee to study anticipated post-war conditions and investigate the possibility of utilizing our plant and staff in various kinds of post-war work." [45]*

The company stressed, however, that meeting wartime demand was its dominant responsibility for the foreseeable future.

> *"'Winning the War' comes first, is foremost in our minds and attention of every member of the Electric Boat organization, and will be until World War II ends in Victory, in Europe and in the Pacific." [46]*

The U.S. government was also seriously engaged in postwar planning. In a report prepared for the U.S. Navy and the U.S. Maritime Commission by the Graduate School of Business Administration at Harvard, the authors made a number of recommendations. Based on the observation that it takes 1.2 million man-hours to build a submarine and 240,000 man-hours to perfect a design, the Harvard researchers concluded that, since these skills were essential to national security, every effort should be made to preserve a nucleus of skilled workers and designers.[47] One recommendation was to preserve a nucleus of active, private shipyards with the following features:

> a) *Ability to expand rapidly.*
> b) *Ability to advance the art of shipbuilding.*
> c) *Versatility.*
> d) *Ability to build ships at the smallest cost to the taxpayer.[48]*

With the surrender of Japan on August 15, 1945, World War II finally came to an end. Electric Boat summarized the company's future mission following the war:

> *"Twice within a single generation America has been forced into a world war, because our enemies considered us unprepared. From bitter experience we in the United States now know that we must maintain the development of key security weapons in proportion to our devotion to a world peace. The responsibility of the Electric Boat Company, as pioneer builders of United States submarines, is to help maintain America's leadership in submarine invention and development through a moderate building program keyed to the proved concept that to keep peace, America must keep pace." [49]*

John Jay Hopkins, 1893-1957, president of Electric Boat Company from 1947 to 1952, was the founder, first chairman and president of General Dynamics Corporation from 1952 to 1957.

CHAPTER VII

Post-World War II

*E*lectric Boat, I've seen it over the years. ... At the end of World War II, it was
a very, very professional, hard-core group of people tremendously dedicated to putting out a very fine product ... That feeling continued.

Vice Admiral Robert Y. Kaufman,
in a 1994 interview

Fiftieth Anniversary
1899-1949

Electric Boat had been thrust into postwar planning as early as 1944 when "there was a major termination of submarine contracts affecting work scheduled for 1946 and 1947."[1] A total of 34 submarine contracts were cancelled in 1944.[2] The company did not want a repeat of their reputation following the First World War—a "Hero in War, Orphan in Peace." While there were no further contract cancellations in 1945, the Navy cancelled the purchase of two submarines in January 1946. Although this was a disappointing development, the local newspaper reported that the future remained bright for Electric Boat.

"Coincident with the announcement by the Navy of the cutback of two submarines at the Electric Boat Co., it was learned today that there are still six submarines under construction and the company understands that the cutback does not alter the basic plan of the navy department to continue the Groton yard as a submarine building plant.

"Two of the six submarines now under construction are on the building ways and four are at the wet dock.

"In addition, the Electric Boat Co. is in the process of decommissioning a substantial number

of submarines which were active in the war and which had such an important part in the destruction of the Japanese fleet and in battering Japan's navy into submission. This process requires a considerable amount of work involving many employees.

"The unexpected cutback means that there will be a reduction in personnel until such time as other activities at the Electric Boat Co., not only submarine construction, but work on numerous postwar civilian projects, builds up, it was pointed out."[3]

Eventually, the two submarines cancelled in January 1946 were "later restored on a partial completion basis."[4] This marked the end of the World War II submarine program. Consequently, "the dollar volume of Company product deliveries in 1946 represented a sharp decrease from the 1945 total."[5] Gross income for 1946 amounted to $14,368,954, a decrease of $31,070,508 from 1945. Approximately $10 million of the 1946 income was from submarines. Still, the company's 1946 annual report notes a "substantial volume of business from new products, although the latter suffered handicaps principally due to shortages of essential materials and, to a lesser degree, from the difficulty of obtaining skilled and productive workmen."

Postwar Planning and Diversification

Electric Boat announced plans for an ambitious program of diversification in its 1945 annual report. "The development of new products and better methods, now being carried on at an unprecedented rate by enterprising American concerns, will keynote this Company's future plans for diversified production."[6] The company also was optimistic that new and emerging technologies would herald a new age of expanded submarine development:

"Tomorrow, in view of the atomic bomb and probable developments in atomic power, the submarine will assume an even greater role in the opinion of many naval experts. Some have gone so far as to predict that submarines will become the capital ships of our future Navy."[7]

An Associated Press story dated January 7, 1946 revealed postwar plans for a U.S. Navy fleet comprised of 319 warships and 90 submarines. According to the report, 39 of the submarines would be assigned to the Pacific fleet and the remaining 51 to the Atlantic fleet.[8] The 90 submarines, however, included boats already on active duty plus the six under construction at Electric Boat.[9] The company thought it wise not to depend solely on submarine construction and to begin diversification in commercial construction. This reasoning proved very beneficial.

"It has often been said, 'if you can build a submarine you can build anything.' In hardly any other product are tremendous strength, complete dependability and mechanical precision so essential. A world in itself, often completely isolated under the most hazardous circumstances, the very lives of all aboard a submarine are dependent upon the reliability of its construction and mechanisms. For personnel with talents for designing and building such a complicated mechanism, automatic machinery for instance presents no insuperable problems."[10]

Three projects were currently under research and development—an electric pin-setter, color offset presses and Armorlite truck bodies.

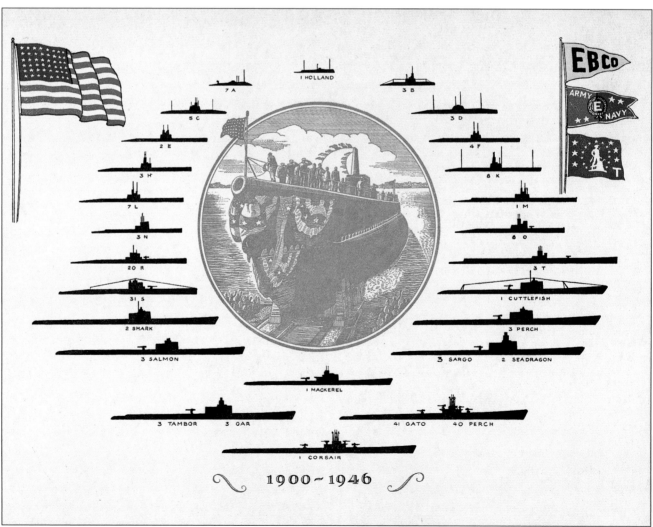

Graphics within the official Electric Boat Christmas card of 1946. Silhouettes depict the classes of boats built by the company.

ELECTRIC BOAT COMPANY

During the post-WWII period, Electric Boat mass-produced Armorlite truck bodies. The photo shows one of the lightweight van panel bodies made from a unique aluminum magnesium construction.

Postwar Commercial Products and Services

Electric Boat was attempting to develop products and services which "would assume a permanent position in its manufacturing program."[11] The company did not want to engage in "stop-gap measures of the type undertaken during the 1930s." One such initiative was to utilize the two foundries at Groton to turn out castings for both commercial and naval work, a program which had begun in 1945.

"Castings being made in the iron foundry and being machined in the shops are destined for such varied and modern uses as package-wrapping machines, package-filling machinery, air conditioning equipment, heavy machine tools, and buffing and polishing machinery. E.B.Co is also fabricating iron pulleys for Pullman car generators, heavy castings for iron presses and punches for the automobile industry, cylinder, piston and cylinder head castings for Diesel engines, and iron castings for oil burners."[12]

Electric Boat also laid keels for the manufacture of steel commercial fishing vessels in 1945, a program they felt well suited to perform.

"The outstanding dependability and strength evidenced by E.B.Co subs in standing terrific water pressures, make the company a natural for the production of these rugged commercial vessels. Built to go out and take any weather, they are also designed for speed, to reduce time spent enroute to and from the fishing banks, an advantage of decided importance to the fishing industry."[13]

Electric Boat pursued new manufacturing ventures which would best utilize the immense pool of skills and resources already existing at the company. The electric Pin-Boy, for example, was seen as a way to use the "same ingenuity which E.B.Co had applied to building submarines"[14] to develop this complex machine, an automatic pin-setting machine used in bowling alleys. Color offset presses were viewed by the company as a way to "exploit its talents in the automatic machinery field." Even Armorlite truck bodies—"constructed with extruded magnesium girders bonded to a metal-clad interior lining"—had the ring of submarine work.

Of course, not every idea came to fruition. In November 1945, Lawrence Y. Spear, the president of Electric Boat, received a preliminary survey, *The Roadside Diner*, prepared by an industrial counseling firm advocating that the company consider building these prefabricated metal structures that commonly housed roadside restaurants. Electric Boat never pursued the idea, although the report indicated that the product's market was good.[15]

Electric Boat's offset printing presses coming off the production line at the Printing Machinery Division.

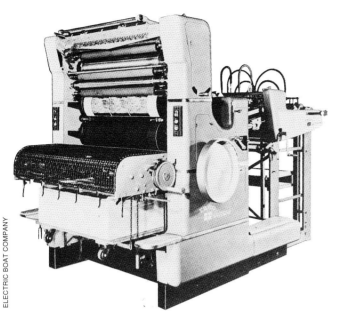

ELECTRIC BOAT COMPANY

The EBCo Willard Offset Press was the first and last of a line of lithographic equipment produced by the company's Printing Machinery Division at Groton. The press was built during the post-WWII period.

The Transition to Peace

Despite Electric Boat's careful planning, the postwar years were not easy ones. Shifting from wartime to peacetime production required a great many readjustments within the company itself. Combined with physical conversion, elimination of artificial wartime controls, and shortages of manpower and materials, disruption is inevitable. The early postwar years were also a time of "frequent and widespread stoppages and prolonged industrial conflict between business, management and workers. Enormous pent up demands have been left unsatisfied, with consequent losses in production and in income, which may never be recovered."[16] Like most American manufacturers, between 1945 and 1947, Electric Boat "faced reconversion delays, shortages and wage increases which originated in forces beyond the Company's control. It suffered, and is still suffering to a lesser degree, unanticipated losses in production and income." Still, the company was able to report a net operating profit for 1946.

Electric Boat had formed a Printing Machinery Division during the year with sales offices in New York and production facilities at the Groton plant. There, workers made ready to produce the E.B.Co 22" x 34" Willard Offset Press, the first of its line of precision-engineered products being built for the lithographing trade. In its annual report, the company said it had already received "scores of inquiries."[17]

The company also established the Commercial Body Division at Groton to build Armorlite truck bodies. The division had already built close to 1,000 "to meet the increasing demand from all sections of the country." The truck bodies came in five standard sizes ranging from 9 feet to 20 feet and offered seven different types of door equipment.[18]

Meanwhile, the E.B.Co Electric Pin-Boy was nearing production. The machine had met the requirements of the National Duckpin Bowling Congress. Furthermore, it had "proved its efficiency in many 'road tests' keeping it in continuous operation for hundreds of frames." The intent was to demonstrate the machine to as many owners of bowling lanes as possible in order to show off its ability to reset pins in only 12 seconds and to remove "dead wood" in only 10 seconds.[19]

Electric Boat was more cautious about the marketability of its steel fishing trawlers in 1946 than it was the year before. Although the trawlers had "aroused great interest in the fishing industry and have earned much favorable comment in the industry's publications," the company questioned whether the trawlers would ever be mass-produced. That would depend "on the stabilization of material and labor costs at practical levels."

Traditional ship overhaul work was continually sought during this period. Electric Boat could boast about its "exceptionally complete and efficient facilities for overhaul and conversion work on ships of many types." Among the many vessels reconditioned at the yard was the *Eagle*, a bark-rigged cadet training ship used by the United States Coast Guard Academy. The company was also still engaged in building automatic machines and producing castings. Forty die-stamping machines with 50-ton capacity and seven machines with 150-ton capacity were built or started during 1946 for a New England manufacturer along with a growing list of other commercial mechanical equipment.[20]

"...plastic molding presses, power driven sheet metal shears, bottle-filling machines with capacities ranging from an ounce to a quart, washing and rinsing machines for glass containers of various sizes, package-filling machines (for soap flakes, cereals, etc.), labeling machines and others."[21]

The Acquisition of Canadair

On March 1, 1946, John Jay Hopkins, vice president of Electric Boat, received a report from Ford, Bacon & Davis, an engineering firm specializing in business evaluations responding to a company request seeking "an investigation of the organization, plant and business of Canadair, Limited." The review had the full

The acquisition of Canadair gave
Electric Boat entre to the skies—
and new business opportunities.

cooperation of Canadair's officers, who also assisted in "brief general inspections of the property." The report included a brief history of the Canadian company, its products, management and facilities, and an analysis which disclosed prospective business, including: "1. Confirmed orders—unfilled. 2. Orders placed or promised but unconfirmed in writing. 3. Probable additional orders." The report advanced no specific recommendation. [22]

Electric Boat management must have sensed Canadair's potential, even though some considered the Canadian company "a white elephant at any price." On April 30, 1946, Electric Boat purchased 10 percent of Canadair's stock with an option to purchase 6,500 additional shares for $2 million Canadian.[23] The agreement also required the addition of Electric Boat officials John Jay Hopkins and O. Pomeroy Robinson to Canadair's board of directors.[24]

This purchase took Electric Boat into a new medium—the skies. Canadair, which was originally operated by Canadian Vickers, Ltd., had begun aircraft construction as early as 1923. By 1945, the Canadian company was converting C-47 military transports into DC-3 commercial transports for Eastern Airlines and Trans-Canada Airlines. By this time, Canadair also acted as a management agent for the Canadian government. Under terms of the agreement with Electric Boat, Canadair was required to initiate negotiations with the Canadian government to return the company to a private enterprise. After dissolving its official relationship with the Canadian government, Canadair Limited became a wholly owned subsidiary of Electric Boat Company on January 20, 1947. Electric Boat also

exercised its option to purchase the additional stock, providing the new acquisition with $2.4 million Canadian in working capital.[25]

The first Willard Offset Press was shipped in May 1947.[26] By year's end, the company had shipped presses to "graphic arts centers in the United States as far west as Chicago, as well as in New Zealand, Argentina, Canada, India, Portugal and Switzerland."[27] Production continued during 1947 for Armorlite truck bodies and automatic equipment. Overhaul work was highlighted by continuing work on the *Eagle*, along with work on the *Atlantis*, a ketch owned by the prestigious Woods Hole Oceanographic Society, and on four commercial trawlers.[28] Electric Boat also became involved during the year in fabricating steel highway bridges on the Wilbur Cross Parkway in Connecticut.[29] Business had steadily improved throughout the year, with employment increasing from 1,520 to 1,724 by the end of the year.[30]

In 1948, Electric Boat renewed its pursuit of defense contracts, although it continued to develop and build presses, fabricate bridges, overhaul ships and make castings.[31] The company secured a submarine order backlog of nearly $30 million on June 30, 1949. The local newspaper characterized the company as "occupied principally with submarine manufacture and modernization."[32] Thanks to the Canadair acquisition, this backlog of defense work rose to an unprecedented $75 million, according to Dow-Jones:

"The service said the company's backlog is expected to get a substantial boost by the signing of a $25,000,000 order with the Canadian government for North American F-86 jet fighters. They will

U.S. Coast Guard training vessel, *Eagle*, on marine railway at Electric Boat for overhaul work in 1945.

be constructed by the company's wholly owned Canadian aircraft subsidiary, Canadair, Ltd.

"Signing of the F-86 order will bring the company's backlog to a new peacetime high of about $75,000,000 . . ."[33]

By 1950, the only commercial product mentioned in the annual report was the offset printing press[34]; by 1951, only this paragraph about commercial work in general was included:

"Commercial work performed by the plant's foundries, machine shops, structural steel fabricating shop and pattern shops continues to meet with customer approval."[35] Electric Boat had relegated commercial manufacture "to the extent practicable under the present volume of defense production."[36]

Electric Boat's New President— John Jay Hopkins

The architect of the Canadair acquisition was John Jay Hopkins, a director of Electric Boat since 1937 who was named a vice president in 1942. In July 1947, Hopkins succeeded Spear as president of the company after Spear was elected chairman of the board.[37] Hopkins would serve

the company for 10 years. During that decade, Electric Boat underwent considerable growth and diversification—not surprising for a man whose motto was, "Grow or die." Making Electric Boat into "a huge, diversified establishment, responsible for not merely one element of the nation's defense but for as many elements or systems as one corporation could handle" was Hopkins' overriding goal. Though criticized by some who thought his acquisitions risky, even reckless, Hopkins had a clear vision of what shape the postwar world would take. He saw that the "need for defense was a permanent need, and not one that could be satisfied by improvisation in a time of crisis."

In his quest to become the foremost defense contractor, Hopkins would accept the challenge issued in 1950 by then Captain Hyman G. Rickover to build a nuclear-powered submarine. His critics insisted that only an organization employing the scientists, engineers and facilities that had originally developed atomic power could design and construct a nuclear submarine. Hopkins also engineered a controlling interest in Consolidated Vultee in 1951, even though that company's future looked uncertain.

One of the bridge frameworks built by Electric Boat during post-WWII period of diversification.

ELECTRIC BOAT COMPANY

ELECTRIC BOAT COMPANY

The WWII submarine, *Halfbeak* (SS-352) in her berth at Electric Boat following Guppy conversion.

In 1952, Hopkins restructured Electric Boat to create General Dynamics Corporation—a new name reflecting a new purpose. It was a skillful move that Electric Boat's first president, Isaac L. Rice, would have undoubtedly admired.

With submarines, aircraft and missiles already combined in the company's manufacturing portfolio, Hopkins established the General Atomic Division in 1955 to "undertake basic research, development and production in nuclear energy." In his last major acquisition, he acquired Stromberg-Carlson in 1955 to add fast-developing electronics technology to the growing corporation. During this phase of acquisition and restructuring, Electric Boat became a division of General Dynamics. [38]

Postwar Submarine Construction and Maintenance

Efforts were refocused on submarine construction even as the company endeavored to establish its presence in the commercial manufacturing arena. In 1947, the U.S. Navy began a program to modify its World War II fleet submarines in order to "increase submerged speed and incorporate results of Navy research and development based on lessons learned during World War II." [39] Known as the Greater Underwater Propulsion Program (or Guppy), the Navy's program focused on three areas—snorkels, propulsion power and streamlining. The snorkel was one of the more important changes made to the submarine because it allowed the underwater craft to operate at periscope depth while running on diesel power. [40] In operation, one snorkel mast supplied fresh air while another vented the exhaust from the diesel engines. The new scheme meant that all the submarine's systems need not rely solely on electric storage batteries, which were quickly depleted while submerged. [41] Recent advances in storage battery design and chemistry significantly increased capacity, enabling batteries to pack more power in the same space and resulting in "higher underwater speed and longer submerged runs without surfacing." [42] Speed was further increased by streamlining the submarine: "reducing the size of its

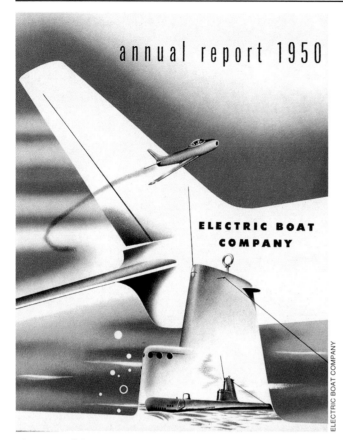

The cover of the 1950 Electric Boat Annual Report reflects a new era of diversification.

superstructure and by removing deck guns and other topside appurtenances which cut down underwater speed."[43]

From 1947 to 1949, Electric Boat completed Guppy modifications on five submarines: the *Corporal, Greenfish, Halfbeak, Cochino* and *Cobbler*.[44] Though additional work was accomplished under this program in the early 1950s, the Guppy program was always viewed as a first step in the Navy's overall postwar modernization program. The Navy was concurrently working toward a future when they could "design and construct the true submarine—a vessel able to cruise around the world with no parts whatsoever exposed above the surface, and capable of launching rockets while still submerged."[45] In 1947, the Navy announced that Electric Boat would receive contracts for four new submarines, "three large fleet-type boats and one of a pioneering nature—an anti-submarine submarine."[46] This last boat was one of the Navy's first steps to assemble a submarine fleet which would some day include boats "for attack, for transport, for oilers, for missile launchers, for minelayers, for radar pickets, and submarines to hunt out and destroy other submarines."[47]

The anti-submarine craft was viewed as vital because of programs—similar to Guppy—initiated by navies of other nations to build "new, long-range submarines capable of high speed underwater and of staying down a long time." The anti-submarine submarine with its "electronic and other locating equipment" was viewed as an advanced prototype, one of several "experimental ships to be used as patterns for full-scale production if needed." In all, the Navy planned to build three. Electric Boat had been contracted to build one of the group. [48]

"The three new anti-submarine submarines will be smaller than any subs built in recent years, but fully equipped to do battle with other submarines on or beneath the surface," said Vice Admiral Earle W. Mills, chief of the bureau of ships.[49]

The keel for the first postwar submarine, the USS *Trigger*, was laid on February 24, 1949.[50] By the end of the year, two more boats were on the building ways under construction. Electric Boat viewed itself in partnership with the U.S. Navy to become the world leaders in submarine design and construction:[51]

> "The Company collaborated with the design agency of the navy in the design and development of these vessels. Security restrictions prevent the release of detailed information with respect to these submarines, but it can be said that they embody the latest features developed from world wide submarine research to achieve important advances in speed, cruising range, maneuverability, hull strength, fire power, efficiency, safety and comfort."[52]

Work continued on the four new submarines throughout 1950. As one of the submarines neared completion in June 1950, the keel for the last of the four was laid. Conversion work on World War II fleet submarines continued throughout the year, along with maintenance and overhaul activity on the four Peruvian submarines which Electric Boat had built in 1926 and 1928 for the Peruvian navy. The boats had remained in "operative status for almost a quarter of a century," a fact which the company provided as an example of its submarines' quality and reliability.[53]

The most significant development for 1950, however, was Electric Boat's participation in "the development of atomic powered submarines":[54]

> "The Groton Plant is now developing basic designs of this vitally important new type of submarine. Working closely with the Navy Department, Westinghouse, and General Electric, the Company's wide submarine experience is being drawn upon to insure complete suitability of the propulsion unit to submarine service. This work is proceeding under the direction of the Atomic Energy Commission, some of whose members, among them Chairman Gordon Dean, visited the Groton Plant last summer. The Company's activity in this revolutionary devel-

opment is another indication of its continuing close association with the evolution of the submarine as an ever more powerful weapon for our country's defense."

In 1951, Electric Boat launched the four submarines which had been under construction since 1948: the USS *K1*, the anti-submarine submarine, the USS *Trigger*, the USS *Trout* and the USS *Harder*.[55]

These launchings were nearly lost in the excitement and tumult of emotions on August 21, 1951, as Electric Boat was chosen to build the *Nautilus*, the world's first nuclear-powered submarine.

Electric Boat's Role in the Early Years of the Cold War

During 1947, John Jay Hopkins' first year as president of Electric Boat, he noted that twice in the "past quarter century this Company has been called upon to give essential aid in meeting national crises." Hopkins described Electric Boat as the "only privately owned shipbuilding organization having the highly experienced staff and specialized facilities needed to meet successfully the requirements of modern submarine construction," and that his perception was that "a long-range submarine program is necessary to preserve the Company's shipbuilding skills."[56]

"Recent international developments indicate that it is by no means clear that a firm basis for permanent peace in the world has yet been found, although every good citizen of this nation cherished the hope that, upon the turn of our country from swords to ploughshares in 1945, a lasting opportunity would be afforded to its people to proceed undisturbed in their peacetime activities and production...

"Apparently not only the whole series of individual freedoms, similar to those guaranteed by our own Bill of Rights, is now at stake throughout the world, but also the entire enlightened civilization for which our ancestors have striven for centuries."

In 1948, Hopkins reaffirmed Electric Boat's commitment to strengthening America's national security.

"Any freedom-loving individual labors under a fearful delusion if he does not recognize that there have been sweeping, far-reaching and fundamental changes in the world since the end of the First World War in 1918. Electric Boat Company, its personnel and its facilities, stands prepared to accept any production responsibility it is capable of discharging in the interest of national defense."[57]

In 1949, the Royal Canadian Air Force executed contracts for 100 F-86A *Sabre* jet fighter planes with Electric Boat's subsidiary, Canadair Limited.[58] Electric Boat began "a series of lectures on atomic energy at its Groton plant in preparation for taking its place in future developments in the field of nuclear ship propulsion."[59]

The government began experimenting with submarine-based guided missiles and rockets, leading up to the launch on November 7, 1949 of a missile from the deck of the submarine *Carbonero*. Traveling at speeds between 400 and 500 miles per hour over a 21-mile course, the missile escaped destruction by the anti-aircraft guns of 35 naval ships and eluded fighter planes.[60]

"A close look at the 'Loon' launching showed the Navy's missile development had reached a stage where submarines could carry a number of jet weapons in normal underseas operations. 'Loon' wings are detachable and the missile and its engine when broken down probably would occupy the same space area in a submarine as three torpedoes.

"The most impressive thing in yesterday's demonstration was the scant launching ramp required to get the bomb into the air with a rocket. After the 'Loon's' jet engine warms up, the rocket jumps the 'Loon' into the air and attains a speed sufficient to develop jet compressive power."

Throughout 1950 rumours continued that Electric Boat was involved in "plans to start construction of what [the United States] hopes to be the world's first atomic-powered submarine."[61] A sense of urgency was in the air, as America viewed itself in a race with Russia to launch the first. In 1951, Hopkins observed that the arms race was accelerating:

"There is nothing in today's world situation—potentially explosive in nearly every segment of the globe—which could conceivably give just cause to relax our vigilance and our efforts. It is only the wishful thinker who believes that aggressor nations can be halted in their plans for world domination by any means other than a well-coordinated progressive program of national and interhemispheric defense—continuing just as long as the present compelling need requires."[62]

Electric Boat, a division of General Dynamics as of April 24, 1952, was ready to win the race. General Dynamics, by then a sprawling, multidisciplinary firm and an integral part of America's military-industrial base, was "engaged in engineering and manufacturing activities wherein nearly every phase of the science of dynamics is applied: hydrodynamics and thermodynamics at the Electric Boat Division, aerodynamics at Canadair Limited, electrodynamics at the Electro Dynamic Division, and the new science of nucleodynamics in the field of industrial applications of atomic energy."[63]

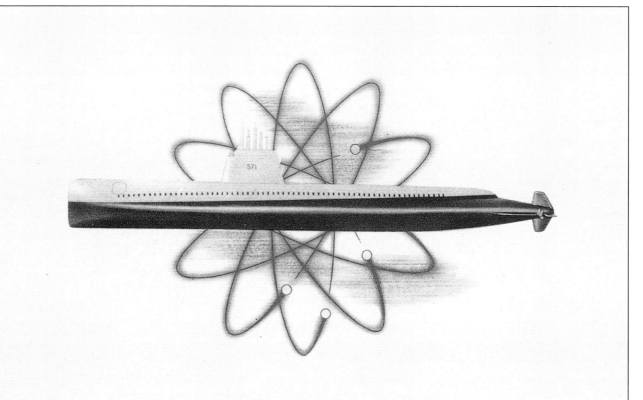

Nautilus

"The NAUTILUS will be able to move under the water at a speed of more than twenty knots. A few pounds of uranium will give her ample fuel to travel thousands of miles at top speed. She will be able to stay under water indefinitely. Her atomic engine will permit her to be completely free of the earth's atmosphere. She will not even require a breathing tube to the surface. . . .

"We are building strength for security. And this ship NAUTILUS is part of that great effort. She is designed to patrol the seas and thus protect our land. She is an answer to the threat of aggression in the world."

HARRY S. TRUMAN
President of the United States

The *Nautilus* was the first submarine to traverse the North Pole submerged. Starting from Pearl Harbor in the Pacific, the *Nautilus* reached the North Pole on August 3, 1958. Thirty-six hours later, the ship resurfaced in the North Atlantic Ocean.

CHAPTER VIII

The Cold War and the Nautilus

*A*ll ships have souls and all men know it, but it takes a while to learn this. *This is why we call them by a personal pronoun and why you'll find one ship is known as the lucky ship, one is the unlucky ship, one is known as the fighting ship ..."*

Captain Edward L. Beach,
first captain of the Triton, in a 1994 interview.

The first half-century of Electric Boat's existence had been filled with wars, financial panics and a depression. There had been lean years and prosperous years. The second half-century would be quieter, but no less momentous. These were the years in which the Cold War heated up to a near-explosive political temperature.

On American shores, signs of a growing international tension began with sightings of mysterious craft off the West Coast in 1950. Early on April 2, observers at two Coast Guard stations simultaneously reported the sighting of a submarine about "eight miles off the rocky edge of Point Arguello and running at 12 knots down the coast." Several others had been reported along the Pacific coast earlier in the year. In the case of the April 2 sighting, the Navy was able to confirm there were "no American submarines in those waters." They immediately responded by sending "dozens of Navy planes" to search the area.[1] Tensions between the Soviet Union and the United States skyrocketed to critical levels. Two years later, in December 1953, Admiral Arthur W. Radford, chairman of the Joint Chiefs of Staff, would graphically de-

scribe the world as "hovering between war and peace."[2]

Coincidentally, on the same day as the sighting in April 1950, congressional defense planners were asking for almost $600 million to be added to defense appropriations. Representative Carl Vinson, a Democrat from Georgia, revealed these plans on the heels of General of the Army Dwight D. Eisenhower's testimony before the Senate that budget increases were necessary. Part of this money was earmarked for anti-submarine warfare which included the conversion of submarines to "sub-killing activity."[3] A month later, Rear Admiral Allan E. Smith, commander of cruisers in the North Atlantic Fleet, was even more adamant about the necessity for a stronger defense posture, saying it was vital for the United States to control the North Atlantic in order to protect Western Europe from a Soviet attack.[4]

"We suffer a weakness for the next five or six years, until Western Europe once again recovers her strength and composure. This gap in time must be filled by the armies, the air force, and above all

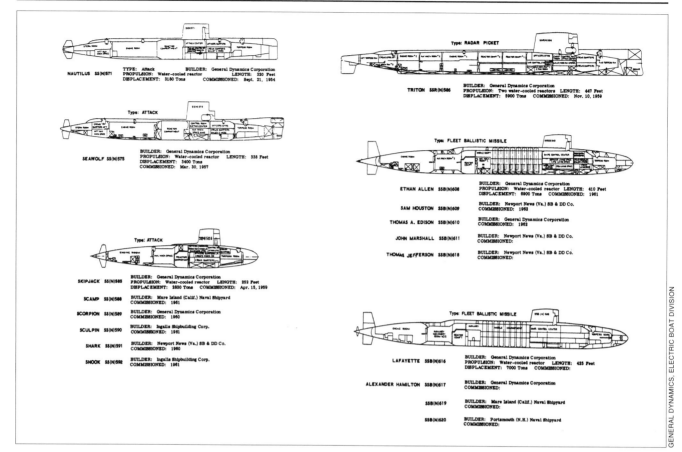

Cutaways of nuclear submarine classes. From top:
Nautilus, Seawolf, Skipjack, Triton, Lafayette, and Ethan Allen

the navies of the non-Communist powers of the world—Great Britain, Canada, Australia, the United States.

"If they misjudge our strength, if their communistic penetration fails, or they believe their country can defend itself against the atom bomb or absorb its damage, if they estimate they can push us out of Western Europe before its recovery—then the temptation may be too great for the Communist leaders to resist."

Others focused on another Soviet threat: frequent "long-range flights across the North Pole and other areas opposite North America's most vulnerable line of defense." These proponents of heightened preparedness cited General Mikhail M. Gromov's *Polar Concept,* which stated that "'the shortest distance between the Soviet Union and the United States is across the top of the world.'" While many in the United States military doubted that the Russians would be capable of mounting an attack across the Arctic for several more years, they were admittedly apprehensive about "the possibility and danger of 'one-shot' air attacks employing the atomic bomb." The United States Air Force was even more apprehensive about Russian transpolar

bombing. General George C. Kennedy, commandant of the University of the Air, was "of the opinion that 'the Communists' will begin such an operation at any time they believe it would be effective."[5]

By the end of 1950, the perceived Russian threat had incited nearly universal anxiety. President Harry S. Truman asked Congress "for $1,050,000,000 with which to multiply the output of atomic weapons." Gordon Dean, chairman of the Atomic Energy Commission, characterized the build-up as representing the most concerted effort since the earlier push to build an atomic bomb. He reported that "there was definitely a high sense of urgency throughout our shop."[6] Meanwhile, Rear Admiral Charles B. Monsen, assistant chief of naval operations for undersea warfare, said that the Navy was less concerned with the Soviet submarine presence in the Pacific than it was with "Russia's long-range submarine building program."[7]

A growing number of advocates in the Navy saw the development of an atomic-powered submarine as the country's best response. Among the strongest and most tenacious was the voice of Captain Hyman G. Rickover.

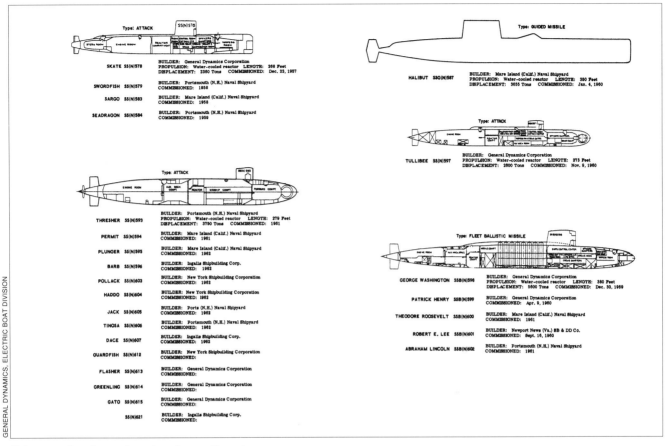

Cutaways of nuclear submarine classes. From top:
Skate, Thresher, Halibut, Tullibee and George Washington.

The Origins of the Nuclear Submarine

Although the submarine had undergone remarkable development in the preceding half-century, the challenge of prolonged submersion was still largely unsolved. The energy generated from storage batteries, regardless of how efficient, could not sustain the craft at high submerged speeds for long periods of time. Using snorkels to discharge and ventilate the exhaust of diesel engines helped to some degree, but their deployment limited submarine maneuverability and tactics. Nuclear power could provide a power source which would allow a submarine to "stay underwater practically indefinitely—there are no diesels that require air; there is no need to surface in order to refuel or recharge batteries." Because nuclear power was more powerful, submarines would be able to travel at speeds over 20 knots. This increased speed, coupled with virtually unlimited range, would make it possible for the submarine to navigate all of the world's oceans, including the Arctic Ocean, which had acquired great strategic significance.[8]

Captain Rickover was among the first naval officers to grasp the importance and implica-tions of submarine atomic power. Soon after World War II, a Navy contingent, led by Rickover, participated in a joint military-civilian team that researched ways in which to use atomic power for practical purposes. Afterward, he submitted a position paper to General Kenneth Nichols, who had headed the Manhattan Project prior to its being absorbed by the civilian-controlled Atomic Energy Commission (AEC). Rickover, with a bravado that would become his hallmark, declared that the Navy "could have a nuclear-powered submarine within five to eight years." Even the Navy considered the estimate impossible, but Rickover was undaunted. He sent a letter to Admiral Chester Nimitz, chief of naval operations, who had faith in Rickover's optimism and who in turn convinced the secretary of the Navy that the Bureau of Ships and the AEC should join forces to design and produce a nuclear submarine. The AEC did not agree and rejected the proposal.[9]

Rickover may have lost the initial skirmish, but he gained command of the Nuclear Propulsion Division of the Navy. In 1949, he became chief of the Naval Reactors Branch of the AEC after the commission reversed its earlier decision about Rickover's ambitious proposal to cooperatively produce a nuclear-powered submarine. This was an enviable power base from which Rickover could advocate his program. A contemporary article summed up this unique position and his inimitable character:

> "Needless to say, the proposals of Rickover of the Navy usually meet with the enthusiastic approval of Rickover of AEC, and vice versa, and this cuts a lot of red tape. He works unconscionable hours and has inspired his little task force—drawn from top scientific talent in the Navy and AEC—to a similar fanaticism. He violates protocol, sasses his superiors, and bullies captains of industry, but he gets things done."[10]

By January 1950, Rickover had Westinghouse working diligently to develop a compact and practical nuclear reactor and he had become anxious to begin plans for the submarine. A story is told that Rickover arrived at the Portsmouth Navy Yard at 0900 and instructed the admiral in charge to begin building a hull to house the reactor under development. The admiral refused. Rickover, with characteristic flair, took matters into his own hands:

> "When the admiral in charge declined, Rickover, in his impudent fashion, picked up the admiral's phone and called O. Pomeroy Robinson Jr., [general manager of the Groton Yard], whom he had never met, at Electric Boat. 'Can you build a hull for an atomic submarine?' he asked him.
> 'Why, sure, sure,' Robby replied, 'but what the hell do we have to do?' 'I don't know myself,' said Rickover, 'but we'll work it out.'"[11]

"Work it out" nearly overwhelmed both Electric Boat and Rickover for the next four years. Among the first initiatives at Electric Boat was to dramatically increase their staff of engineers. The design force, which had peaked at 190 during World War II, grew quickly to 434 to meet the immense engineering challenge. Rickover himself said that building a nuclear submarine was "5 percent physics, 95 percent engineering."[12] In 1951, the company hired Carleton

This composite photo shows the *Nautilus* heading toward the deeper waters of Long Island Sound. Superimposed is the famous dispatch "Underway on Nuclear Power..."

ELECTRIC BOAT DIVISION

First Lady Mamie Eisenhower, breaking the traditional bottle of champagne to launch the *Nautilus* on January 21, 1954.

Shugg, a former deputy commissioner of the AEC, to become the assistant general manager of Electric Boat under O. Pomeroy Robinson Jr. Working with both Rickover and Electric Boat's chief of design, retired Admiral Andrew I. McKee, Shugg "soon energized Electric Boat with his organizational ability, hiring hundreds of engineers and other specialists, and reorganizing the shipyard on a group basis to coordinate hull development with the development of systems and components."[13] Electric Boat even built a "complete wooden mock-up of the ship that serves as a point of reference for every contemplated step."[14]

Development of the *Nautilus*
and its impact on Electric Boat

Electric Boat was selected to work on the development of an atomic-powered submarine because, according to U.S. Senator Brien McMahon (D-Conn.), it was the only private corporation capable of working with Westinghouse to install a nuclear reactor power plant in the hull of a submarine.[15] Electric Boat President John Jay Hopkins agreed. "The company's wide experience is being drawn upon to insure complete suitability of the propulsion unit to submarine service."[16] The atomic submarine was passing from "the experimental to the construction stage." Electric Boat scientists and engineers were advising the AEC, the Navy and other private companies on how to shield the reactor with a protective layer which would not hinder submarine performance with excessive weight.[17]

Beyond the pioneering technical and engineering challenges, Electric Boat felt the weight of a considerable work load which had grown to its highest level since World War II. In March, 1952, General Manager O. Pomeroy Robinson Jr. listed the contracts which were being administered simultaneously:

> *"Complete three Trigger class submarines.*
> *Convert four fleet type boats to Guppies.*

Design and build two training submarines.
Design and build modern streamlined submarines
   for the Peruvian navy.
Design and build the U.S. Navy's first atomic pow-
   ered submarine."[18]

The four years were also hard on the workers. Draftsmen saw their work week at Electric Boat increase from 40 to 48 hours. Employees in the design section began working 54-hour weeks by January 1951.[19] By April, 2,300 additional workers were pressed to work 48-hour weeks.[20] The company graduated 21 men from the apprenticeship program in 1952. Each man had completed a two- to five-year course in one of several shipbuilding trades.[21]

At Rickover's insistence, the company assisted Westinghouse in installing a prototype reactor into a full-sized submarine hull which was missing only the stern and bow sections. This proof-of-concept hull was filled with "all the related machinery that would have anything to do with the reactor and the ship's propulsion."[22] This engineering feat was accomplished at the National Reactor Test Station near Arco, Idaho. The reactor was made "critical" (active) in March 1953, just under a year after the keel for the *Nautilus* had been laid at Electric Boat on June 14, 1952.[23]

On June 23, 1953, the *Mark I* (as the prototype reactor was known) was brought up to full power so that developers could gather information about the reactor's reliability under sustained operation. The plan was to run the reactor at this state for 24 hours.[24] But Rickover, who had been promoted to admiral in the interim, soon changed those plans.

"Admiral Rickover was in Pittsburgh at the time the test began and flew to Idaho immediately.
   "At the scheduled end of the test the Mark I was performing so well that Rickover got the idea of simulating a run across the Atlantic.
   "Charts of the North Atlantic were broken out in the Mark I's control room. The track for a submerged ocean crossing was drawn. A great circle course from Nova Scotia to Ireland was plotted.
   "Competition developed at once among the successive watches to keep the Mark I theoretically plunging ahead in its ocean depths.
   "For the next several days, the Idaho submarine proceeded at top speed. It was never necessary to shut down her reactor or even to 'surface.'
   "Only three times during the entire 'crossing' did the Mark I slow down. Once she was throttled back to two-thirds power for seven minutes and twice to half power for a total of less than an hour and a half. In each case, the crew on duty moved swiftly to make adjustments so their watch would not be responsible for delaying the 'crossing' a moment longer than absolutely unavoidable.
   "Finally, 'landfall' was made on Ireland. The news was flashed to Washington and congratulations went out to those running the submarine in the desert."

From the time President Truman initialed the keel of the *Nautilus* on June 14, 1952 until her launching less than two years later on January 21, 1954, Electric Boat worked at flank speed to construct the world's first nuclear submarine.

While the *Nautilus* was still under construction, there was a changing of the guard at the Groton facility. In 1953, Robinson was promoted to senior vice president of General Dynamics in 1953 and Shugg succeeded him as general manager.

Launching of the *Nautilus*

More than 20,000 people cheered as First Lady Mamie Eisenhower stood on the christening platform with Mrs. Eugene P. Wilkinson, wife of the *Nautilus'* first captain, and christened America's first nuclear submarine on January 21, 1954 by breaking a bottle of champagne on her bow. Among those attending the ceremony were more than 6,000 shipyard employees and another 6,000 members of their immediate families. The remaining invitations went to guests from the Navy, the AEC, other government departments and the suppliers and subcontractors of Electric Boat.[25] In addition to these guests, there were 300 members of the working press, three major radio networks, the three major television networks, five newsreel services, three national photo services, Radio Free Europe, Voice of America, representatives of major foreign press agencies, more than 35 newspapers, representatives of the technical press and the major news magazines of the day—*Life, Time, Newsweek, Look* and *U.S. News and World Report.*

Topping a list of luminaries, John Jay Hopkins, president and chairman of the board of General Dynamics, was first to speak:

"The Nautilus belongs not to General Dynamics, not to Westinghouse, not to the Atomic Energy Commission, not even to the United States Navy! As citizens of the United States, the Nautilus belongs to you! She is your ship! In a still broader sense, however, what our scientists and engineers have already gleaned from her in the broad application of nuclear power—and what they have yet to learn from her in fields of design and dynamics, of propulsion and atomics—should at some future date belong to all free men.
   "But if any one group might be said to have some special claim to the Nautilus, it would be those men and women who brought her into being—the builders who, in these yards, and in the hundreds of mills and factories and offices throughout the nation, have fashioned this mighty shell of steel and in it impressed and put to work the basic power of our universe."[26]

Later in the program, Admiral Robert B. Carney, chief of naval operations, delivered a different perspective of the event:

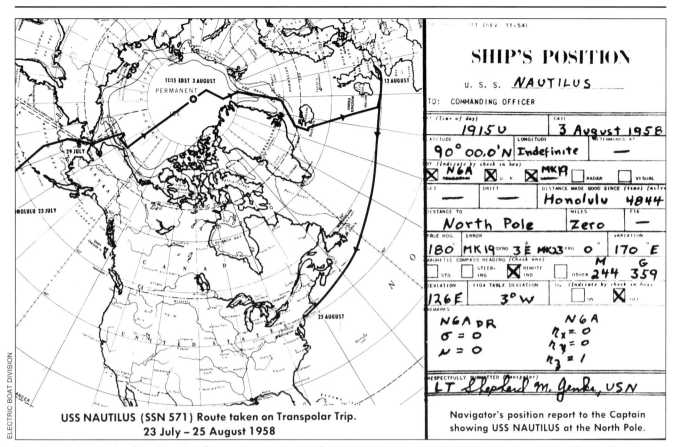

USS NAUTILUS (SSN 571) Route taken on Transpolar Trip.
23 July – 25 August 1958

Navigator's position report to the Captain
showing USS NAUTILUS at the North Pole.

Map depicts the route of the *Nautilus'* famous transpolar trip from July 23 to August 25, 1958. Report on right indicates that the *Nautilus* has reached the North Pole.

"As remarkable as this development seems to us now, Nautilus will probably appear to our sons and grandsons as a quaint old piece of machinery which introduced the transition to a new age of power. This is sure to happen, for this is only the beginning. But I am proud to share this momentous beginning and I believe that we are witnessing one of history's great milestones."[27]

Even untried, the *Nautilus* launched a new era of submarine development. As her sea trials were getting underway in January of the following year, President Eisenhower announced that he was seeking to add three more nuclear-powered submarines to the four already proposed.[28]

The *Nautilus* Begins Sea Trials

After the launching of any submarine, Electric Boat conducted a series of tests, known as builder's trials, to assure that the craft met Navy specifications. Initial tests were accomplished at dockside, followed by sea trials. The *Nautilus* successfully completed her first sea trial on January 17, 1955. Admiral Rickover and Carleton Shugg, Electric Boat's general manager, were on board along with "some 64 observers and technicians" whose job it was "to glean every possible scrap of information from the trials so that the

successors of the *Nautilus* can benefit."[29] The presence of representatives from the Navy, Electric Boat and Westinghouse was unusual since most builder's trials were conducted before a ship was turned over to the Navy.[30] In the *Nautilus'* case, she had been commissioned by the Navy on September 30, 1954, long before her builder's trials were completed.[31]

The first day at sea was nothing less than perfect, according to Commander Wilkinson. He was so excited by the performance of the *Nautilus* that he wanted to proceed immediately with a diving test, but Navy authorities denied the request and the *Nautilus* returned to New London.[32] Only 18 hours later, she was out for another trial during which she made her first test dive on January 20, 1955, remaining submerged for about an hour.[33] The submarine went on to make 50 shallow dives in the period between January 20 and January 24. On February 28, the *Nautilus* made her first deep sea dive off the coast of Maine.[34]

The trials of the *Nautilus* were remarkable for having experienced only a few minor problems: two small electrical fires, a loose screw in a reduction gear box and some damage to the conning tower's sheathing during a storm with 30-knot winds and 12-foot seas.[35] During a press conference after the *Nautilus* returned from the dive, Commander Wilkinson said that he wanted "to emphasize that all new ships have problems which show up during initial trials. Detection and correction of these is one of the main reasons for conducting the Builder's Sea Trials."[36]

Voyages of the *Nautilus*

After the builder's trials, the *Nautilus* went through a great number of tests devised by the Navy. Many of these tests were designed to gather information which would be put to use in the design and operation of future atomic-powered submarines. Along the way, the *Nautilus* accomplished unprecedented feats. In one such operation in 1956, the *Nautilus* left New London for Key West on March 19 for a series of special tests. She sailed back for New London on April 20, making a submerged run totalling 1,152 miles. During the trial, the *Nautilus* was underway for 531 hours, 376 of which were underwater. The boat sailed 7,013 miles, 5,516 of which were under the surface. These figures dwarfed previous records. When, in February 1957, the *Nautilus* was refueled by replacing her nuclear core, she had traveled 62,560 miles on the first one.[37]

On July 18, 1957, Commander Wilkinson was replaced by Commander William R. Anderson as the skipper of the *Nautilus*. Late in the summer of that year, Commander Anderson and his crew made a voyage to 87° north latitude, only 180 miles from the North Pole. While in the Arctic Ocean, the *Nautilus* traveled "1,383 miles under the polar ice cap on three excursions lasting a total of five and one-half days." Obviously a prelude to the famous voyage from the Pacific to the Atlantic Ocean by way of the North Pole, this initial voyage "was of great scientific importance." The crew was able to "gather many times the amount of data on ice characteristics and water depths than previously obtained in the whole of Arctic exploration."[38]

This knowledge was soon put to work. On July 23, 1958, the *Nautilus* left Pearl Harbor, sailing north through the Pacific and through the Bering Straits, which separate Alaska and the Soviet Union. Once through the straits, it surfaced for a brief navigational check and then "dove to start its 2,114 mile journey under the Polar Ice Cap."[39] On August 3, 1958, the *Nautilus* reached 90° north latitude—more commonly known as the North Pole. About 36 hours after that historic event, the boat reached the North Atlantic Ocean. A commemorative brochure described the real impact of that voyage:

> *"A new page has been added to history. And this voyage has also proved America's increased capacity to repel aggression."[40]*

The crew of the *Nautilus* were well aware of the voyage's significance, and published their own mimeographed North Pole Edition of their boat's newspaper, the *Nautilus Express*. It was decidedly less serious in tone. The crew, for instance had its "traditional breakfast on days that we are about the to cross the North Pole": chilled juice, cereal, steak, eggs, bread, butter, toast, jelly, milk and coffee. For the off-duty crew, the rest of the day was spent watching a movie, or one of the activities shown below as described in the *Nautilus Express*:

> *"03_____U (Fill in your own time here). The crew off watch are:*
> *___Eating.*
> *___Playing chess, checkers,*
> *___Cards or acey-ducey*
> *___Listening to the juke box.*
> *___All, or none of the above.*
> *___Sleeping*
> *___Writing letters"[41]*

By 10:50 p.m., the *Nautilus* was 7.7 miles away from the North Pole, and then the countdown began. The excitement can be sensed in the account printed in the "*Nautilus Express:*"

> *"031900U All crew members not on watch, lay into the crew's mess for the North Pole Party.*
> *"And here we all assembled—to await that golden moment in history when we would cross the geographical top of the world, the North Pole, to bring towards its completion the first transpolar voyage in history.*
> *"Remember this part—Aberle as M.C. Marchand the 'Frog' with his movie camera—which he had to stop and rewind every 30 seconds; Old reliable J.J. Krawczyk and his proselytes Larch, Kropp, Aberle, et al with their Brownies, their Polaroids, and other history recording photographic gear—shooting, quiet, lights, stop while I rewind.*
> *"'Mother' Baird's 2 foot by 2 foot North Pole cake, decorated colorfully with a sugary copy of our new 'Transpolar Voyage flag.'*
> *"And in the midst of all this gayety and confusion look—there's our good ship's doctor over in the corner of the mess hall with his ear to the job, trying to crack Krawcyzk's safe. Get a picture of that John."*
> *031912U "'Conn,' sonar has a contact on the North Pole, bearing 000T, range 2000 yards."*
> *031914:55U "Five-Four-Three-Two-One"*
> *031915U "MARK! We've crossed the North Pole. In humble gratitude to God, and in memory of our predecessors who succeeded or failed in attempts to reach this spot by land, we observe one minute silent prayer."*

The Nuclear Fleet Expands— Electric Boat 1951 to 1958

On March 18, 1952—six years before the *Nautilus*' famous voyage—the House Armed Services Committee approved funding for a second atomic submarine.[42] At the time, the *Nautilus* was under construction and it would be two years before her projected launch date. Electric Boat was involved in other submarine development and construction at the same time. During 1951, the company laid the keel for the first of two 250-ton target and training submarines, the *SST-1* and *SST-2*, which were scheduled for completion in 1953. These were the first submarines "ever built primarily for training purposes" as well as "sonar targets for attack submarines." The company also received an order from Peru for two modern submarines. As new submarine orders and the Electric Boat backlog continued to mount, Hopkins predicted that the company would become the nation's foremost shipbuilder.[43]

Sales for General Dynamics—including its Electric Boat and Canadair divisions—reached about $190 million in 1953, a 40 percent increase over the preceding year. By 1954, General Dynamics had secured a backlog of $183 million in scheduled work.[44] Electric Boat, however, could not expect to maintain a monopoly on the construction of atomic submarines for long. Although the company clearly had the most trained and experienced designers and builders at a private yard, it began to face competition from naval shipyards, primarily the yard at Portsmouth, New Hampshire. Senators from both New Hampshire and Maine ambitiously sought contracts for the yard, which lay in and near their states to boost civilian employment. Connecticut congressmen and senators resolutely resisted these efforts.[45] The harmonious relationship between private and naval shipyards was slowly becoming dissonant.[46] Meanwhile, the Peruvian navy took delivery of the *Tiburon* (*Shark*) and *Lobo* (*Wolf*) diesel-electric submarines.

Work began in 1954 on an unusually sophisticated submarine simulator trainer. Controlled by "an electronic computer," the simulator would mimic a submarine's dives, pitches, rolls and turns. The device was designed to be used at the Navy's Submarine School, located just up the Thames River from Electric Boat. The simulator was able to "duplicate in detail the control room of modern attack class submarines." Not only would the simulator accommodate all the features of a modern control room, but it was designed to "simulate all characteristics of the newer craft, even to handling in turns and 'feel' of the various controls when the ship is in motion. If improperly ballasted or trimmed, the ersatz submarine will list or dive in a realistic fashion."[47]

Although the primary purpose for the simulator was to train submariners, ship designers were also interested in observing what would happen during various hypothetical emergencies. To add to the realism, the submariners would "board" the simulator, while observers and trainers remained outside at a control console:

> "It will be fitted with a 'one-way' window so that observers and the instructor can watch the actions of the students operating the control room without detracting from the submarine atmosphere inside.
> "The instructor's control panel will be capable of reproducing almost any problem that is apt to occur in an operating submarine.
> "The synthetic emergencies that the instructor can transmit include failure of the communications system, engine failure, jamming of diving planes or rudder, rough seas, flooding due to malfunctioning valves, and casualties from collision or depth bombing."[48]

Electric Boat's Universal Submarine Simulator was completed and was fully operational by 1956.

A newborn *Nautilus* got its screen debut as the hero in the 1955 motion picture, "It Came from Beneath the Sea." Like many of the genre of science fiction movies produced during the 1950s, the film reflected the public's fascination with atomic weaponry, nuclear power and the effects of radioactivity, all of which play prominently in the plot. The action surrounds the discovery of a giant radioactive octopus in the Pacific Ocean, forced to prey on ships and their crews since its radioactivity apparently scared away normal food such as fish and other sea life.

The movie opens with the actual launching of the *Nautilus* at Electric Boat. The octopus, created by the late Ray Harryhausen, is located by the ship's sonar which detects the sea creature chasing the submarine during sea trials. Ultimately, the giant octopus meets his demise when the *Nautilus* fires an atomic-tipped torpedo into its midsection, of course destroying it immediately and completely.

In a scene that accurately portrays a major operational difference between the *Nautilus* and its predecessors, one of the characters, the ship's captain, remarks that this ship is "quite different from those old iron lungs." Its fictional second officer agrees, saying that the crew has little to do other than eat, sleep and "push buttons when it comes time to work."

In 1955, the Navy requested eight more submarines, three of which were to be nuclear-powered. One of the proposed nuclear submarines was a 4,600-ton craft intended primarily for radar picket duty. Another was specified to be a "guided missile submarine."[49] Electric Boat was already at work on the *Darter*, among the last of the conventional submarines, and on the *Skate*, destined to be the Navy's third nuclear submarine. Work had also begun on another Peruvian boat, the *Atun (Tuna)*.[50]

The Robinson Research and Development Building was also completed at Electric Boat. The building housed a staff of approximately 200 scientists and engineers working in four laboratories "each fully equipped with the most scientific and technical research tools, including a battery of electronic computers." By 1956, the staff was conducting research in "noise and vibration reduction, thermal stress, heat transfer, weapons control and shock resistance." A special research group had begun development on integrated weapons systems, features which would be common to submarines in future decades. Electric Boat had every reason to characterize the nuclear submarine as "the major naval defense in future war," and indicated their level of commitment in the 1956 annual report:[51]

"Prototypes of such future atomic-powered 'weapons systems' are shown in the multiple construction of the world's fastest submarine Skipjack, Skate and the 5,450-ton Triton, world's largest submarine at Electric Boat's South Yard."

The *Seawolf*, the second nuclear submarine, was launched on July 22, 1955. A year later, it had become apparent that the sodium reactor, built by General Electric, was not working as planned. Instead of using water to transfer heat from the core to a steam turbine as in the *Nautilus*, the *Seawolf* used liquid sodium which was supposed to be far more efficient. The problem was that the sodium also had a caustic reaction on the heat exchanger tubing, causing cracks and leaks. As a result, the *Seawolf* operated at speeds far lower than had been planned. Designers working under the direction of Admiral Rickover observed the problem while testing a

The *Skipjack* was a small, remarkably fast submarine. Launched in 1959, she was built alongside the *Triton*, which was, at that time, the U.S. Navy's longest sub, prompting remarks about the *Triton* giving birth.

prototype reactor, but Rickover believed the problems could be solved in the construction phase of the reactor.[52] Eventually the Navy commissioned the 330-foot long, 3,260-ton *Seawolf* on March 30, 1957. The boat would go on to make history by submerging on August 5, 1958 and remain underwater for 60 consecutive days.

The *Skipjack* was designed as a prototype for the "faster, more versatile submarines of the future."[53] This craft featured design advances which would be incorporated in the fleet ballistic missile (FBM) submarines, two of which were under construction at Electric Boat in 1957. The *Skipjack* combined the successful shark-shaped hull of the *Albacore*, an electric-diesel submarine which could exceed 30 knots submerged, with a nuclear propulsion plant. At 252 feet long and a displacement of 2,830 tons, the *Skipjack*

was the fastest and one of the quietest submarines in the world.

Its design was impressive. "Put an *Albacore* hull around a nuclear engine and give it some torpedoes and you've got a ship that will beat the world," observed Captain Edward L. Beach, author of Run Silent, Run Deep, who commanded the *Triton* on her history-making submerged voyage around the world. The *Skipjack* was built alongside the *Triton*—a half-pint 252 feet in length compared to the submarine in the next berth, which, at 447 feet, was the longest made up to that time—spawning "all sorts of cracks about the *Triton* just giving birth," Beach recalled. The "baby" was finished first and launched before her larger kin.[54]

Some of these design enhancements formed the basis of a feasibility study conducted for

First Lady Jacqueline Kennedy launches the 425-foot *Lafayette* (SSBN-616) on May 8, 1962, the lead ship of 32 in its class to be equipped with the new A-3 Polaris missile.

Star II and *Star III* midget submarines, two of a series of research vessels constructed by Electric Boat.

the Maritime Administration of the Department of Commerce on nuclear-powered submarine tankers. Electric Boat studied two models—one of 20,000 tons with a speed of 20 knots and another of 40,000 tons with a speed of 40 knots.[55]

The Polaris Missile and Fleet Ballistic Missile Submarine

Development of missile weapon systems began soon after the close of World War II. By the end of 1949, the Navy had launched a guided missile from the deck of a submarine. During the 1950s, the Polaris program became the Navy's most important development program as it combined the technology of ballistic missiles with nuclear warheads, nuclear submarines and inertial guidance systems. On November 28, 1955, the Navy confidently forecast that nuclear submarines would be capable of firing missiles while submerged by 1962. In 1957, as Cold War tensions intensified, the Department of Defense made this program an urgent priority with an accelerated completion date of 1960.[56] The overall plan was to develop both the missile and the submarine that would launch it concurrently.

Electric Boat was selected to design and build the first two Polaris submarines. The design problem was formidable. The company's engineers and designers had to make room for "a complete missile base as well as a reactor power plant and living quarters for a hundred men, all within the limited space of a submarine." The first step included the redesign of a boat from the Skipjack class:[57]

> *"Because of the high priority of the missile submarine, designers took the plan of the USS Skipjack, cut it immediately aft of the sail, and added a 130-foot missile compartment with sixteen missile-holding tubes, which in effect are pressure vessels penetrating the hull."*

Even the normal design evolution for the equipment was altered to meet the deadline set by the Department of Defense: [58]

> *"Space aboard the submarine was allocated and manufacturers advised to build the equipment to fit the space, an unorthodox procedure that worked because of the close cooperation of the Navy-industry Polaris team—a team of more than 11,000 industries across the country."*

As work on the Polaris project proceeded at a fevered pitch, the Electric Boat team had completed the *Triton* and launched her to start her sea trials off the coast of New London, where she was based. As Captain Beach began planning his shakedown cruise, originally to Scandinavia where she would conduct joint operations with a surface fleet, he received an urgent message requesting his presence in Washington, D.C. Arriving the next day at the assigned place, Beach found the room replete with brass. "They said, 'What shape is your ship in?' And I said, 'Fine. We are about to start our shakedown cruise.' And they said, 'Can you go around the world submerged instead?' It was just like that. As I recall, I said, 'Yes, sir. Fine. Let's plan it.'"[59]

The voyage was called *Operation Magellan*, planned along virtually the same route as that of the early explorer Ferdinand Magellan, a Portuguese navigator who commanded the first expedition to sail around the world in 1519. It took Beach and his crew only 10 days to ready themselves and their ship for what would ultimately be an 84-day journey during which the submarine would never surface. While he was not told of the reason for this assignment, Beach's superiors had given him one mandate that came from President Dwight D. Eisenhower: "You have got to get back by the middle of May."

"I later discovered how it came about," Beach said. "It was asked for by the President. He intended to use it as one of his things to show [USSR Premier Nikita] Khrushchev at this meeting that he had. And the meeting was at the end of May."

Ironically, the *Triton* successfully completed its submerged circumnavigation of the globe shortly after Francis Gary Powers was shot down over the USSR while on a reconnaissance mission in his U-2 spy plane on May 1, 1960. According to Beach, Eisenhower had planned to use photographs from the failed U-2 mission as a demonstration of American military superiority.

On July 20, 1960, Electric Boat's engineering and manufacturing challenge was met when its *George Washington*, the first Polaris class submarine, successfully fired two Polaris A-1 missiles off Cape Canaveral, Florida. The solid-fuel missiles had a range of 1,200 miles. John F. Kennedy, then a candidate for president, witnessed the launches: [60]

> *"It is still incredible to me that a missile can be successfully and accurately fired from beneath the sea. Once one has seen a Polaris firing, the efficacy of this weapons system as a deterrent is not debatable."*

A few months later, on November 15, the *George Washington* made the system operational when she went on patrol with 16 ready-to-fire nuclear-tipped Polaris missiles."[61] She was the lead ship of a class 380 feet long with a displacement of 6,700 tons.

Besides developing submarines as an almost invulnerable deterrent force, Electric Boat was raising undersea warfare to a new level of sophistication—designing and building the *Tullibee*, a

GENERAL DYNAMICS, ELECTRIC BOAT DIVISION

The *Aluminaut* was second in a series of small oceanographic research submarines, preceded by the *Star I*, built by Electric Boat. In 1965, the company completed another research submersible, the *Asherah*, and began construction on two more, the *Star II* and the *Star III*.

FORTY-ONE FOR FREEDOM

Seals of the Polaris submarine fleet.

U.S. Navy's Polaris Submarine Fleet

OFFICIAL U.S. NAVY PHOTO

The *Thomas A. Edison* (SSBN-610) launches a Polaris A-2 missile while submerged during test exercises off Cape Kennedy, Florida in 1964.

new type of hunter-killer submarine launched in 1959 with "more sonar capacity than the entire U.S. submarine navy of World War II."[62]

Within a year, work commenced on an even larger class of Polaris submarines. The lead ship of this class of four boats was the *Ethan Allen* at 410 feet long with a displacement of 6,900 tons. This new class could fire both the Polaris A-1 missile and the newly introduced A-2 missile, which had a range of 1,500 miles. This was the first class to be specifically designed as a Polaris submarine from the keel up. By 1962, Electric Boat had already launched a third class of Polaris submarines, the Lafayette class. These submarines were 425 feet long, displaced 7,000 tons and could fire the latest Polaris missile, the A-3, which had a range of 2,500 miles. The *Lafayette*, lead ship of 32 in this class, was christened by First Lady Jacqueline Kennedy on May 8, 1962. One of the main reasons why this class of submarine was made significantly longer was "to provide more comfort for the crews during prolonged voyages overseas."[63] Patrols that lasted for two or three months became routine as the U.S. submarine force maintained a continuous presence in the world's oceans.

There were 41 Polaris-armed submarines in all, built over a period of seven years. This group earned the moniker, "Forty-one For Freedom."

By the close of 1962, Electric Boat had a backlog of 14 nuclear submarines—10 fleet ballistic missile submarines and four attack submarines. The company had built 11 of the Navy's 28 nuclear submarines in operation by that time.[64] Correspondingly, employment at the company had risen to numbers reached in the peak years of World War II.

This feverish pace continued into 1963. On June 22, 1963, four submarines (three of them Polaris) were launched from three shipyards: Electric Boat launched the *Flasher* (an attack submarine) and the *Tecumseh*, Newport News Shipbuilding and Drydock Company launched the *John C. Calhoun*, and the Navy's Mare Island shipyard launched the *Daniel Boone*.[65] In 1963, Electric Boat launched a total of five nuclear submarines, setting a record for one year. Of the 19 nuclear submarines the company had launched since the *Nautilus* in 1954, nine were prototypes: *Nautilus, Seawolf, Skate, Skipjack, Triton, Tullibee, George Washington, Ethan Allen* and *Lafayette*.[66]

Attack Submarines and Research Submarines—Electric Boat to the End of the Decade

A new class of attack submarines was initiated in 1962 with the authorization of the *Sturgeon* (SSN-637). The 37 boats in this class were designed to be deep-diving and quiet. In 1964, Electric Boat had contracts for 12 nuclear submarines, eight attack class and four ballistic missile class. Four of the attack submarines were being built at the newly acquired shipyard in Quincy, Massachusetts. Work there was underway on three surface vessels designed as instrumentation ships for the Apollo space program.[67] At the Groton plant, employment levels reached an all-time high of 16,373 in 1964.[68] Along with new construction, the facility was responsible for refueling and retrofitting the *George Washington, Patrick Henry, Thedore Roosevelt* and *Abraham Lincoln*, including installation of new Polaris A-3 missiles.[69]

Electric Boat also envisioned a market for small research submarines for use by the government, private industry and research institutions. Designs were discussed for craft ranging in size from 10 feet to more than 200 feet, and for crews of one to 20.[70] The *Star I* was the first of a number of small oceanographic research submarines built by Electric Boat, followed by the *Aluminaut* which was built for the Reynolds Company. In 1965, the company completed another research submersible, the *Asherah*, and began construction on two more, the *Star II* and the *Star III*.[71] The latter were launched in 1966 when work began on the *NR-1*, the first nuclear-powered oceanographic research submarine. Throughout these years, these various research submarines were in constant use for various government and private projects such as the archaeological exploration of the Aegean Sea.[72]

In 1965, Electric Boat launched three Polaris submarines, delivered a fourth and began construction on the last of 41 fleet ballistic missile submarines. Work also continued in refueling and refitting four of the earlier Polaris submarines.[73] This pattern of new construction and conversion continued through 1966 and for some years to follow as the Navy began development of the Poseidon missile. In 1966, work also began on the *Narwhal* (SSBN-671), a unique design which utilized General Electric's S5G power plant. It was an attack submarine that Electric Boat claimed would be technically superior to all that came before it. Kenneth D. Brown, retired vice president of operations for Electric Boat, recalled the corporate philosophy that spawned the *Narwhal*, expected to be a class, rather than just a single boat (as fate would dictate). "In those days, we made a number of single designs—kind of pushing toward the ultimate in submarine design, both in hull form and power plant."[74]

1967 through the end of the decade were halcyon years for Electric Boat. During this time, the company produced 17 fleet ballistic missile submarines, 13 attack and eight research submarines.[75]

Joseph D. Pierce became Electric Boat's general manager in 1967. Pierce joined Electric Boat in 1951, serving as project manager on the *Seawolf* conversion and nuclear project manager on the *Tullibee*. Several former Electric Boat employees described him as a strong shipyard manager.[76]

Getting in the spirit of competition, Electric Boat's workers began racing against their own fine records. In 1968, they completed an overhaul of the *Alexander Hamilton* in a record 53 weeks, months ahead of schedule and six weeks less than the shortest similar maintenance to date. That year, the company also delivered two new attack submarines. According to the company's 1968 annual report, overhaul refueling and conversion work represented a greater proportion of business than ever before and officials expected this trend to continue.[77]

"At the same time we are strengthening our position as the leading designer and builder of new types of undersea craft. Besides the 'quiet' sub contract, we received study contracts in 1968 for formulation of concepts for a new class of attack submarine and for an advanced underwater missile system."

In a grand finish for a decade which saw the *Triton* become the first submarine to circumnavigate the globe while submerged, Electric Boat delivered another prototype: the *NR-1*, the world's first nuclear-powered research submarine. Ken Brown, also an engineer, worked on the *NR-1*. "The *NR-1* was one of Rickover's pride and joys because it was very unique," he recalled. Like other Electric Boat submarines, the *NR-1* performed well its service to the country, which included being one of the first ships to locate debris from the space shuttle *Challenger* after its explosion.[78]

According to Brown, "the Navy broke a lot of traditions on that submarine." Unlike other naval vessels, the *NR-1* used a substantial amount of commercial equipment. It carried a seven-man crew, highly trained in a number of skills. It didn't even serve traditional Navy chow—the crew ate frozen dinners instead. Officers and enlisted men worked side by side.

Throughout the last years of the decade, the company's engineers and designers were researching a new submarine configuration—what was to become the Los Angeles class.

OFFICIAL U.S. NAVY PHOTO

The *George Washington* (SSBN-598), *Patrick Henry* (SSBN-599), *Theodore Roosevelt* (SSBN-600) and *Abraham Lincoln* (SSBN-602) were retrofitted at Groton to launch Polaris A-3 missiles, like the one shown here in a test firing in 1965.

The *Helena* (SSN-725), a Los Angeles class submarine, launches from Electric Boat on June 28, 1986.

CHAPTER IX

Los Angeles and Ohio Classes

Somehow there was a studied deadliness about the smooth black shapes of these new ocean cruisers. They were built for war and they looked it. All other considerations had been subordinated to the requirements of war under the sea.

Edward L. Beach,
Run Silent, Run Deep

Some of the most intense confrontations of the Cold War occurred during the 1970s and 1980s, but they weren't only between the United States and the Soviet Union. Electric Boat, Admiral Hyman G. Rickover and the U.S. Navy were also at odds, provoking and accusing each other of procedural errors and mismanagement. Rumors of a new American attack submarine that were circulated in 1968 were actually the culmination of a struggle between Admiral Rickover and other Navy leadership over the future of the submarine fleet. In early January 1968, U.S. Naval inteligence identified and began to track a Soviet November class submarine patrolling the North Pacific Ocean. The older, twin-reactor design was noisy, making it relatively easy to track with the American underwater Sound Surveillance System (SOSUS) network. Once the Navy determined that the Soviet submarine was enroute to trail the USS *Enterprise*, America's nuclear-powered aircraft carrier, a secret plan was developed to accurately determine the operational speed of the Soviet ship.

Enroute from Alameda near San Francisco to Hawaii, the *Enterprise* gradually increased her speed until her eight nuclear reactors were turning her four large propellers at flank speed–about 31 knots. To the shock of those monitoring the event, including Vice Admiral Rickover, the Soviet submarine kept apace with seeming power to spare. Previously, estimates of the top speed for the November class had been 25 knots, giving American carriers a relative margin of safety to outdistance a submerged Soviet threat. If the Soviet's oldest and presumeably slowest submarines were capable of speeds exceeding America's newest submarines–approximately 31 knots versus 25 knots, what speeds might their latest, Victor class, be able to achieve? The admiral used this new intelligence to lobby for his latest project—a "quiet, high-speed (in excess of 35 knots) attack submarine able to support the carrier battle groups deployed by the U.S. Navy." The Naval Ship Systems Command had a different concept of what the Navy required—coming up with a submarine design which "would recover the speed loss of the Permits and Sturgeons (down from 30 knots to 25 knots) and improve the radiated noise levels."[1]

Admiral Rickover would persevere, but to provide the additional speed that he required, the new attack submarine would have to be powered by the new S6G reactor, which weighed 1,050 tons compared with the 650-ton reactor powering most of the fleet. This required eliminating a substantial amount of weight elsewhere without restricting the submarine's overall mission requirements. Designers recommended removing an auxiliary diesel engine and a supplemental air conditioning system, but Rickover declared this unacceptable. Only one area remained to trim weight—the thickness of the hull itself. Design modifications were successful, and the new submarine would be known as the 688-class, or Los Angeles class, named, as tradition dictates, for the lead boat.

The still larger challenge was cost: A fleet of attack submarines built to Rickover's design would cost billions of dollars. Such was the admiral's power that few dared to ask whether his high-speed submarine was the "best boat to build for the money, or are there alternatives that would increase the speed and performance of the U.S. fleet for less?" Despite opposition, Admiral Rickover prevailed and the design contract was awarded to Electric Boat's principal competitor, the Newport News Shipbuilding and Dry Dock Company in Newport News, Virginia. Although "Newport News had never in its history designed a new submarine from the ground up." They had constructed a number of submarines, but always from Electric Boat's drawings. Of the original twelve Los Angeles class ships autho-

rized, Newport News received contracts to build five and Electric Boat received contracts for seven in early 1971.[2]

In 1970, Electric Boat delivered three Sturgeon class nuclear submarines to the Navy, and continued the construction of two more ballistic missle ships. Design work was also conducted on an experimental electric-drive nuclear submarine (*Glenard P. Lipscomb* SSN-685), to provide extremely quiet operation.

The company's engineers were immersed in designing a submersible strategic deterrent, called the ULMS (Undersea Long-range Missile System) which was to become the Trident submarine fleet.[3] The new system evolved from debates within the Pentagon between the Air Force, which advocated a land- and air-based system, and the Navy, which argued for a sea-based system. Ultimately, the Pentagon recognized the enhanced invulnerability and deterrence of a submarine-based system. Admiral Robert "Yogi" Kaufman (Ret.) recalled that, in the formative years of the ULMS, a proposal surfaced for a "monstrous submarine," with two reactors, two screws, a 38,000-ton displacement and missiles that were equally enormous. The objective was to develop a missile that could effectively acquire a target in a range between 6,500 and 9,000 miles, and a platform that could just as effectively deliver it.[4] What evolved was the Ohio class, the first to carry the powerful Trident missiles.

The nuclear attack submarine, *Groton* (SSN-694), passing the Electric Boat shipyard. The *Groton* is a Los Angeles class submarine, launched in 1976.

ELECTRIC BOAT DIVISION

During years of peak production, Electric Boat had eight submarines under construction. Here, the night shift works on *Michigan* (SSBN-727) and *Florida* (SSBN-728), two Ohio class ships nearing completion.

Electric Boat demonstrated its versatility and ability to juggle a variety of design and construction tasks in 1971. Workers began building the *Glenard P. Lipscomb* (the experimental electric-drive ship), continued the conversion of Polaris submarines to Poseidons, and started on the first of seven Los Angeles class submarines. The company set a target completion date of 1975 for their first Los Angeles class submarine, the *Philadelphia*, with completion of the remainder by late 1977. Engineering and design work also continued on the ULMS with the award of a contract for $13.8 million.[5] By 1972, the design and development contracts for the ULMS, or Trident submarine, amounted to $80 million.[6] The first submarine of the line, the *Ohio*, which was scheduled for completion by the end of 1977, was to be fitted with a Trident missile capable of nearly twice the range of its predecessors, the Polaris and Poseidon. Instead of 16 missiles, the ship would carry 24 Trident I (C-4) and, eventually, Trident II (D-5) missiles.[7] The increased armament and improved navigation and communications equipment called for a considerably larger submarine—one 560 feet long with a displacement of 18,750 tons.[8] The new Ohio class submarines were more than 100 feet longer than the history-making *Triton*, which had been the Navy's longest submarine since she was launched in 1958, with a displacement nearly two-and-a-half times greater than *Triton's*.

During this time, the *Nautilus*, the nation's first nuclear-powered submarine, which was still in active duty status, returned to Electric Boat for a complete overhaul. Henry J. Nardone, a former naval officer who had been the Navy's project officer on the *Nautilus* during its construction, was assigned to head the team. "I was one of the few people around who had experience with the original construction of the ship," he said. The overhaul included completely stripping and refitting the engine room, and installing new machinery and an updated fire control system. "When we finished that ship, it was a good, operating attack ship."[9]

The keel for the *Philadelphia*, the first ship of the Los Angeles class to be built at Electric Boat, was laid on August 12, 1972. In 1973, the company laid keels for three more: the *Omaha*, *Groton* and *New York City*. During the year, engineers and designers worked on the Trident propulsion plant, ship structure and integrated command and control systems.[10]

The first of many conflicts surfaced between Admiral Rickover and Electric Boat management. In an unprecedented action, the admiral first threatened and then ordered the shutdown of Electric Boat's shipyard for what he considered to be breaches in safety procedures in radioactive areas. Electric Boat immediately started a program to retrain workers in radiation safety and, in a little over a month, its authorization to handle radioactive material was restored.[11] But the action had greatly disrupted the shipyard, already working to meet a number of difficult deadlines and concurrently expanding the yard to accommodate Los Angeles class and Trident-armed submarines.[12]

From early in 1971, Electric Boat had been considering expanding its capabilities—and facilities—but had not settled on any particular means of accomplishment. Coincidentally, Governor Philip Noel of Rhode Island was seeking a tenant for the recently closed Quonset Point Naval Air Station. Henry Nardone, who was at the time responsible for overseeing the overhaul of the *Nautilus*, mentioned the company's needs to the governor, who eagerly invited Joseph D. Pierce, then general manager of Electric Boat, to discuss the possibilities. Nardone recalled the meeting between Pierce and Governor Noel. "When the two of them got together, it was like being in the forward battery of the submarine, the language that flew around. They were also kindred souls in that they had a great deal of respect for each other. Their personal relationship had a lot to do with consummating the arrangements at Quonset Point."[13]

By January 1974, the company started revamping the facility, using a lot of ingenuity and very little money. "We started the place on a shoe string," Nardone said. In March 1974, Robert W. McGuffee was named manager of the new Quonset Point facility, untill his replacement in

1976 by Henry Nardone. "We scrounged equipment from all the government and World War II surplus depots all over the world and all over the country. "... By the time I left it in 1977, we had really just started to get some 20th century equipment."

The new construction facility would incorporate mass production knowledge gained from reviewing German submarine-building techniques used in World War II. "The problem in implementing it was there had never been a real submarine building program that was big enough to require that ships be produced in a mass-production manner," Nardone said. With the anticipated construction of the Los Angeles class, this was no longer in question.

Quonset Point's needs gave rise to the concepts of work stations and construction teams. Instead of having expensive skilled labor wandering about collecting the parts they needed to do their jobs, materials were brought to the stations, where teams of workers stood ready to use them.

Unlike other eras, there was a ready and available work force—including sheet metal workers, machinists and electricians—who had been idled by the air station's shutdown. However, the skilled labor pool had worked on aircraft; few of them had ever worked on a ship, let alone a submarine. Construction drawings, which could number in the hundreds, were complex and unfamiliar. The remedy: booklets contain-

A triple threat, submarine style: The *Michigan* (SSBN-727) launches from the Groton shipyard. In the background, another Ohio class ship, the *Florida* (SSBN-728), is still under construction; in the foreground, berthed, is the *Boston* (SSN-703), a Los Angeles class ship.

ELECTRIC BOAT DIVISION

Former General Dynamics Chairman David Lewis, shown here at the launching of the *Hyman G. Rickover* in 1983, was responsible for negotiating a compromise between the company's Electric Boat Division and the U.S. Navy in 1978.

ing all of the drawings needed to complete a particular task. "We called them Mickey Mouse books," Nardone said. "The automobile industry started to do it—you know, flip the pages and build a car. This was flip the pages and build a ship." This paper package—which showed workers what they were building, told them how to build it and what materials it required—was the forerunner of the company's computer-aided design/manufacture electronic network in place today.

By the end of 1974, the company's backlog for work exceeded $2 billion dollars, including a $285 million contract to build the lead ship *Ohio* and contracts for 18 attack submarines.[14]

The company made valiant attempts to increase productivity and improve efficiency at the shipyard, but cost overruns continued to mount. Numerous obstacles deterred the company from making financial headway in 1975.[15]

> "The shipyard was hiring thousands of new workers, but their inexperience was working against efficiency. Absenteeism and turnover in the work force were running at 30 and 40 percent.
>
> "The massive facilities expansion program was disrupting the orderly construction of the ships. Seven different hull-erection plans had been used for the first seven submarines.
>
> "Material shortages were rampant and the materials on hand were not controlled by an inventory system. As a result, the shipyard had hired hundreds of workers to search for materials in the network of Electric Boat warehouses around Groton.

> There was no system that concentrated on getting materials to the right place in the shipyard at the right time when work gangs were ready to install them."

Meanwhile, due to the teamwork inspired by Joseph Pierce, major improvements were accomplished at both the Groton shipyard and Quonset Point facilities, according to General Dynamics' 1975 annual report:[16]

> "Considerable progress was made in 1975 on the $140 million facilities expansion and modernization program, which will provide Electric Boat with the capacity for simultaneous production of the Trident and 688-class submarines.
>
> "Construction of the new ship assembly and launching complex and its adjacent basin is now nearing completion. This land-level facility consists of a huge assembly building, an open outboard platform for hull outfitting and a 100 x 600-foot graving dock with a pontoon for launching and drydocking submarines.
>
> "The 135-foot-high assembly building will be equipped with seven overhead cranes and an unusual railroad-track-type transfer system to position cylinders for assembly to form the ship's hull.
>
> "The new manufacturing facility at the former Quonset Point Naval Air Station, R.I., became fully operational during the year and is rapidly becoming the division's principal center for fabricating hull cylinders, major sub-assemblies and other large components."

In mid-1976, Pierce was replaced as general manager by Gorden E. MacDonald, a financial

SSN688 CLASS
ARRANGEMENT OF COMPARTMENTS AND TANKS

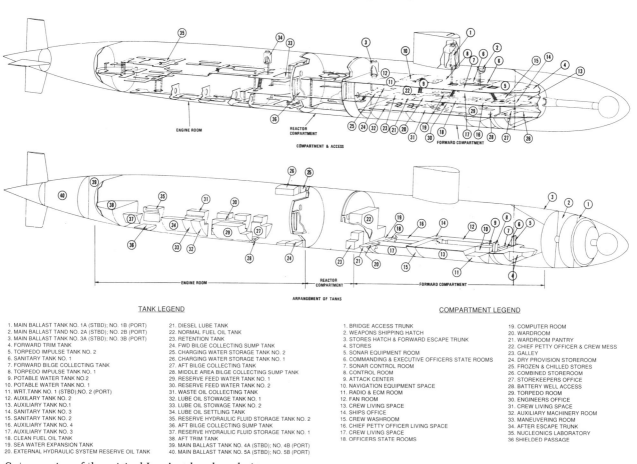

TANK LEGEND

1. MAIN BALLAST TANK NO. 1A (STBD); NO. 1B (PORT)
2. MAIN BALLAST TAND NO. 2A (STBD); NO. 2B (PORT)
3. MAIN BALLAST TANK NO. 3A (STBD); NO. 3B (PORT)
4. FORWARD TRIM TANK
5. TORPEDO IMPULSE TANK NO. 2
6. SANITARY TANK NO. 1
7. FORWARD BILGE COLLECTING TANK
8. TORPEDO IMPULSE TANK NO. 1
9. POTABLE WATER TANK NO.2
10. POTABLE WATER TANK NO. 1
11. WRT.TANK NO. 1 (STBD);NO. 2 (PORT)
12. AUXILARY TANK NO. 2
13. AUXILIARY TANK NO.1
14. SANITARY TANK NO. 3
15. SANITARY TANK NO. 2
16. AUXILIARY TANK NO. 4
17. AUXILIARY TANK NO. 3
18. CLEAN FUEL OIL TANK
19. SEA WATER EXPANSION TANK
20. EXTERNAL HYDRAULIC SYSTEM RESERVE OIL TANK

21. DIESEL LUBE TANK
22. NORMAL FUEL OIL TANK
23. RETENTION TANK
24. FWD BILGE COLLECTING SUMP TANK
25. CHARGING WATER STORAGE TANK NO. 2
26. CHARGING WATER STORAGE TANK NO. 1
27. AFT BILGE COLLECTING TANK
28. MIDDLE AREA BILGE COLLECTING SUMP TANK
29. RESERVE FEED WATER TANK NO. 1
30. RESERVE FEED WATER TANK NO. 2
31. WASTE OIL COLLECTING TANK
32. LUBE OIL STOWAGE TANK NO. 1
33. LUBE OIL STOWAGE TANK NO. 2
34. LUBE OIL SETTLING TANK
35. RESERVE HYDRAULIC FLUID STORAGE TANK NO. 2
36. AFT BILGE COLLECTING SUMP TANK
37. RESERVE HYDRAULIC FLUID STORAGE TANK NO. 1
38. AFT TRIM TANK
39. MAIN BALLAST TANK NO. 4A (STBD); NO. 4B (PORT)
40. MAIN BALLAST TANK NO. 5A (STBD); NO. 5B (PORT)

COMPARTMENT LEGEND

1. BRIDGE ACCESS TRUNK
2. WEAPONS SHIPPING HATCH
3. STORES HATCH & FORWARD ESCAPE TRUNK
4. STORES
5. SONAR EQUIPMENT ROOM
6. COMMANDING & EXECUTIVE OFFICERS STATE ROOMS
7. SONAR CONTROL ROOM
8. CONTROL ROOM
9. ATTACK CENTER
10. NAVIGATION EQUIPMENT SPACE
11. RADIO & ECM ROOM
12. FAN ROOM
13. CREW LIVING SPACE
14. SHIPS OFFICE
15. CREW WASHROOM
16. CHIEF PETTY OFFICER LIVING SPACE
17. CREW LIVING SPACE
18. OFFICERS STATE ROOMS

19. COMPUTER ROOM
20. WARDROOM
21. WARDROOM PANTRY
22. CHIEF PETTY OFFICER & CREW MESS
23. GALLEY
24. DRY PROVISION STOREROOM
25. FROZEN & CHILLED STORES
26. COMBINED STOREROOM
27. STOREKEEPERS OFFICE
28. BATTERY WELL ACCESS
29. TORPEDO ROOM
30. ENGINEERS OFFICE
31. CREW LIVING SPACE
32. AUXILIARY MACHINERY ROOM
33. MANEUVERING ROOM
34. AFTER ESCAPE TRUNK
35. NUCLEONICS LABORATORY
36 SHIELDED PASSAGE

Cutaway view of the original Los Angeles class design.

expert who had come from General Dynamics' corporate office. MacDonald held that position for a year and a half, one of Electric Boat's most turbulent periods. "It was completely adversarial between Electric Boat and the government, led by Rickover pretty much," observed Nardone. "It was a tenuous situation, to say the least."[17]

On December 1, 1976, MacDonald and Electric Boat filed claims against the U.S. Navy for $544 million, declaring that the Navy had provided them with faulty and inadequate design data, which led to delays and cost overruns. The Navy and Rickover reacted predictably, with the admiral vowing "to take those bastards on." Rickover and others in the Navy hierarchy viewed Electric Boat's claims as fraudulent and as an attempt to recover the company's losses and preserve their reputation on Wall Street.[18]

Electric Boat viewed the claims in a much different light. The company pointed out that it was neither responsible for the detail design nor for construction of the Los Angeles class lead ship, and that "problems and errors uncovered during construction should be reflected more rapidly and effectively by correction of detail drawings and other data." The designer and builder of the lead ship was Newport News, which, Electric Boat pointed out, had never before designed a nuclear submarine. The 1977 annual report outlined the company's defense.[19]

"In the case of the SSN688-class, the detail design was still in its earliest stages when Electric Boat received an award for seven follow ships and the design agent received an award for four ships. Two years later, at a time when little additional definitive design data was available, Electric Boat was awarded another contract, this time for 11 ships.

"The Navy's decision to release large numbers of ships to construction before detail design was complete or a prototype or lead ship was available was based on what the Navy considered to be urgent military requirements.

"In the interest of national security, the Navy decided to accept the risks inherent in proceeding concurrently with the design and construction of a very large number of these submarines with two shipbuilders. The success of this kind of operation, risky at best, depends on the quality and timeliness of the design data generated by the design agent and furnished to the other yard. Electric Boat esti-

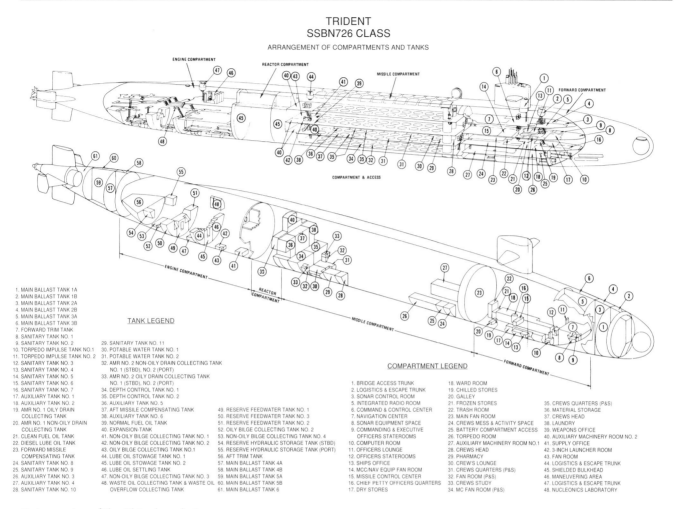

TRIDENT
SSBN726 CLASS
ARRANGEMENT OF COMPARTMENTS AND TANKS

TANK LEGEND

1. MAIN BALLAST TANK 1A
2. MAIN BALLAST TANK 1B
3. MAIN BALLAST TANK 2A
4. MAIN BALLAST TANK 2B
5. MAIN BALLAST TANK 3A
6. MAIN BALLAST TANK 3B
7. FORWARD TRIM TANK
8. SANITARY TANK NO. 1
9. SANITARY TANK NO. 2
10. TORPEDO IMPULSE TANK NO.1
11. TORPEDO IMPULSE TANK NO. 2
12. SANITARY TANK NO. 3
13. SANITARY TANK NO. 4
14. SANITARY TANK NO. 5
15. SANITARY TANK NO. 6
16. SANITARY TANK NO. 7
17. AUXILIARY TANK NO. 1
18. AUXILIARY TANK NO. 2
19. AMR NO. 1 OILY DRAIN
     COLLECTING TANK
20. AMR NO. 1 NON-OILY DRAIN
     COLLECTING TANK
21. CLEAN FUEL OIL TANK
22. DIESEL LUBE OIL TANK
23. FORWARD MISSILE
     COMPENSATING TANK
24. SANITARY TANK NO. 8
25. SANITARY TANK NO. 9
26. AUXILIARY TANK NO. 3
27. AUXILIARY TANK NO. 4
28. SANITARY TANK NO. 10

29. SANITARY TANK NO. 11
30. POTABLE WATER TANK NO. 1
31. POTABLE WATER TANK NO. 2
32. AMR NO. 2 NON-OILY DRAIN COLLECTING TANK
     NO. 1 (STBD), NO. 2 (PORT)
33. AMR NO. 2 OILY DRAIN COLLECTING TANK
     NO. 1 (STBD), NO. 2 (PORT)
34. DEPTH CONTROL TANK NO. 1
35. DEPTH CONTROL TANK NO. 2
36. AUXILIARY TANK NO. 5
37. AFT MISSILE COMPENSATING TANK
38. AUXILIARY TANK NO. 6
39. NORMAL FUEL OIL TANK
40. EXPANSION-TANK
41. NON-OILY BILGE COLLECTING TANK NO. 1
42. NON-OILY BILGE COLLECTING TANK NO. 2
43. OILY BILGE COLLECTING TANK NO.1
44. LUBE OIL STOWAGE TANK NO. 1
45. LUBE OIL STOWAGE TANK NO. 2
46. LUBE OIL SETTLING TANK
47. NON-OILY BILGE COLLECTING TANK NO. 3
48. WASTE OIL COLLECTING TANK & WASTE OIL
     OVERFLOW COLLECTING TANK

49. RESERVE FEEDWATER TANK NO. 1
50. RESERVE FEEDWATER TANK NO. 3
51. RESERVE FEEDWATER TANK NO. 2
52. OILY BILGE COLLECTING TANK NO. 2
53. NON-OILY BILGE COLLECTING TANK NO. 4
54. RESERVE HYDRAULIC STORAGE TANK (STBD)
55. RESERVE HYDRAULIC STORAGE TANK (PORT)
56. AFT TRIM TANK
57. MAIN BALLAST TANK 4A
58. MAIN BALLAST TANK 4B
59. MAIN BALLAST TANK 5A
60. MAIN BALLAST TANK 5B
61. MAIN BALLAST TANK 6

COMPARTMENT LEGEND

1. BRIDGE ACCESS TRUNK
2. LOGISTICS & ESCAPE TRUNK
3. SONAR CONTROL ROOM
4. INTEGRATED RADIO ROOM
5. COMMAND & CONTROL CENTER
6. NAVIGATION CENTER
7. SONAR EQUIPMENT SPACE
8. COMMANDING & EXECUTIVE
     OFFICERS STATEROOMS
9. COMPUTER ROOM
10. OFFICERS LOUNGE
11. OFFICERS STATEROOMS
12. SHIPS OFFICE
13. MCC/NAV EQUIP FAN ROOM
14. MISSILE CONTROL CENTER
15. CHIEF PETTY OFFICERS QUARTERS
16. DRY STORES

18. WARD ROOM
19. CHILLED STORES
20. GALLEY
21. FROZEN STORES
22. TRASH ROOM
23. MAIN FAN ROOM
24. CREWS MESS & ACTIVITY SPACE
25. BATTERY COMPARTMENT ACCESS
26. TORPEDO ROOM
27. AUXILIARY MACHINERY ROOM NO.1
28. CREWS HEAD
29. PHARMACY
30. CREW'S LOUNGE
31. CREWS QUARTERS (P&S)
32. FAN ROOM (P&S)
33. CREWS STUDY
34. MC FAN ROOM (P&S)

35. CREWS QUARTERS (P&S)
36. MATERIAL STORAGE
37. CREWS HEAD
38. LAUNDRY
39. WEAPONS OFFICE
40. AUXILIARY MACHINERY ROOM NO. 2
41. SUPPLY OFFICE
42. 3-INCH LAUNCHER ROOM
43. FAN ROOM
44. LOGISTICS & ESCAPE TRUNK
45. SHIELDED BULKHEAD
46. MANEUVERING AREA
47. LOGISTICS & ESCAPE TRUNK
48. NUCLEONICS LABORATORY

Cutaway view of the Ohio class design.

mated its costs and submitted its bids on the basis that this design data would be both of high quality and delivered on time.

"Unfortunately, as design and construction unfolded, the risks inherent in 'concurrency' came to pass, resulting in extended delays in delivery and tremendous cost growth. Initial drawings were from six to nine months late; the total number of drawings grew significantly and they were replete with errors which led to more than 35,000 revisions to these plans and specifications being imposed on Electric Boat by the design agent through the Navy. Also, the working drawings furnished to Electric Boat frequently did not reflect proven submarine design practices or make possible economical standards of submarine construction. Consequently, the production line operation planned for construction of the submarines at Electric Boat has been completely disrupted and the benefits of serial production have been lost. The Navy, by its actions, has frustrated Electric Boat's efforts to perform under the SSN688 contracts in a professional manner as it always has in the past."

The confrontation between Electric Boat and the Navy resulted in a deadlock. Ultimately, Electric Boat decided at the end of 1977 that it could not profitably continue building Los Ange-les class ships and informed the Navy of its decision to cease construction. Both parties agreed to seek a settlement which would "give fair consideration to the impact of the Navy-directed actions, to the inability of the inflation clauses in the contracts to cope with these actions, and to any cost increases that could be fairly attributed to productivity problems at Electric Boat." In March 1978, no settlement could be reached and Electric Boat informed the Navy that it would halt production on the Los Angeles class program at midnight on April 12, 1978. On March 21, the Navy suggested an extension of two months "to negotiate an equitable solution." In addition, the Navy provided Electric Boat with a provisional cash payment which would "essentially eliminate the negative cash flow of the program for that two-month period."[20]

In early June, only days before the extension ran out, David Lewis, chairman of General Dynamics, and Edward Hidalgo, assistant secretary of the Navy, agreed to a compromise. Electric Boat would reduce its claim to $359 million, and the Navy conceded that they "would consider making an advance payment that would be

The *Baltimore* (SSN-704), a Los Angeles class ship, launches into the Thames River at Groton on December 13, 1980. Sponsored by the Honorable Marjorie S. Holt, the *Baltimore* was formally commissioned on July 24, 1982.

recovered [from progress payments] over the unexpired term of the contract." This advance payment eventually worked out to be $300 million and was, in effect, an interest-free loan for Electric Boat. The settlement agreement also indicated that the Navy would pay 50 percent of any additional overruns up to $100 million.[21]

Meanwhile, General Dynamics named P. Takis Veliotis, then general manager of its Quincy shipyard, general manager of Electric Boat's Groton shipyard in October 24, 1977. Veliotis was a seasoned and respected shipyard manager who immediately took action to increase the efficiency of the shipyard in Groton. He was known as a manager who was "effective against union bosses, demanding customers, and business competitors."[22]

On October 24, 1977, his first day on the job, Veliotis summarily dismissed several thousand mostly salaried employees, gathered the company's managers and outlined his plan of action, which was to "automate the hull-cylinder construction, computerize the shipyard's inventory of steel and parts, and minimize idle time by changing work rules." He maintained a respect-ful demeanor with Admiral Rickover, but refused to cede control of the shipyard to either the Navy or Rickover.[23]

Veliotis and the work force at Electric Boat faced a considerable challenge, but gradually productive practices replaced inefficient ones. In 1978, the company began construction of a $120 million automated frame and cylinder manufacturing facility at Quonset Point. At the facility, which was completed in 1979, huge fabricating and welding machines fashioned hull sections which were then shipped to the Groton yard by barge. The company claimed it was "the most significant breakthrough in submarine-construction technology since EB's development of the welded submarine hull."[24]

After Veliotis arrived, Henry Nardone was sent to the Electro Dynamic facility at Avenel, New Jersey, Elco's successor. Avenel, as the facility is generally known, specializes in the stealthy art of manufacturing extremely quiet electric motors and other noise-sensitive rotating equipment such as fans. Avenel also manufactures other components, such as pipehangers for submarines. "They also had always done

ELECTRIC BOAT DIVISION

The *Augusta* (SSN-710), a Los Angeles class submarine launches from Groton on January 21, 1984 with traditional pomp and flourish.

commercial business—electric motors, generators—so they had commercial work and government work in the same building and that was a real problem. You had to keep the materials separated, you had to keep the workers separated. ... There was always concern about mixing commercial materials and government materials," Nardone explained. The U.S. government, which was paying for material that met stringent military specifications, was concerned about it being mixed in. Segregating and accounting for military-approved materials and workers increased Avenel's overhead expenditures.[25]

In 1979, Electric Boat launched the *Ohio*, the first of its class and the first to carry Trident missiles. Although the ship would not be completed for another two years, Electric Boat was determined to demonstrate that new yard controls were working. Meanwhile, a discouraging problem came to light late in the year. A Navy inspector at the Groton shipyard, aboard the *Bremerton*, a Los Angeles class ship, discovered that a number of welds were either missing or incomplete. Further examination revealed additional welding problems. This resulted in comprehensive inspections being ordered for all Los Angeles class and Ohio class submarines in the shipyard. This difficult and time-consuming inspection program also turned up inferior grades of steel among Electric Boat's inventory, which required further reinspection of the submarine hulls. Work came to a virtual standstill in the shipyard.[26] The year 1980 would be the first year since the construction of the *Nautilus* that not a single nuclear submarine would be delivered to the Navy.

Electric Boat attributed the problems to "the need to incorporate a large number of design changes being directed by the Navy and by problems with government-furnished equipment and components manufactured by outside suppliers."[27] Another conflict developed after Electric Boat made a claim to its insurance underwriter to pay for costs associated with correcting the welding and metallurgical problems. Ironically, Electric Boat's insurance underwriter was the U.S. Navy itself, which had underwritten the shipbuilder's risk insurance to save money on substantial premiums to companies such as Lloyds' of London. Both the Navy and Admiral Rickover were outraged. Veliotis was summoned to testify before Congress concerning Electric Boat's claim for approximately $100 million. He admitted to some deficiencies, but added that Electric Boat had "faced them squarely and put them behind us."[28] As for the defective steel, Veliotis dramatically dumped 50 pounds of steel parts on the table in front of him and told Congress that this was exactly how much had been replaced out of the 23.6 million pounds used in the ships. The confrontation continued,

however, with the Navy withdrawing contracts and Electric Boat refusing to withdraw its claims. Eventually, the two parties reached a resolution. A report in 1981 from a special committee to John F. Lehman Jr., secretary of the Navy, comprised of delegates from both Electric Boat and the Navy, came to these conclusions:[29]

> *Nonconforming Steel* — "The Committee is satisfied that the corrective action is complete and this item will not have an effect on Electric Boat's scheduled delivery dates."
> *Structural and Steel Welding Problem* — "The Committee believes that this item has been satisfactorily restored and that the work remaining on the other submarines will support Electric Boat's scheduled delivery dates."

Work slowly returned to normal at the Groton yard. Electric Boat delivered seven nuclear submarines to the Navy in 1981. During her extensive sea trials, the *Ohio*, Electric Boat's first Trident-armed submarine, "exceeded virtually all of its performance specifications."[30] In November, she officially became part of the U.S. fleet. Six Los Angeles class ships were delivered to the Navy: *Bremerton*, *Jacksonville*, *Dallas*, *LaJolla*, *Phoenix* and *Boston*.

The company also received funding to begin work on three design and development programs. The first program was to provide the Los Angeles class with the ability to launch new Tomahawk cruise missiles vertically as well as from torpedo tubes. The second program was to redesign the Trident submarines so that they could operate the "larger advanced Trident II missile with additional payload, range and accuracy." The third program specified that Electric Boat increase "its design effort in support of the United Kingdom's Trident submarine program."[31]

In 1982, Electric Boat delivered two Los Angeles class submarines, the *Baltimore* and *City of Corpus Christi*, along with a second Ohio class, the *Michigan*. Electric Boat's significant investments and restructuring programs of prior years were beginning to pay dividends in production efficiency:[32]

> "The heavy investment in new machinery, equipment and buildings, particularly at the Quonset Point, R.I., facility, is beginning to make a significant impact on the production man-hours required for the construction work of these extremely complex weapon systems."

In 1982, Fritz Tovar became general manager of Electric Boat. Considered an outstanding manufacturing engineer, Tovar is credited with expanding the modular approach to piping assemblies and the systems area. He was also responsible for investing heavily in "building sophisticated fixtures that could be used for constructing sub-assemblies in the shop and assure that these sub-assemblies really fit the ship." He also allocated funds to construct a transporter that would handle larger and heavier submarine sections, or cylinders, and a barge that could transport the cylinders between Quonset Point and Groton. "He worked very hard at trying to develop good relationships with the Navy, which we really needed after Veliotis," Nardone said.[33] Tovar would remain in this position through 1988, a period during which several of the Trident submarines were built.

During 1982, Electric Boat was awarded contracts for four additional Los Angeles class ships and two more submarines of the Ohio class, increasing the company's backlog of work, which included 11 Los Angeles class and eight Ohio class ships, to $4.6 billion.[34]

In 1984, both Newport News and Electric Boat were asked to submit "preliminary designs to the Navy for a new class of fast-attack submarines, called the SSN-21."[35] Construction of the lead ship of the new Seawolf class, was scheduled to begin in 1989.

Design and Construction of a Nuclear Submarine

Prior to the Los Angeles class, Electric Boat's highly skilled engineers and architects had designed every class of nuclear submarine except the Halibut class (A Navy-Mare Island

design) and Thresher class, (which became known as the Permit class after it's lead ship, the *Thresher*, sank on April 10, 1963).[36] The design cycle begins when the Office of the Chief of Naval Operations (OPNAV) decides, based on operational requirements, to design a new class. In the early days of submarines, this was a simple matter, as the submarine had a rather limited role. But today, submarines are required to perform many exacting missions. They carry ballistic and cruise missiles for launching at enemy land targets; hunt and destroy other submarines; and engage in patrols and special surveillance operations. The selection of missions for a submarine, or combination of missions, has a direct relationship on its design.[37] Consequently, the initial phase of the design cycle is for OPNAV to determine the ship's overall performance characteristics. NAVSEA then writes a request for proposal (RFP) which includes the submarine's mission, speed, diving depth, propulsion power, armament and electronics complement.[38]

In the preliminary design phase, Electric Boat typically devotes 20,000 man-hours to the preparation of specifications, contract drawings and diagrams. This preliminary design package presents the concepts for the ship profile, ship arrangement, weapons systems, navigation, communications and berthing. After these drawings are submitted to the Navy, both sides

The *Helena* (SSN-725), an attack submarine, on sea trials on Long Island Sound. Launched in 1986, the *Helena* was the 62nd Los Angeles class ship.

Each attack submarine has its own unique seal, which is displayed on the ship's bow during launch ceremonies.

work together to define the design and construction of the submarine. This phase can take from 80,000 to 100,000 man-hours and can include 1,200 pages of specifications and 70 drawings. These contract drawings only define the basic design characteristics. The working drawings, or detail design phase, take anywhere from *15 million to 20 million* man-hours to develop. They include 7,500 drawings and up to 33,000 pages of documentation.[39]

There is generally a six-year period between the award of a construction contract and commissioning of the resulting submarine into the fleet. While the end result is one of the most complex pieces of warfare machinery in the world, there is nothing particularly mysterious about the way a modern submarine is built. Much like any other product, standard manufacturing scheduling procedures are generally followed. Items with the longest lead times are ordered first so that they are available when it comes time for installation. These include the nuclear power plant, propulsion machinery and other heavy equipment.

At Electric Boat's Quonset Point facility, the construction process begins with the forming of three-inch thick plates of hardened high-grade steel, forming the metal into curved sections. Critical material has a "pedigree"—traceability of its composition and manufacturing process using a serial number which is identified on each piece, even if subsequently cut into smaller pieces.

The sections are then welded together to form circular cross sections of the submarine's cigar-shaped hull, which are called cylinders. Much of the submarine's major components are set on foundations on the bottom of the circular hulls. In the early days, workers were forced to build these structures, piece by piece in very tight spaces, sometimes becoming contortionists to reach into tiny, hard-to-reach places. Using modern modular techniques, these cylinders are designed to be "end-loaded," giving workers easy access. Accesses and holes are predetermined and cut so that portions of each system, preassembled and tested at a work station, can be installed expeditiously. This design approach also facilitates repair, overhaul and modification work after the submarine has been completed. At Quonset Point, major components such as the heat exchangers and engine room equipment are installed into the hull sections.[40]

A rare look at an Ohio class submarine under construction, as the *Pennsylvania* (SSBN-735) nears completion at Groton.

ELECTRIC BOAT DIVISION

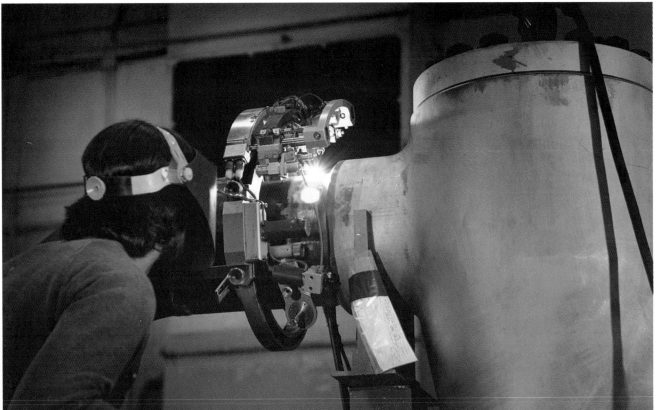

ELECTRIC BOAT DIVISION

Welder at work. Employees at Electric Boat have always taken a great deal of personal pride in the quality of their work.

While the Trident submarines were the first to be entirely built using this approach, the new Seawolf class has advanced modular design and construction techniques.

The modular approach has all but eliminated dreaded, time-consuming mirror welds—welding which required the worker to use a mirror to see what he or she was doing. Referring to the new Seawolf class, former vice president of operations Kenneth D. Brown said, "The idea on this boat is no mirror welds." Much of the welding at Quonset Point is now done using semi-automatic, robotic welders, controlled by master welders—the best of the best. Even though they are using a high-technology tool, it still takes a skilled eye and years of experience to produce an acceptable weld which is later examined by Navy inspectors using radiography, ultrasonic and non-destructive testing techniques.

Combined with prudent use of three-dimensional computer-aided design/manufacturing, the modular approach to design and construction has reduced the amount of effort necessary to build a submarine. According to Brown, the first Trident-armed submarine took *24 million* man-hours. "Now they're down to below 12 [million] and closer to 10 [million]—maybe less," he said. "We essentially cut the labor cost in half."

Each hull cylinder section, fully loaded with its systems and other fittings, weighs as much as 1,400 tons. After completion at Quonset Point,

these sections are shipped by barge to the Groton shipyard for final assembly.

While under construction at Groton, Trident and Seawolf sections are housed inside an immense hangar-like building, protected from the weather. Inside, workers weld the circular sections together to form a pressure hull; as the submarine grows, these dark-orange sections begin to emerge from the building. Even under the best of circumstances the work is hot, dirty and noisy. The metal on each section must be pre-heated to 225°F before it can be welded. Rooster-tails of sparks arc through the hot air. After the pressure hull is finished, the "welds are X-rayed and sold" to scrupulous Navy inspectors.[41]

The ship is then ready to begin the testing stage. While many of the subsystems have been individually put through their paces, testing at Groton focuses on ship-wide operations. Every testing event is carefully documented and tracked. Testing the ship's piping systems—covering the various pipes that carry fluids such as high-pressure hydraulic oil, potable water, and steam for the propulsion system—is one of the most difficult and time-consuming phases of this testing.

Installation of nuclear components takes place at Groton. Electric Boat and Navy personnel strive to stay ahead of construction crews so that the nuclear components are ready for in-

Huge fabricating and welding machines build hull sections at Electric Boat's automated frame and cylinder manufacturing facility in Quonset Point, Rhode Island. The sections with foundations and equipment installed are then shipped by barge to the Groton facility. The company called this plant, which was completed in 1979, "the most significant breakthrough in submarine-construction technology since EB's development of the welded submarine hull."

ELECTRIC BOAT DIVISION

stallation when the ship is ready to receive them. While the heat exchangers and some engine room equipment are installed at Quonset Point, the primary shield tank and reactor compartment components are installed at Groton.

The next stage involves getting the ship into the water. For most of the Electric Boat ships, this meant sliding down the building ways into the river. However, as the ships have gotten larger, the Groton shipyard has turned to "float-offs"—flooding the graving dock in which the ship rests. The *Columbia* (SSN-771), launched on September 24, 1994, was notably the "last to slide."[42]

Electric Boat and Navy personnel conduct operational tests on the stationary submarine, leading up to the dock trials, where the reactor is made "critical" and systems are again tested. Dockside "INSURV" (Board of INspection SURVey) trials, which test the coordination of all systems, follow. The "count-down to the initial *sea trials*" then begins.

During the initial sea trial, the nuclear propulsion plant is tested. There are "noise trials," which measure the ship's noise levels and "electronics trials," which test its electronic systems. When all of these trials are satisfactorily com-

pleted, the ship is delivered, commissioned, and the U.S. Navy puts the submarine into service.

Some trials have demonstrated that they are best conducted at sea. Retired Vice Admiral Yogi Kaufman related an incident that occurred as he conducted test drills aboard the *Will Rogers* while berthed at Electric Boat's Groton facility. "We were going through our whole 'going to sea' routine ... The gold skipper and I were putting the crew through the wringer, so to speak, and giving them drills they would not expect. One of them, of course, was the flooding drill. We have an emergency blow system which is designed to just make sure that we get high pressure air directly into the tanks. Normally, when Electric Boat tests this up the Thames River, they take the boat out in the middle of the stream and blow the emergency blow—and it shoots spray all over the place."

(The "gold skipper" refers to the captain of the gold crew. On all ballistic missile submarines, there are two crews: a gold and a blue. This simply refers to two different complements that will crew the ships on alternating patrols.[43])

The emergency blow test is not done when the ship is docked, simply because of the hazards a highly pressurized spray of air and water

A mammoth, 1200-ton, cylindrical section of the *Wyoming* (SSBN-742) is delivered to the Groton shipyard from Quonset Point. This view shows the advantages of the latest modular construction, with many critical sub-assemblies already in position.

ELECTRIC BOAT DIVISION

can create in civilized surroundings. Kaufman said the crew had been thoroughly briefed that, no matter what the reason for it during the drill, the emergency blow system would not be activated. Unfortunately, one lieutenant, the diving officer, was somehow left out of the briefing. As luck would have it, when the collision alarm sounded during the drill, the lieutenant ordered the chief of the watch, "Blow emergency blow!" The chief, who had been indoctrinated on just why that wasn't prudent, replied, "No, sir." The lieutenant, obviously unaware of why his order had just been refused, turned and, with great conviction and just possibly a bit of rage in his voice, repeated the order. "I said BLOW!" The chief snapped to the order, activated the emergency blow system—and promptly shorted out all electrical power to Electric Boat's docks.

"We had a topside watch and I was sure he was washed over. It was a cold day in January and I rushed to the bridge, Bill (Commander William Cowhill) right behind me. I yelled, 'Topside' ... and this meek little voice said, 'Yes sir, Captain.' He was standing there, water all over everything. ... Then Bill and I looked around and there was water dripping off all the buildings on the waterfront. Power was lost ... Gradually, you would see people peeking out of windows to see what the hell happened. Didn't hurt our power. We were self-sustaining, of course, operating on our reactor. But it sure shut down the waterfront at Electric Boat."[44]

While this long and complicated fabrication and testing procedure might at first appear cold and mechanical, Electric Boat employees take their work personally, say those who have commanded their products. "Probably, without question, they are the highest quality submarines in the world," said Vice Admiral B. M. "Bud" Kauderer, who served aboard the *Skipjack*, the lead ship in its class, and *Ulysses S. Grant*, a Lafayette class submarine.[45]

> "[These ships] are built to exacting standards, with a great deal of personal involvement by workers. They become very attached. In the new construction that I did there I got to see a great deal of personal attachment between the workers and the ship. They just pretend that it's their baby."

During the peak construction years of the Los Angeles class, Brown recalled a time at Groton when they would launch one ship while the tail section of the next, still under construction, hung over the audience—complete with its engine room and equipment, aft ballast tanks and reactor compartment. "When we brought that across the road and down the ways, that was 2,900 tons of a 6,900 ton submarine already put together as a unit," he said. We had four hulls and four tails "so we had eight 688s (Los Angeles class submarines) in manufacture at one time."[46]

A Technological Marvel

The propulsion machinery, reduction gears and nuclear reactor comprise some of the most advanced technologies aboard a modern submarine. The principle behind the propulsion system is relatively straightforward. The reactor generates heat from a controlled nuclear fission when uranium atoms split and produce energy. Neutrons are released when an atom splits and they, in turn, strike and split other uranium atoms which release still more energy and neutrons. Very quickly, a great amount of energy is created. The heat produced from this controlled nuclear reaction is used to generate steam which drives a turbine. The turbines are connected by a set of reduction gears to a propeller shaft which propels the submarine.

The most critical engineering occurs in isolating the radioactive energy from the steam propulsion system. This is accomplished through a primary coolant loop which passes directly through the reactor core. The pressurized water coolant is heated within the core and then transfers this heat to a secondary loop in a heat exchanger outside the reactor. The water in this secondary loop is then converted into steam. The steam contains potential energy which is released as kinetic energy to drive the turbine in much the same manner water built up behind a dam rushes through the turbines of a hydroelectric plant to produce power.

The crew is shielded from the reactor by its placement on the submarine and by layers of protective material. The reactor compartment, situated in the middle of the ship, is only accessible after shutdown. The reactor is controlled from an area called maneuvering, just aft of the reactor compartment. Forward of the compartment is a tank which holds diesel fuel for an auxiliary engine. The fuel assists in shielding. There are also a number of other layers of biological shielding materials surrounding the reactor compartment.

Nuclear power provided a major advance in the quest to make submarines quieter. Now more than ever, evasion and detection of other submarines is a complex function aboard modern nuclear submarine classes such as the Los Angeles or Ohio. Every submarine has a characteristic set of noises which make it both unique and identifiable. Its propeller causes a unique turbulence which can be identified from its characteristic sound "signature" by sophisticated sonar devices. Sounds emanating from inside a ship—such as pumps, machinery, even a tool dropped—can be detected.

The flow of water passing smoothly over the hull creates a noise that is surprisingly loud to an enemy submarine's sensitive sonar detectors. The wake left by a submarine causes detectable thermal and ultraviolet radiation disruptions. The latest detection systems, along with evasion technology are among the most heavily guarded secrets aboard submarines.[47]

Submarine developers have engineered anechoic tiles to thwart some of these detection technologies. These sound-absorbing tiles are made from special plastic compounds designed to absorb active sonar and sound generated within the ship. However, one of the most effective evasion techniques is to dive deeper into the ocean and take advantage of the natural thermal and acoustic shielding there. The most effective shield is the permanent thermocline which reduces the speed of sound by such a large degree that it distorts sonar reports. The permanent thermocline is found at different depths around the world and is affected by a great number of factors such as salinity, presence of minerals and salts, pollution, and the presence of plant and animal life. This thick layer of water, which declines rapidly in temperature, is usually found at 1,000 feet depth in the tropics and at 3,000 feet in higher latitudes.

This illustrates why diving depth is critical to a submarine's undetectability. Some Russian Alpha class submarines are reportedly able to reach depths of almost 3,000 feet.[48] Admiral Kaufman explained why this is not necessarily a disadvantage. "We deliberately changed the depth, made it shallower than the Russian class. We were a little concerned with the overshoot angle and the exceeding depth unless we had better control," he said. "Our point was: Unless you could get down to a depth where you got significant advantages over what you had ... that unless you could get down to the deep sonar channels, deep sound channels, then there was no point. The increments weren't buying you that much.

"You spend a lot of money and a lot of heartache ... Your weapons have to work at depth. All your systems have to be built for depth and you have to do a lot to achieve safety. At that point, safety is usually spelled '$afety.'"[49]

Silence is the most vital strategic and survival characteristic for a submarine. This depends upon what is known as a "fragile technology," called fragile because physical principles which support the technology are widely known to everyone. That makes it relatively easy for engineers and scientists to develop countermeasures and ultimately match their adversaries' performance. Designers at Electric Boat, and at the many other companies and institutions which support detection and evasion technologies, must

ELECTRIC BOAT DIVISION

GENERAL DYNAMICS

Winning Design — House Flag Contest
October 1978

Electric Boat house flag.

work continuously to maintain an increasingly narrow lead. Modern submarines utilize internal noise-monitoring sensors. Any mechanical device not running at perfect efficiency generates noise. "Even with the Cold War over, we don't talk about this much, but they [modern submarines] are significantly quieter by orders of magnitude," Brown said.[50]

At one time, prior to and including World War II, submarines were rather condescendingly called "pig boats," referring to the perceived habitability of the boats. This is not the case in today's submarine fleet. While far from being luxurious or spacious, almost every crewman has his own bunk and space in which to keep his belongings. There are such comforts as showers, laundries and a recreation area for off-duty hours.

One of the most amazing on-board technologies is the submarine's air recirculation system that allows submariners to remain beneath the ocean surface for weeks, even months, at a time. "It's a development possibly as important as nuclear power," said Admiral Kaufman. "In order to really exploit nuclear power, you had to develop air revitalization." Kaufman was on board the *Scorpion* when she and her crew set the world record for submerged time without breathing outside air—a total of 70 days. Kaufman termed the air "better than outside."[51]

Armament

"The modern submarine can launch cruise missiles with a range of the current crop of Tomahawk cruise missiles, reaching targets 750 miles away, which encompasses about 75 percent of all of the targets of interest that might have any military value in the world," said Admiral Kauderer. The missiles can travel 500

USS AUGUSTA

USS GEORGIA

USS MINNEAPOLIS-SAINT PAUL

USS HENRY M. JACKSON

USS HYMAN G. RICKOVER

Leading The Way At Electric Boat
58,200 TONS OF SUBMARINES DELIVERED IN 1984

GENERAL DYNAMICS
Electric Boat Division

GENERAL DYNAMICS, ELECTRIC BOAT DIVISION

Submarines delivered to the U.S. Navy by Electric Boat in 1984 included *Augusta, Georgia, Minneapolis-St. Paul, Henry M. Jackson* and the *Hyman G. Rickover.*

miles to a target and still have an error radius of only a few feet.[52]

Kauderer described a number of missions that would utilize today's submarines: Covertly inserting and extracting Navy SEALs and Special Forces troops. Laying and detecting mines covertly. Attacking surface ships or simply making an appearance in port to let people know it is there.

"It is usually the first one on station if you have a crisis," Kauderer said.

Submarines are armed with two classes of missiles—ballistic missiles and cruise missiles. Cruise missiles, deployed by Los Angeles class submarines, are basically pilot-less aircraft.[53] They can be launched either from torpedo tubes or from the vertical launch system (VLS) located in the bow just aft of the sonar dome. The Harpoon cruise missile with a range of 155 miles, is launched from the torpedo tubes, accelerating to the ocean's surface where a small rocket engine ignites which launches it into the air. The

rocket is then ejected and a turbojet propels the missile to its target at a speed of approximately 550 knots.[54]

The Tomahawk cruise missile, with a range of up to 1,019 miles, can deliver either a 200-kiloton, W-88 nuclear warhead or a 1,000-pound high-explosive conventional warhead. It can be launched from either the torpedo tubes or the vertical launch system, where up to twelve missiles can be stored. The Tomahawk missile travels at approximately 500 knots.[55]

The missiles most commonly identified with submarines are the ballistic missiles carried by the Ohio class. These missiles are true rockets, which trace a trajectory through space enroute to a land target. They are all equipped with multiple warheads of two types—MIRVs (Multiple Independently targetable Reentry Vehicles) which are deployed in flight to independently hit programmed targets and MARVs (MAneuverable Reentry Vehicles), which can be steered to their

OFFICIAL U.S. NAVY PHOTO

The nuclear-powered strategic missile submarine *Michigan* (SSBN-727) launches a Trident missile during a demonstration and shakedown operation in 1982.

OFFICIAL U.S. NAVY PHOTO BY TGS TECHNOLOGY INC.

The first developmental flight test model of the Trident II D5X-1 missile launches from a flat pad. The missile was designed to be fired from the ninth Trident submarine, *Tennessee* (SSBN-734), and subsequent Ohio class ballistic missile submarines.

targets by on-board guidance systems. The Trident I has an accuracy of 500 yards, meaning that half its warheads will fall within 500 yards of their target after having traveled almost 5,000 miles.[56] The Trident II has a range of 6,000 miles and can match the accuracy of any land-based missile—an amazing feat for a weapon launched from a moving platform.[57]

There are three major torpedoes in the Navy's arsenal: the Mark (MK-)48 heavyweight, the Mark (MK-)46 lightweight and the Mark (MK-)50 advanced lightweight. The most advanced torpedo deployed by Trident and Los Angeles class submarines today is the MK-48 ADvanced CAPability (ADCAP) torpedo. The MK-48 ADCAP is 21 inches in diameter and 19 feet long, and powered by a piston-driven engine that operates like a pump jet. This propulsion system gives the weapon a range of more than 5 miles at speeds greater than 28 knots (32.2 miles per hour). The torpedo delivers a warhead containing 650 pounds of PBXN-103, a high explosive. The warhead is rigged with an electromagnetic fuse which allows for the precise detonation of the charge where it will do the most damage. This could be at the point of impact or within the hull of the targeted ship. The MK-48 is

designed to terminate deep-diving nuclear submarines and high-performance surface ships and is carried by all Navy submarines. The MK-48 ADCAP is carried by submarines of the Los Angeles and Ohio classes and will be carried by the Seawolf class attack submarine. Both versions of the MK-48 can operate with or without wire guidance (a wire connection between the submarine and the torpedo) and use active and/or passive homing. When launched, the torpedoes execute programmed target search, acquisition and attack procedures. Both can conduct multiple re-attacks if they miss the target.[58]

Mines are a weapon that the public normally does not associate with modern submarines. Although aircraft are responsible for most mine-laying activities, submarines excel where stealth and precision are required. Mines either lie on the ocean floor or float at the ends of cables attached to anchors on the bottom. Either variety is detonated when a passing ship sets off one of the mine's sensors. Sensors can be triggered by magnetic fields, acoustic variables, pressure waves or combinations of all three. Some mines are even programmed to explode only when a certain type of submarine passes near them.[59]

The latest Los Angeles class submarines can carry as many as 40 of these specialized mines.

The Improved Los Angeles Class

The Los Angeles class has evolved since the first of the class, the *Los Angeles*, was launched. Starting with the *Providence* (SSN-719), Electric Boat began installing the vertical launch system (VLS) for Tomahawk missiles. More improvements followed in the mid- to late-1980s when the improved Los Angeles class (designated as SSN-688I, with the *I* meaning "improved") were launched. A new combat system, which integrated all of the boat's weapons and sensors, was installed. The superstructure was strengthened; the sail planes were removed and replaced with retractable bow diving planes to improve the SSN-688I's ability to surface through ice. These submarines are also covered in anechoic tiles, making them orders of magnitude quieter and less detectable than their predecessors.[60]

The SSN-688I class is 360 feet long, displacing 6,080 tons surfaced and 6,927 tons submerged. They are 33 feet in diameter with a draft of 32.3 feet. They can reach speeds of more than 30 knots while submerged, and carry a complement of 127 crew members.[61]

The Ohio Class

The Ohio class submarine is larger than a World War II cruiser and positively more lethal. According to the U.S. Navy, "Deterrence of nuclear war has been the sole mission of the fleet ballistic missile submarine (SSBN) since its inception in 1960."[62] The first eight Ohio class submarines were designed to carry 24 Trident I C-4 ballistic missiles. Beginning with the *Tennessee* (SSBN-734), the ships were equipped with advanced Trident II D-5 missiles. The submarine is also equipped with four torpedo tubes and armed with MK-48 torpedoes.

The Ohio class' mobility, quietness and speed have made it an integral part of America's defensive triad. As Electric Boat declared, it is "more capable of surviving attack than any of the nation's other strategic weapons systems."[63]

OFFICIAL U.S. NAVY PHOTO

Technicians perform maintenance on a Mark 48 Advanced Capabilities (MK-48 ADCAP) torpedo.

The 1,000-pound conventional warhead of a BMG-109 Tomahawk cruise missile detonates over its target, a revetted aircraft, during a test conducted by the Joint Cruise Missiles Project. The missile was launched from a submerged submarine 400 miles off the coast of California.

"Trident can also remain at sea longer than its predecessors, requiring less time between patrols, less maintenance and fewer overhauls.

"The ship's command and control systems are integrated, employing the most sophisticated digital computer system in a submarine, and its sonar system is the most sensitive ever installed.

"Being at sea for long periods is also more comfortable for Trident's crew. Nine-person staterooms for enlisted personnel include hanging lockers and stereo headsets at each bunk. Two libraries and an exercise area provide luxuries unheard of in earlier designs."

The Ohio class dwarfs most earlier submarine designs. Ships in its class are 560 feet long and 42 feet in diameter. The boat displaces

18,750 tons submerged, has a draft of 36.5 feet, and carries a crew of between 157 and 160.[64]

This class is intended to replace Poseidon-equipped submarines, which are being retired throughout the decade of the 1990s.

The Seawolf Class

As the 1980s came to a close, James E. Turner Jr. was named vice president, general manager of Electric Boat, whose professionals were already at work on the next stage in submarine development—the SSN-21, or Seawolf class. The Seawolf class was designed to be "the fastest, quietest, deepest diving and most heavily armed attack submarine ever built by the United States."[65]

PERHAPS OUR SUBMARINES
ARE TOO QUIET.

You don't hear much concerning the role of America's "Silent Service" in bringing an end to the Cold War. But for nearly 40 years, the submarine community provided one of the most powerful deterrents to aggression.

Operating independently, unseen and unheard for months at a time, American submarines were on station, unsupported, and served notice to potential adversaries. And all the while, we were developing the advanced technologies in propulsion, quieting and weaponry that make today's submarines even more formidable.

Now there's a new mission for our submarine force. In an era of force reductions, submarines become an increasingly valuable force multiplier. Strategically deployed, attack submarines can quickly respond to regional conflicts virtually anywhere in the world. They combine the element of surprise with the ability to engage enemy forces at sea as well as over land with cruise missiles. Submarines also provide the ideal platform for covert surveillance and special warfare operations.

Maintaining a viable submarine force requires the preservation of the unique infrastructure of manufacturers and suppliers that has been developed over the past 45 years.

The United States' submarine force has long been known as the "Silent Service" but the need to preserve this vital capability must now be heard loud and clear.

Electric Boat Division, Groton, CT.

GENERAL DYNAMICS
Electric Boat Division

This Electric Boat advertisement in *Sea Power* describes the importance of America's "Silent Service" and its vital role in the country's defense strategy.

CHAPTER X

Electric Boat's Second Century

As always, the future of the submarine force will be different than the past. But, as always, the gold and silver dolphins will mark sailors who are a breed apart—those who sail with courage beneath the distant seas. We will continue to build the most capable submarines in the world and crew them with the most capable sailors. That will not change.

John H. Dalton, Secretary of the Navy
in remarks on June 16, 1994

World events at the beginning of this decade—having a tremendous impact on the military and its budget—were largely unanticipated. The fall of the Berlin Wall in 1989 touched off a chain of events that dramatically changed the world's political dynamics, culminating with the dissolution of the Soviet Union in 1992.

Initially, the changes were greeted with nearly universal euphoria in the west. Certainly, the threat of spontaneous, global nuclear war had significantly diminished, but the evolving new world order has unleashed other hostilities to threaten world peace and new flashpoints of conflict continually emerge throughout the world. There is also a growing fear, accompanied by some evidence, that organized crime in the former Soviet Union is stealing nuclear weapons and is now seeking to sell them to bellicose factions. The director of the FBI declared that this problem poses "the greatest long-term threat to the security of the United States."[1]

"We now live in a world where a handful of people with a well-placed explosive charge can cause untold difficulties, so in terms of people's sense of security, even though the fear of nuclear holocaust has diminished substantially, there is heightened anxiety over renegade states that don't see their position in the new political alignment and that are willing to sacrifice substantial portions of their population for some particular purpose," said Connecticut Senator Christopher Dodd.[2]

In 1990, Electric Boat General Manager James E. Turner Jr. began the last decade of the 20th century with cautious optimism. Less than 10 years before the company would commemorate its centennial anniversary in 1999, it was celebrating the commencement of construction on the lead ship of the Seawolf class, to be delivered to the Navy in 1996. The Navy proudly announced that the *Louisville* (SSN-724), a Los Angeles class ship built at the Groton shipyard, had been the platform for the first-ever combat launch of a Tomahawk cruise missile during the Gulf War. Remnants of the Cold War remained, at least in the minds of the American people. The company was in the process of dealing with "some difficult contracts from the heydays of the head-to-head competition in the 1980s."[3]

Two more Los Angeles class ships had been delivered to the Navy in 1989, bringing the total of ships in that class built by Electric Boat to 25—more than half of the 42 boats in this class produced thus far, not including Electric Boat's backlog of eight ships. Electric Boat also secured a contract during the year for its 17th Ohio class

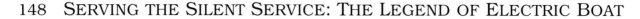

An artist's conception of a Seawolf (SSN-21) on the attack while running at periscope depth.

submarine, giving the company "sole procurement and logistics support responsibilities for the Trident through the first quarter of the next century." The Navy's five-year plan included delivery of one Ohio class submarine every year until a fleet of 21 was completed.

Turner, a prudent businessman who had come to Electric Boat from its competitor Newport News Shipbuilding, realized that the cooling of the Cold War and warming of international relations would ultimately result in a reduction in submarine orders. Responding to an antici-

Electric Boat announces the *Seawolf* contract to the world.

pated loss of critical business, he began streamlining company operations, setting a direction in which his successor, Roger E. Tetrault, would continue when he took over in 1991. "An awful lot of attention had been paid to technical aspects and the building of the product, versus the running of the business," Turner said. "So we started broadening it into building on the strengths, addressing the weaknesses and bringing all the employees on board."[4]

The company accelerated programs associated with increased productivity, enhanced cost management and improved scheduling. "These programs have resulted in successive annual reductions to overhead spending of more than 10 percent compared with budget levels both in 1989 and 1990," the company said in its 1990 annual report.[5]

By August 1990, it became evident that the Seawolf program was going to be cut back from its planned 29 ships in the class. Although the Navy had originally planned for 12 contracts to be awarded through 1998,[6] talks began, first reducing the number to eight, followed by discussions that ended in even fewer numbers.[7] Several permutations were offered: One Seawolf every other year with construction of a new attack submarine to begin in 1998. A combination of the two. No more Seawolf class submarines, just more Los Angeles class boats.[8]

Seawolf was envisioned as replacing the Los Angeles class. The new ship had "revolutionary

Groton in mid-1960s was building attack submarines and delivered the *George Washington* (SSBN-598), the first fleet ballistic missile (FBM) submarine.

PHOTOS ELECTRIC BOAT DIVISION

Groton in 1994. Today's facility can handle construction of several different classes of submarines at one time. In the upper left corner, a Trident submarine nears completion while another's front half emerges from a construction building.

ELECTRIC BOAT DIVISION

The ballistic submarine *Maine* (SSBN-741) lies in its berth awaiting launch on July 16, 1994. This ship is of the Ohio class, whose members are 560 feet long with a displacement of 18,750 tons—the largest submarines ever built in America.

improvements in submarine warfighting capability" according to Navy officials.[9] These included higher speed, quieter running, improved detection capabilities and greater firepower.

Of greatest concern to Electric Boat was what percentage of work it might be awarded in a shrinking pool of potential contracts. According to one naval analyst, Congress not only had to decide what type of submarine it wanted, but what "[constituted] an adequate submarine construction base and then determine what, if anything, should be done to preserve it."[10] In October 1991, the Navy declared that it wanted "to maintain EB as a submarine builder and let Newport News continue its work on surface ships."[11]

Much discussion about the design and construction of advanced submarines began during this time at Electric Boat and the Pentagon. The company was "participating in several programs that explore stealth, mobility and endurance in current and future ships." One of Electric Boat's design challenges was to convert the Los Angeles class USS *Memphis* (SSN-691) into "the Navy's first research and development submarine." The submarine will become a "platform for testing technology advances in an at-sea environment while the ship still retains its warfighting capabilities." The strategy was to accelerate the introduction of new technologies throughout the submarine fleet.[12]

The company had already begun downsizing to adjust to the market's initial changes; now, management realized, more drastic action would be required. "That's when we began in earnest to do the reengineering," Turner said. "Reengineering has been a detailed evaluation of what our strengths and resources are, as well as defining what they needed to be in order to be successful in the late 1990s time frame."[13]

The company also began working on methods to "improve hydrodynamic design in submarine construction, reduce ship weight and noise, and improve ship construction automation technologies." The Seawolf class had been designed to maximize the benefits of modular construction methods.[14]

Electric Boat expressed confidence that greater accessibility and improved material flow afforded by the modular construction method would boost productivity while reducing costs.[15] These innovations were combined with the implementation of computer-aided design/ manufacture (CAD/CAM) for the Seawolf class[16] as Electric Boat geared up for anticipated future construction based on the Navy's estimates:[17]

"The submarine force is the dominant element of the nation's strategic and tactical deterrence. The Navy strongly supports a force of 100 attack submarines through the year 2010, requiring an

ELECTRIC BOAT DIVISION

The president of Electric Boat, James E. Turner Jr.

added procurement of about three ships annually for Fiscal Years 1991 through 2004."

Faced with a diminishing budget, the U.S. Navy sought ways to reduce costs while maintaining its effectiveness and ability to meet strategic and tactical threats. In June 1991, the Navy announced plans for a new submarine that would be as quiet as a Seawolf, but with reduced speed and weaponry—a new class code-named Centurion—and that Electric Boat was already working on the preliminary designs. The Centurion was expected to displace between 5,000 and 6,000 tons—much less than the Seawolf class' 9,100 tons or Los Angeles class' 6,900 tons. The Centurion would complement the Seawolf rather than replace it. The Navy's primary goals were to maintain fleet effectiveness as Los Angeles class ships begin retirement and to deploy a cost-effective submarine that could deter existing nuclear submarines and respond to an increasing number of regional conflicts throughout the world.[18]

Meanwhile, Electric Boat's new general manager, Roger Tetrault, was seeking new, non-military clients to boost revenues. His efforts were timely, as six months later, in early 1992, President George Bush announced his decision to reduce the Seawolf program to the single submarine already under construction at Electric Boat and rescind funding for the second and third ships. Only two years before, the U.S.

The *Columbus* (SSN-762), a Los Angeles class submarine, was launched on August 1, 1992 and commissioned on July 24, 1993. 1992 was a busy year for launchings at Groton—four attack submarines slid down the building ways to prepare for active duty in the U.S. Navy.

Navy's confident projection that there would be contracts for 29 ships in the class to be built fueled the Groton shipyard's long-term planning. Now, Electric Boat would fight alongside its shipyard unions and congressional delegations "to at least prevent cancellation of the second and third Seawolfs."[19]

It was a very real possibility that the Groton shipyard would be shut down if the company could not find work to cover the period between the completion of existing construction programs and the start of the proposed Centurion program in 1998. Electric Boat believed the cancellation order unfair, especially since Congress had already approved funding for two more Seawolf class boats. Kenneth J. DelaCruz, president of the Metal Trades Council, the major shipyard union, felt that the decision to halt production was wrong. "EB's production line is not something that can be turned off and on like a faucet," he said. Connecticut Senators Christopher Dodd and Joseph Lieberman began to gather statistics about various production exigencies "in preparation for a fight in Congress over the program."[20] In discussing alternative markets which would best utilize the company's skilled labor force, Senator Dodd pointed out that making the change from a highly sophisticated, "big ticket" machine like a nuclear submarine to something more salable and universal, like a household appliance, would take massive revamping and retraining—not to mention the fact that it would take selling "something like a billion" toasters for Electric Boat to stay in business.[21]

Congress debated the Seawolf program vigorously. Funding for the second ship in the class was saved. Congress also approved an "additional $540 million specifically for preservation of the submarine industrial base."[22] Construction of a third Seawolf remained uncertain. During this protracted process, Newport News Shipbuilding contested the award of a contract for the second Seawolf to Electric Boat, taking the matter to court. After much emotional debate, a federal appeals court upheld the Navy's award of the second Seawolf contract (SSN-22) to Electric Boat, and work ultimately resumed on the craft in June 1992.

Another setback occurred in the program when welding cracks were discovered during construction of the SSN-21, the first ship in the Seawolf class. The conditions resulted from using existing specifications, which were inappropriate to a new type of high-grade steel (HY-100) being used. Electric Boat devised and implemented new welding procedures immediately.[23]

Grave concern remained over the reinstatement of the third Seawolf. Electric Boat believed that "full funding for the third Seawolf class submarine mentioned above would be in the best interest of the nation." Furthermore, the company observed that a considerable investment in the future of the program had already been expended:

> "With about half of the needed funding already spent or allocated ($450 million in sunk costs and the $540 million earmarked for industrial base preservation), continued Seawolf production is the most cost effective alternative consistent with Secretary of Defense Aspin's policy of selected low-rate production for preservation of capabilities vital to national defense, and is in keeping with the support for additional Seawolf production expressed by President Clinton during the recent election."[24]

ELECTRIC BOAT DIVISION

The *Columbus* (SSN-762), is underway in open waters in this unusual view of the bridge. The ship's periscopes and masts are located just aft of where the crew is standing.

The crew of the *Santa Fe* (SSN-763) braces for the sharp ocean spray as this powerful ship is underway. The *Santa Fe* was the third and last Los Angeles class submarine to launch from Groton in 1992. It was commissioned into active duty a year later, on January 8, 1994.

Diversification

Anticipating fewer submarine contracts, Electric Boat considered diversifying its product line. It had sought other marketplaces after World War I and World War II to keep its work force intact, but the character of submarine production had changed profoundly since those early years. Submarine design and construction had become an extraordinarily complex enterprise, one requiring many years to move from concept to completion. To build the world's most technologically advanced platforms, the company had dedicated 100 percent of its plant and human resources.

Electric Boat had thoroughly investigated means to "supplement [its] core submarine design and construction business with the establishment of a market-extension business initiative."[25] The initiative addressed work in four areas centered around heavy industrial manufacturing and marine systems, chosen to allow the company to "capitalize on our existing skills and capabilities in an effort to land new customers in new markets." The principal objective was not to consider becoming a non-defense company, but "to help maintain the work force we need to stay in business over the long term as a full-service submarine builder." In a report released in May 1993, even the Pentagon was not optimistic about Electric Boat's—or any critical defense contractor's—potential for market extension, diversification or conversion, saying that "there aren't enough non-defense uses of submarines and submarine technology to make diversification a panacea for shipyards like EB." The report added the assertion that it was "up to the Defense Department to sustain companies that build submarines and other 'defense-unique' weapons."[26]

"Instead of diffusing our attention we should retain our concentration on the very demanding business of nuclear submarine construction," said James Turner, who returned as president of Electric Boat and executive vice president of General Dynamics Corp. in 1993.[27] However, one such market-extension effort did make it to the construction stage: Electric Boat built eight huge, egg-shaped digester tanks at its Charleston, South Carolina facility for a Boston sewage treatment facility during 1993 and early 1994. The venture, however, proved unprofitable.[28]

The fixed costs of running a complex shipyard like Groton are very high, making it difficult to compete with non-specialized, commercial yards. In addition, specialization leads to a level of complexity which makes it nearly impossible to convert the yard to other purposes. Turner described submarine building as "high technology heavy manufacturing in its most complex form."[29]

> "The ships themselves are astounding examples of applied and integrated technology. Over a six-year, 12 million-manhour period, we integrate into each submarine an array of weapons and life-support systems that span the technological spectrum. In the case of a Trident ballistic-missile submarine, for example, there are embodied some 265 subsystems, 25,000 components and 350,000 parts numbers. Propulsion is supplied by compact, reliable nuclear reactors so safe that crew members working only a few feet away for extended periods are exposed to no more radiation than they would be while strolling down a city block.
>
> "The design and engineering capabilities for nuclear submarines are unique resources that, combined, are nothing short of a national asset...
>
> "The production capabilities of the submarine industrial base derive from unique and specialized facilities that must be maintained and kept up to date. These largely one-of-a-kind facilities represent an immense investment and have a replacement value well in excess of $1 billion...
>
> "...But the real key to our national capability is a work force dedicated to the design and construction of nuclear submarines.
>
> "The highly skilled work force is the product of years of extensive and specialized training—and most importantly, hands-on application."

Among the last, yet most influential, arguments against diversification is the inevitable violation of U.S. Navy confidentiality and national security by attempting to combine classified and non-classified work under one roof.[30] By early 1994, the market extension program was largely discontinued.

Preserving the Submarine Industrial Base

Perhaps the "Silent Service" has been too silent in the face of taxpayer rebellions calling for massive governmental budget-cutting. As U.S. Representative Ronald K. Machtley pointed out to the U.S. Navy in 1994, "it's always been the silent submarine force. We have not publicly talked about what we have been able to achieve, what we are doing. We don't tell people what our mission is. We don't even put a hull number on the submarines. We don't tell people—for classified reasons—where they are, what they are doing. If the American people had the access that I've had to see what we have been able to do and accomplish with submarines, they would not only be supportive, but they would say, 'What nut would even think of interrupting this industrial base.'

"But that is unfortunately the classified nature of submarine work that we can't get into, but it is the most important platform, in my opinion, to preserve the future security of our sea-lanes..."[31]

Indeed, while the United States ponders what the "right size" is for its military forces, other countries—big and small—are improving their fleets, making them as powerful as they can. Submarines are playing a major role in those plans.

"One of the concerns that the American public should have now, and it's not well-publicized, is that the Russians ... have decided that, if they're going to have any navy at all, ... it's going to be a submarine navy," asserted Vice Admiral B. M. "Bud" Kauderer. "Although they're letting the rest of their fleet deteriorate and run it up on the beach so it won't sink, they are continuing to build high-performance submarines and indications are clear that well into the next century they are going to continue building high-performance submarines, both ballistic and attack."[32]

Kauderer pointed out that China, Iran and North Korea are currently purchasing submarines from Russia, while the South Koreans are buying similar ships from Germany. India, with its extensive coastline, also deploys a large submarine force and reportedly is seeking to build its first nuclear submarine. Most countries operate diesel-electric submarines; only the United States, Great Britain, France, Russia and China possess nuclear submarines.

Germany is making a business of selling its 209-type submarines to qualified buyers, Kauderer said. Sweden also builds "some fine submarines," and have recently assisted Australia in the development of its Collins class submarine; the first of that class launched in 1993. "It's going to sea this year, and it's going to be, probably, the very best of the diesel submarines in the world."

Secretary of the Navy John H. Dalton has repeatedly affirmed his confidence in the U.S. Navy's submarine fleet and its integral role in this nation's defense force.

> "Our submarine force remains our trump card in retaining command of the seas—an absolute necessity for the defense of our maritime nation and the bedrock prerequisite for being able to carry out our '... From the Sea' strategy. Our submarine force is critical in ensuring that no other nation can challenge us at sea. And, indeed, our submarines can perform missions in support of all future operations that are only limited by imagination."[33]

In 1993, President Bill Clinton called for a comprehensive review of the armed services in an attempt to tailor the United States military to fit the post-Cold War world. President Clinton outlined his commitment to national security and the role of the U.S. Navy in a May 1994 address to the graduating class of the U.S. Naval Academy.[34]

"At the end of the Cold War it was right to reduce our defense spending. But let us not forget that this new era has many dangers. We have replaced a Cold War threat of a world of nuclear gridlock with a new world threatened with instability, even abject chaos, rooted in the economic dislocations that are inherent in the change from communism to market economics; rooted in religious and ethnic battles long covered over by authoritarian regimes now gone; rooted in tribal slaughters, aggravated by environmental disasters, by abject hunger, by mass migration across tenuous national borders. And with three of the Soviet Union's successor states now becoming non-nuclear and the tension between the United States and Russia over nuclear matters declining, we still must not forget that the threat of weapons of mass destruction remain in the continuing disputes we have over North Korea, and elsewhere with countries who seek either to develop or to sell or to buy such weapons.

"So we must—we must do better. For this generation to expand freedom's reach, we must always keep America out of danger's reach.

"Last year, I ordered a sweeping review—we called it the Bottom-Up Review—to ensure that in this new era we have a right-sized Navy, Marine Corps, Army and Air Force for the post-Cold War era. That is especially important for our naval forces. For even with all the changes in the world, some basic facts endure: We are a maritime nation. Over 60 percent of our border is sea coast. Over 70 percent of the world is covered by water. And over 90 percent of the human race lives within our Navy's reach from the sea. Now, as long as these facts remain true, we need naval forces that can dominate the sea, project our power and protect our interests.

"We've known that lesson for over 200 years now, since the time Admiral John Paul Jones proclaimed, 'Without a respectable Navy, alas America.'"

Kenneth D. Brown, retired Electric Boat vice president of operations, put it simply and succinctly. "If you don't continue to build submarines and have a steady industrial base, those people will go somewhere else. Then, where will you go to get them? The Navy doesn't want anybody testing a nuclear system unless they have experience. Nowadays, they aren't making any more commercial nuclear plants—so where are they going to get that kind of talent?"[35]

Economic Survival for Electric Boat and the Third Seawolf

Responding to its changing marketplace and economic environment, Electric Boat embarked on a course to ensure its survival. In 1993, the Department of Defense announced its decision to "keep the shipyard in business by building a third Seawolf class submarine and by designing and building the first of a new generation of attack submarines."[36] Based on this commitment, the company in January 1994 announced a major restructuring of operations that was designed to create a more efficient management structure, combined with a selective mothballing of certain areas of the yard, a move the company expects will reduce overhead and maintenance costs. "We're changing because if we don't, we won't be here," said Electric Boat Division President Turner.[37]

"The real focus on technology for the new attack submarine is really in the area of affordability," said John K. Welch, Electric Boat's vice president-programs. The company is taking measures to squeeze "excess" costs from all phases of submarine design and production, Welch said. It is streamlining procedures where possible and using high technology, computer-aided design/manufacture and three-dimensional visualization to reduce design time and increase productivity. Many of these design tools are similar to those the Boeing Company used to design its 777 airliner, which was completely digitally designed, component by component.[38]

"One important tool is the design technology that allows us to use 3-D models, a common data base and fully integrated design analysis tools, and then roll that right into manufacturing a critical element. ... You have the customer, the Navy, involved in those teams so that if there's excessive bureaucracy or red tape in the approval process ... you are able to identify it up front and just get it out of the process.

"In many ways, the end of the Cold War and how you retain critical mass of skills and capabilities in a low-production-rate environment has really forced Electric Boat to reinvent the business. It's with great irony that you are reinventing the business ... it's been a tremendous success over a 100-year history. Yet, we are going to enter into the second century of the history of the company looking a lot more like a small business-being a lot more entrepreneurial, having a lot more teamwork in the whole design-building process and hopefully establishing a whole new method for designing and building ships that will carry into the 21st century."

"Cost is the number one thing we're looking at," said Leslie A. Morse Jr., Electric Boat's deputy program manager for the new attack submarine. "Today it's how do we make this product more affordable for the government, knowing that the defense budget is going to be downsized dramatically. How do you maintain the ability to provide the most technologically advanced products to the government and still reduce the cost?"[39]

Cutting the amount of time and cost of materials to design and produce new submarines is the key to reducing the price tag, Morse said. "The design period is about nine years long to design a ship. We're trying to cut that down to five or six years." The company's goal is to reduce construction time to four years, primarily focusing on having a complete design that accommodates 100 percent modular construction and testing.

ELECTRIC BOAT DIVISION

The *Rhode Island* (SSBN-740) is put through her paces during sea trials several months after her launch on July 17, 1993. This Ohio class submarine was sponsored by Kati Machtley, wife of Representative Ronald K. Machtley of Rhode Island.

While most Americans' perception of virtual reality is grounded in Hollywood motion picture creations like "Lawnmower Man," Electric Boat's multidisciplinary team of operations, planning, quality, design and engineering personnel is using this high technology tool to reduce costs and development time. They are utilizing the software to create the design and then to walk through it before it is built. Outfitted with a helmet and using a 12-foot by 12-foot screen which displays a digital image that Morse described as "very clear and lifesize," the team can view a potential design and evaluate it in terms specific to each one's expertise. It allows the ability to "walk through" the design and see first-hand how the "human factor"—builders, maintenance workers, equipment operators—will interact with the design. "You can go down and see how it is to operate a valve station," Morse said.

By the year 1998—when work on the new class of attack submarines is scheduled to begin—Electric Boat expects to have downsized, going from a $1.7 billion enterprise with 17,000 employees, to "one with $800 million in sales and a work force of no more than 7,000."[40] Further-

more, the company projects that its sources of revenue will shift from being 72 percent new construction/23 percent engineering to a 50/50 contribution from each area.

"The overall target is to cut overhead spending by more than half," Turner said. "None of these cuts will come easy. But we must have an affordable new attack submarine that meets the Navy's requirement in order for us to have more business."[41]

In the middle of implementing the universally unpopular cutback measures, apprehension at Electric Boat flared anew when the Pentagon announced delays in its design review of the new attack class. Concern mounted that delays might further extend the 1998 start of construction of the New Attack Submarine (NAS), formerly codenamed Centurion. A delay of a year could mean that the shipyard would be without work between finishing construction on existing Seawolfs and starting on the new attack submarine.

Secretary of the Navy Dalton emphasized the importance of maintaining the nation's shipbuilding skills. "The submarine, the most revolutionary naval weapon developed and perfected in this century, was not developed by the Navy.

It was developed by *private* industry. It was perfected by a cooperative, productive partnership between the Navy and private industry.

"As a former submariner and private businessman now in government, I really like the image of this partnership. And I know this partnership is vital for the health of the Navy."[42]

In a statement made in 1994, Dalton noted that losing the skills of those shipbuilders who have been partners with the government in building submarines, like Electric Boat, would be improvident.

> "The submarine industrial base is a national resource and today's nuclear submarines are not overnight products ... The companies involved in nuclear submarine construction developed today's technical base through steady evolutionary progress ... 48 years of evolution.
>
> "This has been an enormous national investment that required ongoing training and upgrade of the necessary skills. To allow it to dissolve, to starve, to dissipate is to throw away a national resource that simply cannot be recreated when a crisis arrives."[43]

Representative Sam Gejdenson, Connecticut's congressman from the district in which Electric Boat is located, arranged for tours of the plant for members of the Defense Appropriations Subcommittee to assist in preserving the funding for the third Seawolf and retain the "$507 million in research and development for the new class of submarine requested in the fy'95 Defense Budget."[44] The visit prompted strong support from the chairman of the subcommittee, Representative John P. Murtha of Pennsylvania, who said, "I will personally do everything possible to make sure we have this capability available to our country."[45]

Admiral Stanley R. Arthur, the vice chief of Naval Operations and the Navy's second-in-command, declared that the administration was solidly behind the proposals of the Bottom-Up Review. Arthur further suggested that it was incumbent upon submariners and submarine builders to let the public know that "the silent service is not silent anymore," and that efforts had to be made to "increase the public's understanding of their mission and importance," such as "the use of submarines to transport special forces to trouble spots around the globe."[46]

Answering critics' suggestions that future submarine programs be abandoned, along with the country's ability to build the ships, a coalition of congressional supporters replied, "the cost of halting submarine production and then restarting it would be greater than maintaining 'low-rate production.'"[47] Estimates provided by Representative Gejdenson predicted that restarting the submarine industrial base would cost between $4 billion and $6 billion.[48]

In April 1994, Electric Boat announced its new management structure. "Our objective has been to develop and put in place an organization that has the proper mix of skills, talents and resources to design and build affordable submarines for the Navy," Turner said.[49]

At the end of 1994, Electric Boat has three Ohio class Trident submarines, one Los Angeles class attack submarine and two Seawolfs under construction. In addition, the company is "doing detailed design work on the forward and aft ends of a new attack submarine."[50]

First Lady Hillary Rodham Clinton launches the *Columbia* (SSN-771) on September 24, 1994. Notably the "last to slide" down American ways, the *Columbia* is also the last Los Angeles class submarine to be built by Electric Boat. Pictured from left to right: John Dalton, Secretary of the Navy, Chelsea Clinton, Maid of Honor, Nora Slatkin, Assistant Secretary of the Navy, Hillary Rodham Clinton, sponsor, James E. Turner, Jr., President, Electric Boat Division.

As the sun rises off the coast of Groton, the crew of the *Maryland* (SSN-738) prepare to face a new day.

In August 1994 the company received an affirmation of the country's commitment to strengthening its submarine fleet and maintaining its vital submarine construction industrial base:[51]

> *"Electric Boat Division is extremely pleased with the results of today's Defense Acquisition Board Milestone I Review for the New Attack Submarine.*
>
> *"Today's DAB recommendations track precisely with the position Electric Boat has put forward regarding the need to proceed with the NSSN as a follow-on to a three ship Seawolf Submarine Program. Our reengineering initiatives to be the submarine designer and builder of choice for the U.S. Navy are being validated in a most positive way,' stated Jim Turner, president of Electric Boat Division.*
>
> *"Milestone I approval of the New Attack Sub gives EB the OK to proceed with detailed design that 'can move beyond the conceptual stage, to be on target for construction in 1998.'"*

The *Columbia* (SSN-771), a Los Angeles class submarine, became the "last to slide" on September 24, 1994 as it was launched into the river from the building ways at Groton. First Lady Hillary Rodham Clinton honored the crowd estimated at 22,000 by christening the *Columbia* with the traditional bottle of champagne. Mrs. Clinton became only the third first lady to launch a submarine at Electric Boat, following Mamie Eisenhower (*Nautilus* in 1954) and Jacqueline Kennedy (*Lafayette* in 1962). To the roaring approval of all assembled she declared, "The men and women who work in this shipyard are the best in the world and they deserve the support of every citizen of the United States of America," and "...all Americans are grateful for your skills and patience, your perseverance and your dedication to the vital national industry. On behalf of the president, and all of our citizens, I salute and thank you–those who work here, for contributing to the security of us all." As have all Ohio class submarines, the dock on which all future submarines are built will be flooded and the ships will float into open waters.

In 1995, the company projects that it will lay off nearly 2,500 people and continue annual reductions at a similar rate until the work force at Groton and Quonset Pointe numbers approximately 6,500 employees. The company has been forthright in discussing its plans and policies with the unions that represent workers, trying to let all concerned understand what the effects of low-rate production will be on the shipyard so that steps can be taken to reduce the impact on their lives. Electric Boat's "increased communication with its unions is part of an effort to change the company's corporate culture by putting the emphasis on cost control as a means of survival."[52]

Electric Boat and the thousands of men and women who have worked with the company throughout nearly a hundred years have confronted similar challenges in the past. Both Electric Boat and its dedicated employees will continue to play a vital role in safeguarding America's submarine fleet.

Electric Boat President Turner described his company's commitment to its business—and the Silent Service—succinctly:[53]

> *"On one hand, we're pursuing a goal that is worthy from a business point of view, that provides a challenging employment opportunity for people as we go forward, providing a product that is specifically spelled out and needed in the defense arsenal of the United States.*
>
> *"We feel we've come a long way in the last few years, defining what we need to be, defining the talents and skills and capabilities that we must have in order to serve this market in the future in an affordable manner."*

Appendix A: Electric Boat Chronology

2/5/1891 — Holland Torpedo Boat Co. incorporated

1896 — Work begun on the *Holland* at Crescent Shipyard, Elizabethport, N.J.

7/4/1898 — Captain Frank T. Cable demonstrates *Holland* to Isaac L. Rice in New York harbor

2/7/1899 — Electric Boat Co. incorporates; Isaac L. Rice becomes first president

4/11/1900 — *Holland* delivered to U.S. Navy to become the Navy's first submarine

1902 — Lawrence York (L.Y.) Spear joins Electric Boat

1903 — Six A-class submarines and the second *Plunger* delivered to the U.S. Navy. Built at Crescent Shipyard, Elizabethport, N.J. and Union Iron Works, San Francisco, Calif.

1904 — Navy trials commence between Simon Lake's *Protector* and Electric Boat's *Fulton*

John Holland leaves Electric Boat Co.

1906 — U.S. Navy orders four more Electric Boat submarines, including the *Octopus*. Three of the boats built at Fore River Shipbuilding Co., Quincy, Mass.

5/1907 — Navy conducts trials between Electric Boat *Octopus* and Simon Lake's *Lake* at Newport, R.I.

1910-11 — Subsidiary, New London Ship and Engine Co., organized at Groton, Conn. to build submarine diesel engines and other machinery and parts for submarines

1912 — Marine diesel engines introduced in Electric Boat's E-class submarines. Construction of these engines, the first marine diesels built in the U.S., was started at Fore River Shipyard and completed at the Groton Plant

1913 — L. Y. Spear introduces partial double hull for submarines

1914 — John P. Holland dies

World War I begins

During World War I and just after, Electric Boat builds 85 submarines under wartime contracts for the U.S. Navy

ELCO builds 722 submarines chasers, including 550 ML boats in 488 days for Great Britain

Submarine Boat Co. builds 118 Liberty ships at Port Newark, N.J.

8/15/1915 — Isaac L. Rice resigns as Electric Boat's first president; dies in November. Henry R. Carse is elected president

1918 — Submarine Boat Co. purchases Port Newark shipyard, 32 uncompleted Liberty ships and prefabricated material on order with aim of completing the ships for use as merchant vessels. This venture, and an attempt to operate some of the ships, proved unprofitable

3/1922 — Marine railway built at Groton and completed in 1923. Thirty S-class submarines are overhauled at Groton

1924 — Peruvian government awards contract to Electric Boat for construction of two submarines, the first ever to be built at Groton Shipyard. (Launched in 1926)

1925 — Last delivery of Electric Boat submarines to U.S. Navy under WWI contracts. No new U.S. submarine contracts from 1918 to 1931

1928 — New London Ship and Engine Co. becomes NELSECO Division of Electric Boat Co.

1929 — Electric Boat pioneers welding in ship construction

1931 — *Cuttlefish* becomes first submarine order from U.S. Navy since 1918

1934 — *Cuttlefish* delivered to U.S. Navy. First welded submarine and first Navy submarine built at Groton shipyard

1937 — John Jay Hopkins becomes a director of Electric Boat

1940 — Electric Boat North Yard at Groton expanded with four additional building ways, bringing total to nine

1941 — World War II begins

From beginning of hostilities on Dec. 7, 1941 to end of World War II, Electric Boat builds 74 submarines, 398 PT boats, 7,667 electric motors, 33,378 smoke cylinders and 113 quadruple, 20-millimeter gun turrets

1942 — Victory shipyard built at nearby Groton Iron Works plant with 10 shipways

Henry R. Carse, Electric Boat's second president, dies and is replaced by Lawrence Y. Spear. John Jay Hopkins becomes vice president

1945 — Electric Boat develops other products, including electric Pin-Boy and Armorlite truck bodies

6/1945 — Last submarine is launched from the Victory Yard at Groton

5/1946 — Last submarine of World War II program launched at Electric Boat

1947 — Electric Boat gets contract from U.S. Navy to modify World War II fleet submarines under Guppy program, or Greater Underwater Propulsion Program

1/25/1947 — Electric Boat acquires Canadair Ltd. John Jay Hopkins becomes chairman of the board of Canadair

O. Pomeroy Robinson Jr. becomes president of Electric Boat

7/1947 — L.Y. Spear becomes chairman of the board of Electric Boat; John Jay Hopkins becomes president

5/1948 — Delivery of first EBCo printing presses

1949 Electric Boat receives $25 million order from Canadian government for F-86 jet fighters to be built by wholly owned subsidiary, Canadair

11/7/1949 Guided missile launched from deck of the submarine *Carbonero*

1950 Captain Hyman G. Rickover challenges Electric Boat to build a nuclear-powered submarine

8/21/1951 Electric Boat announces contract to build the *Nautilus*, the world's first nuclear powered submarine

1952 John Jay Hopkins restructures Electric Boat into General Dynamics Corp. to reflect new multifaceted business purpose

6/14/1952 Keel laid for *Nautilus* bearing the initials of President Harry S. Truman

1953 Carleton Shugg becomes general manager of Electric Boat Division

1/21/1954 First Lady Mamie Eisenhower christens the *Nautilus* (SSN-571), launching the world's first nuclear-powered submarine

1/17/1955 *Nautilus*, world's first nuclear-powered submarine, flashes historic message: "Underway on nuclear power"

2/1957 *Nautilus* refueled after traveling 62,560 miles on her first core

12/1957 Electric Boat begins work designing a new submarine and weapon system known as Polaris

8/3/1958 *Nautilus* reaches the North Pole on her 2,114 mile journey under the Polar Ice Cap

8/7/ 1958 to 10/6/1958 *Seawolf* (SSN-575), world's second nuclear-powered submarine, remains submerged for 60 days, traveling 13,761 miles in the Atlantic Ocean

3/17/1959 *Skate* (SSN-578) becomes first submarine to surface at North Pole, leading the way toward opening up the Arctic as a year-round operational area

4/15/958 *Skipjack* (SSN-585), world's fastest and most maneuverable submarine, commissioned. First submarine with whale-shaped hull, teardrop nose and diving planes on sail

12/30/1959 *George Washington* (SSBN-598), first fleet ballistic submarine (FBM), commissioned

2/1960 to 5/1960 Electric Boat-built *Triton* (SSN-586), world's largest submarine, circumnavigates the globe submerged. The journey, which required only 84 days, was along the route the explorer Ferdinand Magellan took in his three-year voyage. *Triton* is the only submarine equipped with two nuclear reactors

7/20/1960 *George Washington*, lead ship of its class and first Polaris-armed submarine, becomes first to successfully fire two Polaris missiles. Flashes historic message: "From out of the depths to target—perfect"

8/1960 *Seadragon* surfaces at North Pole. Crew plays famous baseball game

11/15/1960 *George Washington* goes on patrol with 16 ready-to-fire Polaris missiles

5/8/1962 *Lafayette*, lead ship of a new class carrying the Polaris A-3 missile, is launched

8/2/1962 *Skate* and *Seadragon* rendezvous at North Pole to conduct simulated dogfights and develop tactics for coordinated operations

1963 J. W. Jones becomes general manager of Electric Boat Division

2/26/1966 *Sturgeon* (SSN-637), first of its class, is launched

1967 C. G. Holschuh temporarily named general manager of Electric Boat Division, followed by Joseph D. Pierce

1971 Electric Boat begins converting Polaris submarines to carry new Poseidon missiles

Fabrication begins on first Los Angeles class attack submarines

1972 Electric Boat receives contracts for design and development of Ohio-class submarines to carry new Trident missiles

8/12/1972 Keel laid for Electric Boat's first Los Angeles-class attack submarine, the *Philadelphia* (SSN-690).

1976 Gorden E. MacDonald becomes general manager of Electric Boat Division

1977 P. Takis Veliotis becomes general manager of Electric Boat Division

1978 Electric Boat begins construction of automated frame and cylinder manufacturing facility at Quonset Point, R.I.

1979 Electric Boat launches the *Ohio* (SSBN-726), lead ship of the class bearing the same name and the first Trident-armed submarine

1982 Fritz G. Tovar becomes general manager of Electric Boat Division

1988 James E. Turner Jr. becomes general manager of Electric Boat Division

1989 Electric Boat begins construction on the lead ship of the new Seawolf class

1991 Roger E. Tetrault becomes general manager of Electric Boat Division

1992 President George Bush cuts 29-ship Seawolf class to one

Congress restores contract for second ship of Seawolf class and awards $540 million to preserve submarine industrial base

1993 Defense department urges building of third Seawolf-class ship and the design and construction of a class of new attack submarines

James E. Turner Jr. returns to Electric Boat Division as president

Appendix B: U.S. Navy Submarines

Name	Hull No.	Building Yard	Commission date
Holland	SS-1	CS	1900
Plunger (A-1)	SS-2	CS	1903
Adder (A-2)	SS-3	CS	1903
Grampus (A-3)	SS-4	UIW	1903
Moccasin (A-4)	SS-5	CS	1903
Pike (A-5)	SS-6	UIW	1903
Porpoise (A-6)	SS-7	CS	1903
Shark (A-7)	SS-8	CS	1903
Octopus (C-1)	SS-9	FR	1908
Viper (B-1)	SS-10	FR	1907
Cuttlefish (B-2)	SS-11	FR	1907
Tarantula (B-3)	SS-12	FR	1907
Stingray (C-2)	SS-13	FR	1909
Tarpon (C-3)	SS-14	FR	1909
Bonita (C-4)	SS-15	FR	1909
Snapper (C-5)	SS-16	FR	1910
Narwhal (D-1)	SS-17	FR	1909
Grayling (D-2)	SS-18	FR	1909
Salmon (D-3)	SS-19	FR	1910
Seal (G-1)	SS-19a	LTB	1912
Carp (F-1)	SS-20	UIW	1912
Barracuda (F-2)	SS-21	UIW	1912
Pickerel (F-3)	SS-22	Moran	1912
Skate (F-4)	SS-23	Moran	1913
Skipjack (E-1)	SS-24	FR	1912
Sturgeon (E-2)	SS-25	FR	1912
Thrasher (G-4)	SS-26	Cramp	1914
Tuna (G-2)	SS-27	LTB	1915
Seawolf (H-1)	SS-28	UIW	1913
Nautilus (H-2)	SS-29	UIW	1913
Garfish (H-3)	SS-30	Moran	1914
Turbot (G-3)	SS-31	LTB	1915
Haddock (K-1)	SS-32	FR	1914
Cachalot (K-2)	SS-33	FR	1914
Orca (K-3)	SS-34	UIW	1914
Walrus (K-4)	SS-35	Moran	1914
K-5	SS-36	FR	1914
K-6	SS-37	FR	1914
K-7	SS-38	UIW	1914
K-8	SS-39	UIW	1914
L-1	SS-40	FR	1916
L-2	SS-41	FR	1916
L-3	SS-42	FR	1916
L-4	SS-43	FR	1916
L-5	SS-44	LTB	1918
L-6	SS-45	Craig	1917
L-7	SS-46	Craig	1917
M-1	SS-47	FR	1917
L-8	SS-48	PNS	1917
L-9	SS-49	FR	1916
L-10	SS-50	FR	1916
L-11	SS-51	FR	1916
T-1	SS-52	FR	1920
N-1	SS-53	SCD	1917
N-2	SS-54	SCD	1917
N-3	SS-55	SCD	1917
N-4	SS-56	LTB	1918
N-5	SS-57	LTB	1918
N-6	SS-58	LTB	1918
N-7	SS-59	LTB	1918
T-2	SS-60	FR	1922
T-3	SS-61	FR	1920
O-1	SS-62	PNS	1918
O-2	SS-63	PS	1918
O-3	SS-64	FR	1918
O-4	SS-65	FR	1918
O-5	SS-66	FR	1918
O-6	SS-67	FR	1918
O-7	SS-68	FR	1918
O-8	SS-69	FR	1918
O-9	SS-70	FR	1918
O-10	SS-71	FR	1918
O-11	SS-72	LTB	1918
O-12	SS-73	LTB	1918
O-13	SS-74	LTB	1918
O-14	SS-75	CSC	1918
O-15	SS-76	CSC	1918
O-16	SS-77	CSC	1918
R-1	SS-78	FR	1918
R-2	SS-79	FR	1919
R-3	SS-80	FR	1919
R-4	SS-81	FR	1919
R-5	SS-82	FR	1919
R-6	SS-83	FR	1919
R-7	SS-84	FR	1919
R-8	SS-85	FR	1919
R-9	SS-86	FR	1919
R-10	SS-87	FR	1919
R-11	SS-88	FR	1919
R-12	SS-89	FR	1919
R-13	SS-90	FR	1919
R-14	SS-91	FR	1919
R-15	SS-92	UIW	1918
R-16	SS-93	UIW	1918
R-17	SS-94	UIW	1918
R-18	SS-95	UIW	1918
R-19	SS-96	UIW	1918
R-20	SS-97	UIW	1918
R-21	SS-98	LTB	1919
R-22	SS-99	LTB	1919
R-23	SS-100	LTB	1919
R-24	SS-101	LTB	1919
R-25	SS-102	LTB	1919
R-26	SS-103	LTB	1919
R-27	SS-104	LTB	1919
S-1	SS-105	FR	1920
S-2	SS-106	LTB	1920
S-3	SS-107	PNS	1919
S-4	SS-109	PNS	1919
S-5	SS-110	PNS	1920
S-6	SS-111	PNS	1920
S-7	SS-112	PNS	1920
S-8	SS-113	PNS	1920
S-9	SS-114	PNS	1921
S-10	SS-115	PNS	1922
S-11	SS-116	PNS	1923
S-12	SS-117	PNS	1923
S-13	SS-118	PNS	1923
S-14	SS-119	LTB	1921
S-15	SS-120	LTB	1921
S-16	SS-121	LTB	1920
S-17	SS-122	LTB	1921
S-18	SS-123	B(Q)	1924
S-19	SS-124	B(Q)	1923
S-20	SS-125	B(Q)	1922
S-21	SS-126	B(Q)	1923
S-22	SS-127	B(Q)	1924
S-23	SS-128	B(Q)	1923
S-24	SS-129	B(Q)	1923
S-25	SS-130	B(Q)	1923
S-26	SS-131	B(Q)	1923
S-27	SS-132	B(Q)	1924
S-28	SS-133	B(Q)	1923
S-29	SS-134	B(Q)	1923
S-30	SS-135	B(Q)	1924
S-31	SS-136	B(SF)	1920
S-32	SS-137	B(SF)	1923
S-33	SS-138	B(SF)	1923
S-34	SS-139	B(SF)	1922
S-35	SS-140	B(SF)	1923
S-36	SS-141	B(SF)	1923
S-37	SS-142	B(SF)	1923
S-38	SS-143	B(SF)	1923
S-39	SS-144	B(SF)	1923
S-40	SS-145	B(SF)	1923
S-41	SS-146	B(SF)	1924
H-4*	SS-147	PS	1918
H-5*	SS-148	PS	1918
H-6*	SS-149	PS	1918
H-7*	SS-150	PS	1918
H-8*	SS-151	PS	1918
H-9*	SS-152	PS	1918
S-42	SS-153	B(Q)	1924
S-43	SS-154	B(Q)	1924
S-44	SS-155	B(Q)	1925
S-45	SS-156	B(Q)	1925
S-46	SS-157	B(Q)	1925
S-47	SS-158	B(Q)	1925
S-48	SS-159	LTB	1925
S-49	SS-160	LTB	1925
S-50	SS-161	LTB	1925
S-51	SS-162	LTB	1925
Barracuda	SS-163	PNS	1924
Bass	SS-164	PNS	1925
Bonita	SS-165	PNS	1926
Argonaut	SS-166	PNS	1928
Narwhal	SS-167	PNS	1930
Nautilus	SS-168	MI	1930
Dolphin	SS-169	PNS	1932
Cachalot	SS-170	PNS	1933
Cuttlefish	SS-171	EB	1934
Porpoise (P-1)	SS-172	PNS	1935
Pike (P-2)	SS-173	PNS	1935
Shark (P-3)	SS-174	EB	1936
Tarpon (P-4)	SS-175	EB	1936
Perch (P-5)	SS-176	EB	1936
Pickerel (P-6)	SS-177	EB	1937
Permit (P-7)	SS-178	EB	1937
Plunger (P-8)	SS-179	PNS	1936
Pollack (P-9)	SS-180	PNS	1937
Pompano (P-10)	SS-181	MI	1937
Salmon (S-1)	SS-182	EB	1938
Seal (S-2)	SS-183	EB	1938
Skipjack (S-3)	SS-184	EB	1938
Snapper (S-4)	SS-185	PNS	1937
Stingray (S-5)	SS-186	PNS	1938
Sturgeon (S-6)	SS-187	MI	1938
Sargo (S-7)	SS-188	EB	1939
Saury (S-8)	SS-189	EB	1939
Spearfish (S-9)	SS-190	EB	1939
Sculpin (S-10)	SS-191	PNS	1939
Sailfish (S-11)	SS-192	PNS	1940
Swordfish (S-12)	SS-193	MI	1939
Seadragon (S-13)	SS-194	EB	1939
Sealion (S-14)	SS-195	EB	1939
Searaven (S-15)	SS-196	PNS	1939
Seawolf (S-16)	SS-197	PNS	1939
Tambor	SS-198	EB	1940
Tautog	SS-199	EB	1940
Thresher	SS-200	EB	1940
Triton	SS-201	PNS	1940
Trout	SS-202	PNS	1940
Tuna	SS-203	MI	1941
Mackerel	SS-204	EB	1941
Marlin	SS-205	EB	1941
Gar	SS-206	EB	1941
Grampus	SS-207	EB	1941
Grayback	SS-208	EB	1941
Grayling	SS-209	PNS	1941
Grenadier	SS-210	PNS	1941
Gudgeon	SS-211	MI	1941
Gato	SS-212	EB	1941
Greenling	SS-213	EB	1942
Grouper	SS-214	EB	1942
Growler	SS-215	EB	1942
Grunion	SS-216	EB	1942
Guardfish	SS-217	EB	1942
Albacore	SS-218	EB	1942
Amberjack	SS-219	EB	1942
Barb	SS-220	EB	1942
Blackfish	SS-221	EB	1942
Bluefish	SS-222	EB	1943
Bonefish	SS-223	EB	1943
Cod	SS-224	EB	1943
Cero	SS-225	EB	1943
Corvina	SS-226	EB	1943
Darter	SS-227	EB	1943
Drum	SS-228	PNS	1941
Flying Fish	SS-229	PNS	1941
Finback	SS-230	PNS	1942
Haddock	SS-231	PNS	1942
Halibut	SS-232	PNS	1942
Herring	SS-233	PNS	1942
Kingfish	SS-234	PNS	1942
Shad	SS-235	PNS	1942
Silversides	SS-236	MI	1941
Trigger	SS-237	MI	1942
Wahoo	SS-238	MI	1942
Whale	SS-239	MI	1942
Angler	SS-240	EB	1943
Bashaw	SS-241	EB	1943
Bluegill	SS-242	EB	1943
Bream	SS-243	EB	1944
Cavalla	SS-244	EB	1944
Cobia	SS-245	EB	1944
Croaker	SS-246	EB	1944
Dace	SS-247	EB	1943
Dorado	SS-248	EB	1943
Flasher	SS-249	EB	1943
Flier	SS-250	EB	1943
Flounder	SS-251	EB	1943
Gabilan	SS-252	EB	1943
Gunnel	SS-253	EB	1942
Gurnard	SS-254	EB	1942
Haddo	SS-255	EB	1942
Hake	SS-256	EB	1942
Harder	SS-257	EB	1942
Hoe	SS-258	EB	1942
Jack	SS-259	EB	1943
Lapon	SS-260	EB	1943
Mingo	SS-261	EB	1943
Muskallunge	SS-262	EB	1943
Paddle	SS-263	EB	1943
Pargo	SS-264	EB	1943
Peto	SS-265	MAN	1942
Pogy	SS-266	MAN	1943
Pompon	SS-267	MAN	1943
Puffer	SS-268	MAN	1943
Rasher	SS-269	MAN	1943
Raton	SS-270	MAN	1943
Ray	SS-271	MAN	1943
Redfin	SS-272	MAN	1943
Robalo	SS-273	MAN	1943
Rock	SS-274	MAN	1943
Runner	SS-275	MAN	1942
Sawfish	SS-276	MAN	1942
Scamp	SS-277	PNS	1942
Scorpion	SS-278	PNS	1942
Snook	SS-279	PNS	1942
Steelhead	SS-280	PNS	1942
Sunfish	SS-281	MI	1942
Tunny	SS-282	MI	1942
Tinosa	SS-283	MI	1943
Tullibee	SS-284	MI	1943
Balao	SS-285	PNS	1943
Billfish	SS-286	PNS	1943
Bowfin	SS-287	PNS	1943
Cabrilla	SS-288	PNS	1943
Capelin	SS-289	PNS	1943
Cisco	SS-290	PNS	1943
Crevalle	SS-291	PNS	1943
Devilfish	SS-292	Cramp	1944
Dragonet	SS-293	Cramp	1944
Escolar	SS-294	Cramp	1944
Hackleback	SS-295	Cramp	1944
Lancetfish	SS-296	Cramp	1945
Ling	SS-297	Cramp	1945
Lionfish	SS-298	Cramp	1944
Manta	SS-299	Cramp	1944
Moray	SS-300	Cramp	1945
Roncador	SS-301	Cramp	1945
Sabalo	SS-302	Cramp	1945
Sablefish	SS-303	Cramp	1945
Seahorse	SS-304	MI	1943
Skate	SS-305	MI	1943
Tang	SS-306	MI	1943
Tilefish	SS-307	MI	1943
Apogon	SS-308	PNS	1943
Aspro	SS-309	PNS	1943
Batfish	SS-310	PNS	1943
Archerfish	SS-311	PNS	1943
Burrfish	SS-312	PNS	1943
Perch	SS-313	EB	1944
Shark	SS-314	EB	1944
Sealion	SS-315	EB	1944
Barbel	SS-316	EB	1944
Barbero	SS-317	EB	1944
Baya	SS-318	EB	1944
Becuna	SS-319	EB	1944
Bergall	SS-320	EB	1944
Besugo	SS-321	EB	1944
Blackfin	SS-322	EB	1944
Caiman	SS-323	EB	1944
Blenny	SS-324	EB	1944
Blower	SS-325	EB	1944
Blueback	SS-326	EB	1944
Boarfish	SS-327	EB	1944
Charr	SS-328	EB	1944
Chubb	SS-329	EB	1944
Brill	SS-330	EB	1944
Bugara	SS-331	EB	1944
Bullhead	SS-332	EB	1944
Bumper	SS-333	EB	1944
Cabezon	SS-334	EB	1944
Dentuda	SS-335	EB	1944
Capitaine	SS-336	EB	1945
Carbonero	SS-337	EB	1945
Carp	SS-338	EB	1945
Catfish	SS-339	EB	1945
Entemedor	SS-340	EB	1945
Chivo	SS-341	EB	1945
Chopper	SS-342	EB	1945
Clamagore	SS-343	EB	1945
Cobbler	SS-344	EB	1945
Cochino	SS-345	EB	1945
Corporal	SS-346	EB	1945
Cubera	SS-347	EB	1945
Cusk	SS-348	EB	1945
Diodon	SS-349	EB	1946
Dogfish	SS-350	EB	1946
Greenfish	SS-351	EB	1946
Halfbeak	SS-352	EB	1946
Golet	SS-361	MAN	1943
Guavina	SS-362	MAN	1943
Guitarro	SS-363	MAN	1944
Hammerhead	SS-364	MAN	1944
Hardhead	SS-365	MAN	1944
Hawkbill	SS-366	MAN	1944
Icefish	SS-367	MAN	1944
Jallao	SS-368	MAN	1944

Name	Hull No.	Building Yard	Commission date
Kete	SS-369	MAN	1944
Kraken	SS-370	MAN	1944
Lagarto	SS-371	MAN	1944
Lamprey	SS-372	MAN	1944
Lizardfish	SS-373	MAN	1944
Loggerhead	SS-374	MAN	1945
Macabi	SS-375	MAN	1945
Mapiro	SS-376	MAN	1945
Menhaden	SS-377	MAN	1945
Mero	SS-378	MAN	1945
Sand Lance	SS-381	PNS	1943
Picuda	SS-382	PNS	1943
Pampanito	SS-383	PNS	1943
Parche	SS-384	PNS	1943
Bang	SS-385	PNS	1943
Pilotfish	SS-386	PNS	1943
Pintado	SS-387	PNS	1944
Pipefish	SS-388	PNS	1944
Piranha	SS-389	PNS	1944
Plaice	SS-390	PNS	1944
Pomfret	SS-391	PNS	1944
Sterlet	SS-392	PNS	1944
Queenfish	SS-393	PNS	1944
Razorback	SS-394	PNS	1944
Redfish	SS-395	PNS	1944
Ronquil	SS-396	PNS	1944
Scabbardfish	SS-397	PNS	1944
Segundo	SS-398	PNS	1944
Sea Cat	SS-399	PNS	1944
Sea Devil	SS-400	PNS	1944
Sea Dog	SS-401	PNS	1944
Sea Fox	SS-402	PNS	1944
Atule	SS-403	PNS	1944
Spikefish	SS-404	PNS	1944
Sea Owl	SS-405	PNS	1944
Sea Poacher	SS-406	PNS	1944
Sea Robin	SS-407	PNS	1944
Sennet	SS-408	PNS	1944
Piper	SS-409	PNS	1944
Treadfin	SS-410	PNS	1944
Spadefish	SS-411	MI	1944
Trepang	SS-412	MI	1944
Spot	SS-413	MI	1944
Springer	SS-414	MI	1944
Stickleback	SS-415	MI	1945
Tirj	SS-416	MI	1943
Tench	SS-417	MI	1944
Thornback	SS-418	PNS	1944
Tigrone	SS-419	PNS	1944
Tirante	SS-420	PNS	1944
Trutta	SS-421	PNS	1944
Toro	SS-422	PNS	1944
Torsk	SS-423	PNS	1944
Quillback	SS-424	PNS	1944
Trumpetfish	SS-425	Cramp	1944
Tusk	SS-426	Cramp	1946
Corsair	SS-435	EB	1946
Argonaut	SS-475	PNS	1945
Runner	SS-476	PNS	1945
Conger	SS-477	PNS	1945
Cutlass	SS-478	PNS	1945
Diablo	SS-479	PNS	1945
Medregal	SS-480	PNS	1945
Requin	SS-481	PNS	1945
Irex	SS-482	PNS	1945
Sea Leopard	SS-483	PNS	1945
Odax	SS-484	PNS	1945
Sirago	SS-485	PNS	1945
Pomodon	SS-486	PNS	1945
Remora	SS-487	PNS	1946
Sarda	SS-488	PNS	1946
Spinax	SS-489	PNS	1946
Volador	SS-490	PNS	1948
Amberjack	SS-522	BNS	1946
Grampus	SS-523	BNS	1949
Pickerel	SS-524	BNS	1949
Grenadier	SS-525	BNS	1951
Barracuda	SSK-1	EB	1951
Bass	SSK-2	MI	1952
Bonita	SSK-3	MI	1952
Tang	SS-563	PNS	1951
Trigger	SS-564	EB	1952
Wahoo	SS-565	PNS	1952
Trout	SS-566	EB	1952
Gudgeon	SS-567	PNS	1952
Harder	SS-568	EB	1952
Albacore	AGSS-569	PNS	1953
Nautilus	SSN-571	EB	1954
Sailfish	SS-572	PNS	1956
Salmon	SS-573	PNS	1956

Name	Hull No.	Building Yard	Commission date
Grayback	LPSS-574	MI	1958
Seawolf	SSN-575	EB	1957
Darter	SS-576	EB	1956
Growler	SS-577	PNS	1958
Skate	SSN-578	EB	1957
Swordfish	SSN-579	PNS	1958
Barbel	SS-580	PNS	1959
Blueback	SS-581	ING	1959
Bonefish	SS-582	NYS	1959
Sargo	SSN-583	MI	1958
Seadragon	SSN-584	PNS	1959
Skipjack	SSN-585	EB	1959
Triton	SSN-586	EB	1958
Halibut	SSN-587	MI	1960
Scamp	SSN-588	MI	1961
Scorpion	SSN-589	EB	1959
Sculpin	SSN-590	ING	1961
Shark	SSN-591	NNS	1960
Snook	SSN-592	ING	1961
Thresher	SSN-593	PNS	1961
Permit	SSN-594	MI	1962
Plunger	SSN-595	MI	1962
Barb	SSN-596	ING	1963
Tullibee	SSN-597	EB	1960
George Washington	SSBN-598	EB	1959
Patrick Henry	SSBN-599	EB	1960
Theodore Roosevelt	SSBN-600	MI	1961
Robert E. Lee	SSBN-601	NNS	1960
Abraham Lincoln	SSBN-602	PNS	1961
Pollack	SSN-603	NYS	1964
Haddo	SSN-604	NYS	1964
Jack	SSN-605	PNS	1967
Tinosa	SSN-606	PNS	1964
Dace	SSN-607	ING	1964
Ethan Allen	SSBN-608	EB	1961
Sam Houston	SSBN-609	NNS	1962
Thomas A. Edison	SSBN-610	EB	1962
John Marshall	SSBN-611	NNS	1962
Guardfish	SSN-612	NYS	1966
Flasher	SSN-613	EB	1966
Greenling	SSN-614	EB	1967
Gato	SSN-615	EB	1968
Lafayette	SSBN-616	EB	1963
Alexander Hamilton	SSBN-617	EB	1963
Thomas Jefferson	SSBN-618	NNS	1963
Andrew Jackson	SSBN-619	MI	1963
John Adams	SSBN-620	PNS	1964
Haddock	SSN-621	ING	1967
James Monroe	SSBN-622	NNS	1963
Nathan Hale	SSBN-623	EB	1963
Woodrow Wilson	SSBN-624	MI	1963
Henry Clay	SSBN-625	NNS	1964
Daniel Webster	SSBN-626	EB	1964
James Madison	SSBN-627	NNS	1964
Tecumseh	SSBN-628	EB	1964
Daniel Boone	SSBN-629	MI	1964
John C. Calhoun	SSBN-630	NNS	1964
Ulysses S. Grant	SSBN-631	EB	1964
Von Steuben	SSBN-632	NNS	1964
Casimir Pulaski	SSBN-633	EB	1964
Stonewall Jackson	SSBN-634	MI	1964
Sam Rayburn	SSBN-635	NNS	1964
Nathaniel Greene	SSBN-636	PNS	1964
Sturgeon	SSN-637	EB	1967
Whale	SSN-638	GD(Q)	1968
Tautog	SSN-639	ING	1968
Benjamin Franklin	SSBN-640	EB	1965
Simon Bolivar	SSBN-641	NNS	1965
Kamehameha	SSBN-642	MI	1965
George Bancroft	SSBN-643	EB	1966
Lewis & Clark	SSBN-644	NNS	1965
James K. Polk	SSBN-645	EB	1966
Grayling	SSN-646	PNS	1969
Pogy	SSN-647	NYS/ING	1971
Aspro	SSN-648	ING	1969
Sunfish	SSN-649	GD(Q)	1969
Pargo	SSN-650	EB	1968
Dolphin	AGSS-555	PNS	1968
Queenfish	SSN-651	NNS	1966
Puffer	SSN-652	ING	1969
Ray	SSN-653	NNS	1967
George C. Marshall	SSBN-654	NNS	1966
Henry L. Stimson	SSBN-655	EB	1966
George Washington Carver	SSBN-656	NNS	1966
Francis Scott Key	SSBN-657	EB	1966
Mariano G. Vallejo	SSBN-658	MI	1966

Name	Hull No.	Building Yard	Commission date
Will Rogers	SSBN-659	EB	1967
Sand Lance	SSN-660	PNS	1971
Lapon	SSN-661	NNS	1967
Gurnard	SSN-662	MI	1968
Hammerhead	SSN-663	NNS	1968
Sea Devil	SSN-664	NNS	1969
Guitarro	SSN-665	MI	1972
Hawkbill	SSN-666	MI	1971
Bergall	SSN-667	EB	1969
Spadefish	SSN-668	NNS	1969
Seahorse	SSN-669	EB	1969
Finback	SSN-670	NNS	1970
NR-1	NR-1	EB	delivered
Narwhal	SSN-671	EB	1969
Pintado	SSN-672	MI	1971
Flying Fish	SSN-673	EB	1970
Trepang	SSN-674	EB	1970
Bluefish	SSN-675	EB	1971
Billfish	SSN-676	EB	1971
Drum	SSN-677	MI	1972
Archerfish	SSN-678	EB	1971
Silversides	SSN-679	EB	1972
William H. Bates	SSN-680	ING	1973
Batfish	SSN-681	EB	1972
Tunny	SSN-682	ING	1974
Parche	SSN-683	ING	1974
Cavalla	SSN-684	EB	1973
Glenard P. Lipscomb	SSN-685	EB	1974
L. Mendel Rivers	SSN-686	NNS	1975
Richard B. Russell	SSN-687	NNS	1975
Los Angeles	SSN-688	NNS	1976
Baton Rouge	SSN-689	NNS	1977
Philadelphia	SSN-690	EB	1977
Memphis	SSN-691	NNS	1977
Omaha	SSN-692	EB	1978
Cincinnati	SSN-693	NNS	1978
Groton	SSN-694	EB	1978
Birmingham	SSN-695	NNS	1978
New York City	SSN-696	EB	1979
Indianapolis	SSN-697	EB	1980
Bremerton	SSN-698	EB	1981
Jacksonville	SSN-699	EB	1981
Dallas	SSN-700	EB	1981
La Jolla	SSN-701	EB	1981
Phoenix	SSN-702	EB	1981
Boston	SSN-703	EB	1982
Baltimore	SSN-704	EB	1982
City of Corpus Christi	SSN-705	EB	1983
Albuquerque	SSN-706	EB	1983
Portsmouth	SSN-707	EB	1983
Minneapolis-St. Paul	SSN-708	EB	1984
Hyman G. Rickover	SSN-709	EB	1984
Augusta	SSN-710	EB	1985
San Francisco	SSN-711	NNS	1981
Atlanta	SSN-712	NNS	1982
Houston	SSN-713	NNS	1982
Norfolk	SSN-714	NNS	1983
Buffalo	SSN-715	NNS	1983
Salt Lake City	SSN-716	NNS	1984
Olympia	SSN-717	NNS	1983
Honolulu	SSN-718	NNS	1985
Providence	SSN-719	EB	1985
Pittsburgh	SSN-720	EB	1985
Chicago	SSN-721	NNS	1986
Key West	SSN-722	NNS	1987
Oklahoma City	SSN-723	NNS	1988
Louisville	SSN-724	EB	1986
Helena	SSN-725	EB	1987
Ohio	SSBN-726	EB	1981
Michigan	SSBN-727	EB	1982
Florida	SSBN-728	EB	1983
Georgia	SSBN-729	EB	1984
Henry M. Jackson	SSBN-730	EB	1984
Alabama	SSBN-731	EB	1985
Alaska	SSBN-732	EB	1986
Nevada	SSBN-733	EB	1986
Tennessee	SSBN-734	EB	1988
Pennsylvania	SSBN-735	EB	1989
West Virginia	SSBN-736	EB	1990
Kentucky	SSBN-737	EB	1991
Maryland	SSBN-738	EB	1992
Nebraska	SSBN-739	EB	1993
Rhode Island	SSBN-740	EB	
Maine	SSBN-741	EB	
Wyoming	SSBN-742	EB	
Louisiana	SSBN-743	EB	

Name	Hull No.	Building Yard	Commission date
Newport News	SSN-750	NNS	1989
San Juan	SSN-751	EB	1988
Pasadena	SSN-752	EB	1989
Albany	SSN-753	NNS	1990
Topeka	SSN-754	EB	1989
Miami	SSN-755	EB	1990
Scranton	SSN-756	NNS	1991
Alexandria	SSN-757	EB	1991
Asheville	SSN-758	NNS	1991
Jefferson City	SSN-759	NNS	1992
Annapolis	SSN-760	EB	1992
Springfield	SSN-761	EB	1993
Columbus	SSN-762	EB	1993
Santa Fe	SSN-763	EB	1994
Boise	SSN-764	NNS	1992
Montpelier	SSN-765	NNS	1993
Charlotte	SSN-766	NNS	
Hampton	SSN-767	NNS	1993
Hartford	SSN-768	EB	
Toledo	SSN-769	NNS	
Tucson	SSN-770	NNS	
Columbia	SSN-771	EB	1994
Greeneville	SSN-772	NNS	
Cheyenne	SSN-773	NNS	
Seawolf	SSN-21	EB	
Connecticut	SSN-22	EB	

Ship names in **bold** indicate those built for or by Electric Boat or the Holland Torpedo Boat Co., its predecessor. Those ships denoted with an * were sold in knocked-down condition and assembled elsewhere.

SHIPBUILDER'S ABBREVIATIONS

EB	Electric Boat, Groton, Conn. (a division of General Dynamics since 1954)
GD(Q)	General Dynamics Quincy Shipbuilding Division, Quincy, Mass.
BNS	Boston Naval Shipyard, Boston, Mass.
B(Q)	Bethlehem Steel, Quincy, Mass.
B(SF)	Bethlehem Steel, San Francisco, Calif.
Craig	Craig Shipbuilding Co., Long Beach, Calif.
Cramp	William Cramp & Sons, Philadelphia, Penn.
CS	Crescent Shipyard, Elizabethport, N.J.
CSC	California Ship Building Co., Long Beach, Calif.
F	Fairchild Engine & Airplane Co., Farmingdale, N.Y.
FR	Fore River Shipbuilding Co., Quincy, Mass.
ING	Ingalls Shipbuilding Corp., Pascagoula Miss. (a division of Litton Ind. since 1962)
LTB	Lake Torpedo Boat Co., Bridgeport, Conn.
MAN	Manitowoc Shipbuilding, Manitowoc, Wisc.
MI	Mare Island Naval Shipyard, Vallejo, Calif.
Moran	The Moran Co., Seattle, Wash.
NNS	Newport News Shipbuilding & Dry Dock Co.
NYS	New York Shipbuilding Corp., Camden, N.J.
PS	Puget Sound Naval Shipyard, Bremerton, Wash.
PNS	Portsmouth Naval Shipyard, Portsmouth, N.H.
SCD	Seattle Construction & Dry Dock Co., Seattle, Wash.
UIW	Union Iron Works, San Francisco, Calif.

NAVAL IDENTIFICATION SYMBOLS

SSN	Attack submarine, nuclear
SSBN	Ballistic submarine, nuclear
SSGN	Guided missile submarine, nuclear
AGSS	Auxiliary research submarine

Appendix C: U.S. Navy Submarine Losses

Name Cause of Loss	Date Lost	Loss of Life
F-4 Crushed hull due to plates weakened by leaking sulphuric acid from forward battery tank.	3/25/15	21
F-1 Accidentally rammed by *F-3* in low visibility conditions during engineering runs.	1917	19
S-51 Rammed and sunk by the steamship *City of Rome*.	9/25/25	33
S-4 Rammed and sunk by Coast Guard destroyer *Paulding* while surfacing.	12/17/27	40
S-11 (Squalus) Unknown.	5/23/39	26

World War II Losses

Name Cause of Loss	Date Lost	Loss of Life
O-9 Inconclusive. Probably met with some kind of accident during deep-submergence test.	6/20/41	Not determined
Sealion (SS-195) Sunk by enemy aircraft attack at the dock.	12/10/41	5
S-26 (SS-131) Rammed and sunk by friendly escort vessel.	1/24/42	46
Shark (SS-174) Inconclusive. Probable cause—enemy depth charge attack.	2/11/42	58
Perch (SS-176) Scuttled after enemy fire from three destroyers. Men taken as prisoners of war; nine died in prison camps.	3/3/42	9
Grunion (SS-216) Unknown.	8/16/42	70
Argonaut (SS-166) Hit by depth charge and sunk by fire from enemy destroyers upon surfacing.	1/10/43	105
Amberjack (SS-219) Either by depth charges or enemy aircraft attack.	2/16/43	74
Grampus (SS-207) Inconclusive. Probable cause—sunk by fire from enemy destroyers.	3/6/43	71
Triton (SS-201) Sunk by enemy destroyers.	3/15/43	74
Pickerel (SS-177) Enemy depth charge attack.	4/3/43	74
Grenadier (SS-210) Scuttled after enemy aircraft attack. 76 men taken prisoner, of which 4 died in prison camp.	4/22/43	4
Runner (SS-275) Inconclusive. Probable cause—destroyed by mines	7/20/43	78
R-12 (SS-89) Inconclusive. Probable cause—flooding through torpedo tube.	6/12/43	42
Grayling (SS-209) Operational or unrecorded enemy attack.	9/30/43	76
Pompano (SS-181) Inconclusive. Probable cause—enemy mines.	10/15/43	76
Cisco (SS-209) Inconclusive. Probable cause —attack by enemy aircraft and surface craft.	9/28/43	76
S-44 (SS-149) Attack by enemy destroyer. Two men were picked up in the water and sent to prison camp, which they survived.	10/7/43	55
Wahoo (SS-238) Inconclusive. Probable cause—enemy aircraft attack.	10/11/43	80
Dorado (SS-248) Inconclusive. Probable cause—friendly aircraft fire.	10/12/43	76
Corvina (SS-226) Enemy submarine attack.	11/16/43	82
Sculpin (SS-191) Enemy depth charge attack. 43 men were killed, 41 taken prisoner. 20 prisoners died when the enemy carrier was torpedoed and sunk	11/19/43	43

Name Cause of Loss	Date Lost	Loss of Life
by USS *Sailfish*. 21 men survived prison camp.		
Capelin (SS-289) Inconclusive. Probable cause—destroyed by mines.	12/9/43	78
Scorpion (SS-278) Inconclusive. Probable cause—destroyed by mines.	2/24/44	76
Grayback (SS-208) Attack by enemy aircraft and surface craft.	2/26/44	80
Trout (SS-202) Enemy surface craft.	2/29/44	81
Tullibee (SS-284) Lone survivor picked up by enemy and put in prison camp. After release at end of war, the survivor said that the *Tullibee* was sunk by a circular run of one of its own torpedoes.	3/26/44	79
Gudgeon (SS-211) Unrecorded enemy attack.	6/7/44	78
Herring (SS-233) Counterattack by enemy shore battery.	6/1/44	84
Golet (SS-361) Enemy surface craft attack.	6/14/44	82
S-28 (SS-132) Operational.	7/4/44	50
Robalo (SS-273) Destroyed by enemy mine.	7/26/44	81
Flier (SS-250) Destroyed by enemy mine. Eight crew members survived and swam to safety.	8/13/44	78
Escolar (SS-294) Destroyed by enemy mine.	10/17/44	82
Albacore (SS-218) Destroyed by enemy mine.	11/7/44	86
Growler (SS-215) Unknown.	11/8/44	85
Scamp (SS-277) Attack by enemy aircraft and surface craft.	11/16/44	83
Swordfish (SS-193) Either enemy depth charge attack or destroyed by enemy mine.	1/12/45	89
Barbel (SS-316) Enemy aircraft attack.	2/4/45	81
Kete (SS-369) Unknown.	4/16/45	87
Trigger (SS-237) Attack by enemy aircraft and surface craft.	3/28/45	89
Snook (SS-279) Unknown.	5/16/45	84
Lagarto (SS-371) Attack by enemy surface craft.	5/3/45	85
Bonefish (SS-223) Enemy depth charge attack.	6/18/45	85
Bullhead (SS-332) Attack by enemy aircraft.	8/6/45	84

Post-World War II

Name Cause of Loss	Date Lost	Loss of Life
Thresher (SSN-593) Inconclusive. Lost while conducting initial deep-dive test.	4/10/63	129
Scorpion (SSN-589) Unknown.	5/21/68	99

Sources:
R.H. Barnes, *United States Submarines*, New Haven, CT: H.F. Morse Associates Inc., 1944.
United States Submarine Losses: World War II, Washington, DC: Naval History Division, 1963
United States Ship Thresher: In Memoriam, Submarine Force, U.S. Atlantic Fleet, April 1964.
United States Ship Scorpion: In Memoriam, Washington, DC: U.S. Government Printing Office, 1969.

Appendix D: U.S. Navy Nuclear Fleet Statistics

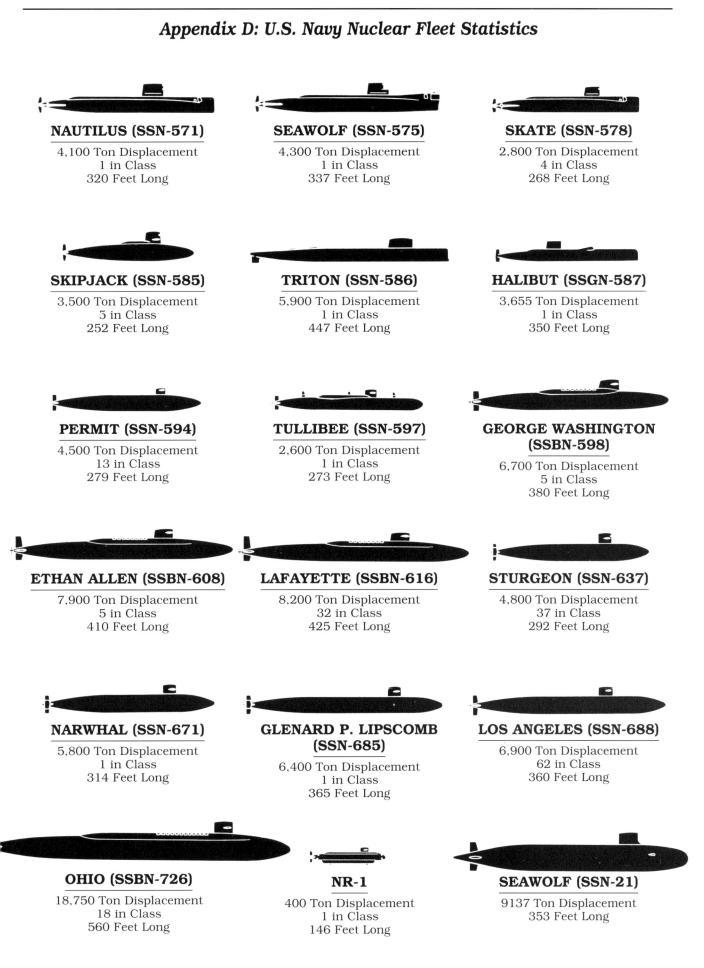

NAUTILUS (SSN-571)

4,100 Ton Displacement
1 in Class
320 Feet Long

SEAWOLF (SSN-575)

4,300 Ton Displacement
1 in Class
337 Feet Long

SKATE (SSN-578)

2,800 Ton Displacement
4 in Class
268 Feet Long

SKIPJACK (SSN-585)

3,500 Ton Displacement
5 in Class
252 Feet Long

TRITON (SSN-586)

5,900 Ton Displacement
1 in Class
447 Feet Long

HALIBUT (SSGN-587)

3,655 Ton Displacement
1 in Class
350 Feet Long

PERMIT (SSN-594)

4,500 Ton Displacement
13 in Class
279 Feet Long

TULLIBEE (SSN-597)

2,600 Ton Displacement
1 in Class
273 Feet Long

GEORGE WASHINGTON (SSBN-598)

6,700 Ton Displacement
5 in Class
380 Feet Long

ETHAN ALLEN (SSBN-608)

7,900 Ton Displacement
5 in Class
410 Feet Long

LAFAYETTE (SSBN-616)

8,200 Ton Displacement
32 in Class
425 Feet Long

STURGEON (SSN-637)

4,800 Ton Displacement
37 in Class
292 Feet Long

NARWHAL (SSN-671)

5,800 Ton Displacement
1 in Class
314 Feet Long

GLENARD P. LIPSCOMB (SSN-685)

6,400 Ton Displacement
1 in Class
365 Feet Long

LOS ANGELES (SSN-688)

6,900 Ton Displacement
62 in Class
360 Feet Long

OHIO (SSBN-726)

18,750 Ton Displacement
18 in Class
560 Feet Long

NR-1

400 Ton Displacement
1 in Class
146 Feet Long

SEAWOLF (SSN-21)

9137 Ton Displacement
353 Feet Long

Introduction

1. President Bill Clinton, in remarks at the U.S. Naval Academy's graduation ceremony, Annapolis, MD, May 25, 1994.
2. Adm. Robert Y. "Yogi" Kaufman, USN (Ret.), in an interview with the author, May 26, 1994.
3. Frank T. Cable, *History of the Famous Submarine Torpedo Boat "Holland"* (unpublished paper), 17

Chapter I

1. Excerpt from *La vraie histoire d'Alexandre*, a 13th century book, reprinted in *Little Known Facts about the Submarine* (Groton, CT: Electric Boat Division, General Dynamics, June 1977).
2. Edward Horton, *The Illustrated History of the Submarine*. (Garden City, NY: Doubleday & Co. Inc., 1974).
3. Ibid.
4. Ibid.
5. Richard Compton-Hall, *Submarine Boats: The Beginnings of Underwater Warfare* (New York: Arco Publishing Inc, 1983).
6. Richard Humble, *Undersea Warfare* (Secaucus, NJ: Basinghall Books Ltd., 1981), 21.
7. Stephen Howarth, *To Shining Sea: A History of the United States Navy.* (New York: Random House, 1991).

Chapter II

1. Richard Compton-Hall, *Submarine Boats: The Beginnings of Underwater Warfare* (New York: Arco Publishing Inc., 1983).
2. Frank T. Cable, *The Birth and Development of the American Submarine* (1924).
3. Ibid.
4. Edward Horton, *The Illustrated History of the Submarine* (Garden City, NY: Doubleday & Co. Inc., 1974).
5. Cable, *Birth*, 13.
6. "Development of Submarines in the United States" (unpublished paper), 2.
7. Cable, *Birth*, 13-14.
8. Cable, *Birth*, 14.
9. *History of the Electric Boat Company*, internal company document, written circa 1949, p. 12.
10. Compton-Hall, *Submarine Boats*.
11. Frank T. Cable, *History of the Famous Submarine Tor-*

pedo Boat "Holland" (unpublished paper), 2.
12. Robert Hatfield-Barnes, *United States Submarines* (New Haven, CT: H.F. Morse Associates Inc., 1944), 20.
13. Stuart J. Barnes, *A Connecticut Yankee: Pioneer Submarine Builder* (unpublished paper, 1918), 3.
14. *History of the Electric Boat Company*, 14.
15. Letter from Norman G. Johnson, attorney for the Holland Torpedo Boat Co. to Robert C. Pruyn, Esq., dated Dec. 15, 1897.
16. Ibid.
17. Jonathan Crane, *Submarine* (London: British Broadcasting Corp., 1984).
18. *History of the Electric Boat Company*, 15.
19. Cable, *History of the Holland*, 9.
20. Letter from Elihu B. Frost to C.E. Creecy, Esq., March 26, 1898.
21. Letter from Elihu B. Frost to Capt. W. H. Jacques, March 28, 1898.
22. Cable, *History of the Holland*, 10.
23. Letter from Elihu B. Frost to Theodore Roosevelt, assistant secretary of the Navy, April 23, 1898.
24. Cable, *History of the Holland*, 16.
25. Ibid.
26. Ibid., 17.
27. Ibid.
28. Ibid., 19.
29. Ibid.
30. Ibid., 20.
31. Ibid., 24.
32. Ibid., 29.
33. Letter from Elihu B. Frost to Isaac L. Rice, dated Jan. 31, 1900.
34. Ibid.
35. Letter from Elihu B. Frost to Isaac L. Rice, dated March 2, 1900.
36. Ibid.
37. Frank T. Cable, *Exhibition Run of the Submarine Torpedo Boat "Holland,"* 5-6.
38. Addition by John P. Holland to letter from Elihu B. Frost to Capt. F. M. Barber, USN, dated March 17, 1900.
39. Letter from Elihu B. Frost to M.A. Cruden, dated April 2, 1900.
40. Letter from Elihu B. Frost to Hon. Edward Brown, Dec. 23, 1899.
41. Letter from Elihu B. Frost to Charles H. Allen, acting secretary of the Navy, April 4, 1900.
42. Letter from Elihu B. Frost to Messrs. Gibson, May 2, 1900.
43. Letter from Elihu B. Frost to F.W. Brady, May 14,

1900.
44. Letter from Elihu B. Frost to Union Iron Works, July 17, 1900.
45. Cable, *History of the Holland*, 39.
46. Ibid.
47. Ibid.
48. Letter from O.S. Lyford, assistant to the president of Electric Boat, to Charles Blizzard, manager, sales department, Electric Storage Battery Co., dated May 11, 1901.
49. Hatfield-Barnes, *United States Submarines*, 26.

Chapter III

1. Letter from Elihu B. Frost to Messrs. Murrill and Keizer dated Jan. 15, 1900
2. Letter from Elihu B. Frost to Captain Henry R. Lemley dated Jan. 31, 1900.
3. Letter to General Reyes, Minister of War, Mexico from Elihu B. Frost, Holland Torpedo Boat Company dated July 7, 1900.
4. Letter from Elihu B. Frost to Captain William Hougaard, Royal Danish navy dated Aug. 17, 1900 .
5. Letter from E.B. Frost to Isaac L. Rice dated Aug. 21, 1900 .
6. Letter from Elihu B. Frost Aug. 22, 1900.
7. Letter from M. Artanjour, vice president, Holland Torpedo Boat Company, to L.T. Paul, vice president, Electro-Dynamic Company, dated Aug. 27, 1901.
8. Cablegram from Isaac Rice to Vickers Maxim and Sons Ltd. dated February 19, 1904.
9. Letter from Issac Rice to Basil Zaharoff, Esq., dated May 27, 1904.
10. Letter from Basil Zaharoff, Esq., to Isaac Rice dated May 20, 1904.
11. Frank T. Cable, *Smuggling a Submarine* (unpublished paper, 1904), 1.
12. Letter from Isaac Rice to Messrs. Mitsui & Company dated May 25, 1904.
13. Letter from Isaac Rice to Fore River Ship and Engine Company dated June 14, 1904 .
14. J.D. Scott, *Vickers: A History* (Shenval Press), 63.
15. Ibid., 65.
16. Letter from M. Artanjour to Elihu B. Frost dated July 11, 1901 .
17. Letter from Isaac Rice to S. Loewe, Esq., dated June 6, 1902.
18. Ibid.

19. Scott, *Vickers*, 65.
20. Letter from Isaac Rice to Lt. A.T. Dawson dated Dec. 6, 1905 .
21. "Bringing Invention to Market," *Invention & Technology* (spring 1987): 14.
22. Letter from Isaac Rice to Albert Vickers, Esq., dated Jan. 7, 1907.
23. Letter from Isaac Rice to Albert Vickers, Esq., dated Dec. 2, 1909
24. Ibid.
25. Cablegram from Isaac Rice to Basil Zaharoff dated June 23, 1904.
26. Cablegram from E.B. Frost to Isaac Rice dated Aug. 3, 1904
27. Letter from Isaac Rice to Lt. A.T. Dawson dated Jan. 9, 1905 .
28. "The Peace-Making Terror of the Sea," *Woman's Home Companion* (October 1904), 49.
29. Ibid.
30. Letter from Isaac Rice to Lieutenant A.T. Dawson dated Jan. 22, 1904.
31. September 18, 1903 letter from A. Treadwell, assistant to the president of Electric Boat, to Mathieu Albert, Esq., director, Usines Nevesky.
32. "Bringing Invention to Market."
33. A history of the Electric Boat Company, written circa 1929, p. 28
34. Letter from Isaac Rice to John P. Holland, Esq., dated Dec. 22, 1904.
35. Letter from Isaac Rice dated Jan. 6, 1905 .
36. Electric Boat Company history, 34.
37. Electric Boat Company history, 38-39.
38. Electric Boat Company history, 39.
39. Letter from Isaac Rice to Lieutenant Paul Koster, Messers. Whitehead & Company dated March 3, 1908.
40. Letter from Isaac Rice to Captain Paul Koster, Messrs. Whitehead & Company dated Feb. 28, 1910 .
41. Electric Boat Company history, 40.
42. Robert Barnes-Hatfield, *United States Submarines* (New Haven, CT.: H.F. Morse Associates, Inc., 1946), 40.
43. Ibid., 41.
44. Ibid.
45. General Dynamics, *Dynamic America* (New York: General Dynamics and Doubleday & Co. Inc., 1958), 101
46. Electric Boat Company history, 43

47. General Dynamics, *Dynamic America*, 101
48. Barnes-Hatfield, *United States Submarines,* 41.
49. General Dynamics, *Dynamic America*, 101.
50. Lawrence York Spear, "The Development of the Submarine" (Paper no. 11), 23
51. Electric Boat Company history, 42.
52. Electric Boat Company history, 43.
53. *A comparison of the Holland and Laurenti types of submarine boats.* Electric Boat document probably written by Lawrence Y. Spear in 1912. No publisher identified.
54. Electric Boat Company history, 41
55. Electric Boat internal memo dated May 13, 1912.
56. 1914 Electric Boat advertisement.
57. March 18, 1912 letter from W.H. Parsons of *Janes's Fighting Ships* to Electric Boat.
58. Barnes-Hatfield, *United States Submarines,* 41.
59. Lawrence York Spear, *The Submarine: An Economical Coast Defense*(December 1906), 7-8.
60. Ibid., 9.
61. Ibid., 12-13.
62. Ibid., 18.
63. Barnes-Hatfield, *United States Submarines*, 62.
64. Ibid., 62-63.
65. Ibid., 63.
66. Ibid., 63-65.

Chapter IV

1. Lieutenant M-P-S, *Hounding the Hun from the Seas* (New York: Underwood & Underwood, 1919). This Royal Navy booklet was subtitled, *A Tale of the British M.L.'s on the High Seas.*
2. Early draft, circa 1929, on the history of Electric Boat and its founders, pp. 51-52.
3. Ibid., p. 52.
4. Stuart J. Barnes, *A Connecticut Yankee: Pioneer Submarine Builder*(unpublished paper, 1918), 16.
5. *Dynamic America* (New York: General Dynamics and Doubleday, 1958), 107.
6. Barnes, *A Connecticut Yankee,* 17.
7. Ibid.
8. Ibid.
9. *Dynamic America*, 109.
10. Ibid., 157.
11. Ibid., 109.
12. Electric Boat Company history, 48.
13. Ibid., 109.
14. *Dynamic America*, 109.

15. Ibid., 103.
16. Ibid., 109.
17. "The British 'MLs,'" *Motor Boat,* 7.
18. Ibid.
19. *Hounding the Hun from the Seas.*
20. *Dynamic America*, 104.
21. "The British 'MLs,'" *Motor Boat,* 8.
22. D. Hickey and G. Smith, *Seven Days to Disaster: The Sinking of the Lusitania,* (New York: G.P. Putnam's Sons, 1982), 263.
23. *Hounding the Hun from the Seas.*
24. Ibid.
25. General Dynamics, *Dynamic America*, 113.
26. Ibid.
27. *Wall Street Journal*, May 9, 1915.
28. *New York Herald*, July 14, 1915.
29. *New York Press*, July 14, 1915.
30. *Dynamic America*, 113.
31. *Financial Chronicle*, Aug. 14, 1915.
32. *Dynamic America*, 168.
33. Electric Boat Company history, 56.
34. *Dynamic America*, 168.
35. Electric Boat Company history, 56.
36. *Wall Street Journal*, February 9, 1916.
37. *Financial America*, February 9, 1916.
38. Electric Boat Company history, 47.
39. Ibid., 48.
40. Ibid., 51.
41. Barnes, *A Connecticut Yankee,* 17.
42. House of Representatives Document No. 389, 64th Congress, 1st Session, Letter from the Secretary of the Navy, p. 5.
43. Ibid.
44. Speech of Hon. James L. Slayden of Texas in the House of Representatives, Jan. 29, 1915, pp. 3-4
45. Ibid., 5.
46. Ibid., 6.
47. Ibid., 14.
48. Ibid., 23.
49. Robert Hatfield Barnes, *United States Submarines*, 105.
50. Ibid.
51. *The Submarine in the United States Navy*, Naval History Division, 8.
52. Barnes, *United States Submarines*, 106.
53. Ibid.
54. Ibid.
55. Ibid., 108.
56. Ibid.
57. Ibid., 110.
58. Ibid., 108.
59. Ibid.
60. Ibid., 110.
61. Ibid.

62. Ibid.
63. Chuck Lawliss, *The Submarine Book,* 62.
64. Ibid., 63.
65. Electric Boat Company history, 50.
66. *Development of Submarines in the United States,* 8-9.
67. Ibid., 10.
68. Ibid., 11.
69. Ibid., 12.
70. Ibid., 13.
71. Ibid., 13-14.
72. Electric Boat Company history, p. 49.
73. Lawliss, *The Submarine Book,* 49.
74. *Development of Submarines in the United States,* 17.
75. Ibid., 19-20.

Chapter V

1. Anonymous draft of the history of the Electric Boat Company, printed internally circa 1929, p. 58
2. 1919 company advertisement.
3. *Dynamic America* (New York: General Dynamics and Doubleday, 1958), 185.
4. Electric Boat Company history, 69.
5. Ibid., 69-70.
6. Ibid., 70-71.
7. *Development of Submarines in the United States* (unpublished paper), p. 7.
8. Electric Boat Company history, 67.
9. *Development of Submarines in the United States,* pp. 7-8.
10. Ibid.
11. Electric Boat Company history, 63-64.
12. Ibid.
13. Ibid.
14. "A Submarine Mother Ship," *Motorship*, February 1923.
15. Ibid.
16. "Schedule Maintained for Two Seasons," *Motorship*, April 1924.
17. *EB Scope*, 1955.
18. Electric Boat internal memorandum, Jan. 1, 1929.
19. Electric Boat Company history, 64.
20. Ibid., p. 65.
21. *The 'Scope*, July 17, 1955, p. 6.
22. Electric Boat Company history, 65.
23. *The 'Scope*, July 17, 1955, p. 8.
24. *The 'Scope*, July 17, 1955, p. 8.
25. *Dynamic America*, 187.
26. Letter from H.E. Page to L.Y. Spear, May 17, 1932.
27. Letter from L.Y. Spear to H.E. Page, May 20, 1932.
28. Letter from Alexander Stefanidi to L.Y. Spear, Feb.

14, 1939.
29. Letter from L.Y. Spear to Alexander Stefanidi, Feb. 14, 1939.
30. Letter from L.Y. Spear to Alexander Stefanidi, Feb. 14, 1939.
31. *Dynamic America*, 187.
32. Electric Boat Company history, 68.
33. Contract between Peru and Electric Boat Company, March 19, 1924.
34. Letter from Sir Trevor Dawson to L.Y. Spear, Nov. 16, 1927.
35. Letter from L.Y. Spear to Sir Trevor Dawson, Dec. 19, 1927.
36. Ibid.
37. Letter from L.Y. Spear to Henry Carse, May 31, 1933.
38. Letter from Henry Carse to L.Y. Spear, June 2, 1933.
39. Letter from L.Y. Spear to Sterling Joyner, June 3, 1933.
40. Memo from Sterling Joyner, June 6, 1933.
41. Letter from L.Y. Spear to Paul Koster, Dec. 7, 1933.
42. Letter from E. Nibbs to C.J. O'Neill, Dec. 28, 1933.
43. Spear, Lawrence Y., *The Submarine of Today* (Groton, CT: Electric Boat Company, 1927), 4-5.
44. Ibid., 1-2.
45. Ibid.
46. Ibid., 6
47. Ibid., 12-13
48. Ibid., 13
49. Ibid., 14
50. Ibid., 15
51. Ibid.
52. Ibid.
53. Robert Barnes-Hatfield, *United States Submarines* (New Haven, CT: H.F. Morse Associates, Inc., 1944), 45-46
54. Ibid., 44
55. Ibid.
56. Ibid., 44-45
57. Ibid., 45
58. Lawrence York Spear, *United States Submarines - 'S' Class*, Aug. 22, 1927, pp. 3-4,.
59. *Dynamic America*, 226
60. *The 'Scope*, November 20, 1958.
61. Ibid.
62. Ibid.
63. Electric Boat Company history, 77.
64. *Dynamic America*, page 226.
65. Electric Boat Company history, 77.
66. *Dynamic America*, page 226.
67. *Dynamic America*, page 189.
68. Electric Boat Company history, 78-79.
69. Ibid., 79.
70. *Dynamic America*, page

189.

71. Electric Boat Company history, 82.
72. Ibid.
73. Ibid., p. 83.
74. Ibid., p. 84.
75. "Union Calls Sit-Down Strike In Electric Boat Shipyard," *The New London Day* (CT), Feb. 23, 1937.
76. Ibid.
77. Ibid.
78. "Employee Activities at the Electric Boat Co.," *The Association Mirror*, June 6, 1938, 15.
79. "They Fear 'Bloodshed,' Leave Shipyard Gates," *The New London Day* (CT), Feb. 25, 1937.
80. "National Board To Have Hearing in Boat Co. Strike," *The New London Day* (CT), May 4, 1937.
81. "N.L.R.B. Rules For Submarine Plant Strikers," *New York Herald Tribune*, June 2, 1938.
82. "Electric Boat Co. Says It Will Recognize Union," *The New London Day* (CT), Aug. 5, 1938.

Chapter VI

1. *History of the Electric Boat Company*, page 92. This is an unpublished, internally generated draft, written circa 1949.
2. Ibid., 88.
3. *History of the Electric Boat Company*, Chapter II, page 3. This is a second unpublished draft of company history, written circa 1949.
4. *Dynamic America* (General Dynamics Corp. and Doubleday & Co. Inc.,1958), 283.
5. *History of the Electric Boat Company*, 90.
6. *Dynamic America*, 285.
7. *History of the Electric Boat Company*, Chapter II, 4.
8. *History of the Electric Boat Company*, 94.
9. *History of the Electric Boat Company*, Chapter II, 4.
10. *History of the Electric Boat Company*, 93.
11. *History of the Electric Boat Company*, Chapter II, 4.
12. 1943 Electric Boat Company Annual Report (Groton, CT: Electric Boat Company, 1944), 4.
13. 1944 Electric Boat Company Annual Report (Groton, CT: Electric Boat Company, 1945), 3.
14. Ibid., 26.
15. Ibid., 27.
16. Ibid., 24.
17. Ibid., 38.
18. Ibid.
19. *History of the Electric Boat Company*, 91.

20. Ibid.
21. Ibid., 86.
22. Ibid., 104.
23. Ibid., 105.
24. Ibid.
25. Ibid., 106.
26. Naval History Division, *The Submarine in the United States Navy* (Washington DC: Author, 1963), 12.
27. *History of the Electric Boat Company*, 86.
28. Naval History Division, *The Submarine in the United States Navy*, 12.
29. 1945 Electric Boat Company Annual Report (Groton, CT: Electric Boat Company, 1946), 22.
30. *History of the Electric Boat Company*, 86-87.
31. 1945 Electric Boat Annual Report, 20-21.
32. Naval History Division, *The Submarine in the United States Navy*, 14.
33. 1945 Electric Boat Company Annual Report, 22.
34. Ibid.
35. *History of the Electric Boat Company*, 100-101.
36. Naval History Division, *The Submarine in the United States Navy*, 13-14.
37. Chuck Lawliss. *The Submarine Book* (New York and London: Thames and Hudson, 1991) 83.
38. Robert Barnes-Hatfield, *United States Submarines* (New Haven, CT: H.F. Morse Associates, Inc., 1944), 153.
39. Ibid., 150.
40. Richard Garrett, *Submarines* (Boston, Toronto: Little, Brown and Company, 1977), 104-105.
41. 1945 Electric Boat Company Annual Report, 22-25.
42. Ibid., 25.
43. Chris R. Schlidz, "WWII Tautog Sank Most Enemy Ships" (in *General Dynamics World*, August 1987), p. 8.
44. 1943 Electric Boat Company Annual Report, 2.
45. Ibid., 7.
46. Electric Boat Company Annual Report 1944, 21.
47. Harvard University, Graduate School of Business, *The Use and Disposition of Ships and Shipyards at the End of World War II* (Washington, DC: United States Government Printing Office), 160 - 162.
48. Ibid., 191.
49. 1945 Electric Boat Annual Report, 25.

Chapter VII

1. 1944 Electric Boat Annual Report (Groton, CT: Electric Boat Company, 1945),

10.

2. *History of the Electric Boat Company*, page 121. This is an unpublished, internally generated draft, written circa 1949.
3. "Electric Boat Co. Still Has Six Submarines Under Construction," *The New London Day* (CT), Jan. 9, 1946.
4. 1945 Electric Boat Annual Report (Groton, CT: Electric Boat Company, 1946), 18.
5. 1946 Electric Boat Annual Report (Groton, CT: Electric Boat Company, 1947), 7.
6. Ibid., p. 30.
7. Ibid.
8. "Plan Postwar Fleet of 319 Warships," *The New London Day* (CT), Jan. 7, 1946.
9. "Active Subs for Atlantic Fleet Listed," *The New London Day* (CT), Feb. 9, 1946.
10. 1945 Electric Boat Annual Report, 30.
11. *History of the Electric Boat Company*, 123.
12. 1945 Electric Boat Annual Report, 33.
13. Ibid.
14. Ibid., 30.
15. Harry W. Alexander, "The Roadside Diner" (preliminary survey, Nov. 9, 1945).
16. 1946 Electric Boat Annual Report, 7.
17. Ibid., 27.
18. Ibid., 27.
19. Ibid., 32.
20. Ibid., 29.
21. Ibid.
22. Ford, Bacon & Davis, "Letter Report: Canadair, Limited," March 1, 1946, p. 1.
23. *Dynamic America* (General Dynamics Corp. and Doubleday & Co. Inc.,1958), 343.
24. *History of the Electric Boat Company*, 115.
25. Ibid., 116-117.
26. "EBCo Continues Its Diversified Commercial Work," *The New London Day* (CT), Dec. 31, 1947.
27. 1947 Electric Boat Annual Report, 27.
28. Ibid., 29.
29. Ibid.
30. "EBCo Continues It's Diversified Commercial Work," *The New London Day* (CT), Dec. 31, 1947.
31. 1948 Electric Boat Annual Report (Groton, CT: Electric Boat Company, 1949), 16-19.
32. "E.B. Backlog Here About $29,400,000," *The New London Day* (CT), Sept. 13, 1949.
33. Ibid.
34. 1950 Electric Boat Annual Report (Groton, CT: Electric Boat Company, 1951),

12.

35. 1951 Electric Boat Annual Report (Groton, CT: Electric Boat Company, 1952), 25.
36. 1952 Electric Boat Annual Report (Groton, CT: Electric Boat Company, 1953), 22.
37. *History of the Electric Boat Company*, 111-112.
38. *Dynamic America*, 337-338
39. 1947 Electric Boat Annual Report, 24.
40. *History of the Electric Boat Company*, 121.
41. 1947 Electric Boat Annual Report, 24.
42. *History of the Electric Boat Company*, 121.
43. 1947 Electric Boat Annual Report, 24.
44. *History of the Electric Boat Company*, 122.
45. 1947 Electric Boat Annual Report, 24.
46. *History of the Electric Boat Company*, 122.
47. Naval History Division, *The Submarine in the United States Navy* (Washington, DC: U.S. Government Printing Office, 1963) 16.
48. "Anti-Sub Submarines To Be Tiny," *The New London Day* (CT), Oct. 25, 1948.
49. Ibid.
50. 1948 Electric Boat Annual Report, 16.
51. 1949 Electric Boat Annual Report, 21.
52. Ibid.
53. 1950 Electric Boat Annual Report, 12.
54. Ibid., 11-12.
55. 1951 Electric Boat Annual Report, 24-25.
56. 1947 Electric Boat Annual Report, 18.
57. 1948 Electric Boat Annual Report, 13.
58. *Dynamic America*, 345.
59. 1949 Electric Boat Annual Report, 5.
60. "Navy Fails to Down Submarine Rocket," *The New York Times*, Nov. 9, 1949.
61. "U.S. Plans Atomic-Powered Sub; EBCO Figuring in Discussions," *The New London Day* (CT), Feb. 20, 1950.
62. 1951 Electric Boat Annual Report, 5.
63. 1952 Electric Boat Annual Report (Groton, CT: Electric Boat Company, 1953), 6.

Chapter VIII

1. "Another Submarine Seen Off California," *The New York Times*, April 2, 1950.
2. "Military Puts Stress on Air, Atom Power," *Washington Post*, Dec. 15, 1953.
3. "Defense Planners Ask $583,000,000 For More

Planes," *The New York Times*, April 2, 1950.

4. "Navy's Task Seen To Deter Russia," *Washington Post*, May 4, 1950.

5. "Russian Route Over North Pole Developed in Repeated Flights," *New York Herald Tribune*, May 8, 1950.

6. "Speed-Up On Atom Laid To Red Drives," *The New York Times*, Dec. 3, 1950.

7. "Submarines on Paper: Navy Fears Russia's Projected Fleet, Not One Now Operating," *New York Herald Tribune*, Jan. 14, 1951.

8. "So They Named It General Dynamics," *Fortune*, April 1953, 7.

9. Chuck Lawliss, *The Submarine Book* (New York: Thames and Hudson, 1991), 91.

10. "So They Named It General Dynamics," 7.

11. Ibid.

12. Ibid.

13. *Dynamic America* (General Dynamics Corp. and Doubleday & Co. Inc., 1958), 351.

14. "So They Named It General Dynamics," 7.

15. "Says Ebco Know-How Figures in Atomic Submarine Plans," *The New London Day* (CT), April 27, 1950.

16. "Atomic-Powered Sub Work Significant Event at E.B.," *The New London Day* (CT), April 2, 1951.

17. "Ebco to Build Atomic Sub; Robinson Sees Increase Of 1,000 in Work Force," *The New London Day* (CT), Aug. 22, 1951.

18. "Robinson Reports Ebco Work Load Greatest Since War," *The New London Day* (CT), March 12, 1952.

18. "Robinson Reports Ebco Work Load Greatest Since War," *The New London Day* (CT), March 12, 1952.

19. "54-Hour Week for Ebco Unit," *The New London Day* (CT), Jan. 6, 1951.

20. "2,300 Ebco Workers Put on 48 Hours," *The New London Day* (CT), March 8, 1951.

21. "Record Number to End Apprentice Training Course at Electric Boat," *The New London Day* (CT), Dec. 10, 1952.

22. "So They Named It General Dynamics," 7.

23. Lt. Dean L. Axene, *School of the Boat for the* Nautilus (United States Naval Institute Proceedings, November, 1955), 1231.

24. Lewis L. Strauss, *The Sub in the Desert* (unpublished paper) p. 8.

25. *Nautilus* background material from General Dynam-

26. Text of remarks by John Jay Hopkins at launching ceremonies on Jan. 21, 1954.

27. Address by Adm. Robert B. Carney, USN made at *Nautilus* launching ceremonies on Jan. 21, 1954.

28. "Eisenhower Asks Seven Atom Subs," *The New London Day* (CT), Jan. 17, 1955.

29. "Nautilus Goes to Sea for Trials," *The New London Day* (CT), Jan. 17, 1955.

30. Ibid.

31. "History of the USS *Nautilus*" from the General Dynamics press kit created for the *Nautilus* launching.

32. "Nautilus Skipper Says Test 'Perfect,'" *Montreal Star*, Jan. 19, 1955.

33. "Nautilus Down Hour in Making First Dive," *The New York Times*, Jan. 21, 1955.

34. "A-Sub Makes First Ocean Dive Today," *The Long Island Press*, Feb. 26, 1955.

35. "'Bugs' Gave Crew a Scare During *Nautilus* 1st Dive," *New York Herald Tribune*, March 31, 1955.

36. Cmdr. Eugene P. Wilkinson's statement at press conference on March 30, 1955.

37. "History of the USS *Nautilus*," General Dynamics press kit.

38. Ibid.

39. "A Voyage of Importance," Westinghouse's commemorative brochure created for the USS *Nautilus* launching.

40. Ibid.

41. Cmdr. R.F. Dobbins, MC, USN, "T.D.T.N.C.T.P. (The Day the *Nautilus* Crossed the Pole) Day," (August 3, 1958), 13.

42. "2nd A-Sub OK'd by House Group," *Daily Mirror*, March 19, 1952.

43. "Boat Co. Has Record $$ Year; Hopkins Predicts Firm Will Lead Nation's Shipbuilders," *The New London Day* (CT), April 1, 1952.

44. "General Dynamics Has $183,000,000 Backlog," *The New London Day* (CT), Jan. 4, 1954.

45. "Congressman Seel-Brown Renews Pledge to Work for Third Nuclear Submarine for Electric Boat as Portsmouth Makes Bid," *Norwich Bulletin*, May 7, 1954.

46. "First Atomic Submarine to Be Armed With Fast 14,522-pound Guided Missile," *The New York Times*, June 13, 1954.

47. "Electric Boat Building Mock-Up Trainer-Sub," *Marine News*, September 1954.

48. Ibid.

49. "Eight Submarines Asked in Navy Program; One Would Be Half Again Size of *Nautilus*," *The New London Day* (CT), Feb. 25, 1955.

50. 1955 General Dynamics Annual Report (New York: General Dynamics Corp., 1956), 33.

51. 1956 General Dynamics Annual Report (New York: General Dynamics Corp., 1957), 23-25.

52. "Sea Wolf, 2nd U.S. Atom Sub, Giving Trouble; Sodium-Type Reactor May Have To Be Removed," *The Bridgeport Post*, November 14, 1956.

53. 1958 General Dynamics Annual Report (New York: General Dynamics Corp., 1959).

54. Capt. Edward L. Beach, USN (Ret.) in an interview with the author, May 27, 1994. Capt. Beach is the author of *Run Silent, Run Deep*, among a number of other books.

55. 1958 General Dynamics Annual Report, 18.

56. "Polaris Submarines in Brief," General Dynamics/ Electric Boat public information document, p. 2.

57. 1959 General Dynamics Annual Report (New York: General Dynamics Corp., 1960), 16.

58. "Polaris Submarines in Brief," General Dynamics/ Electric Boat, p. 2.

59. Beach interview, May 27, 1994.

60. *From Holland to Ohio* (Groton, CT: General Dynamics/Electric Boat Division), 8.

61. Naval History Divison, *The Submarine in the United States Navy* (Washington, DC: U.S. Government Printing Office, 1963) 21..

62. 1960 General Dynamics Annual Report (New York: General Dynamics Corp., 1961), 5.

63. 1962 General Dynamics Annual Report (New York: General Dynamics Corp., 1963), 11.

64. Ibid.

65. "A-Sub Double-Header Set Today at Groton," *Hartford Courant*, June 22, 1963.

66. 1963 General Dynamics Annual Report (New York: General Dynamics Corp., 1964), 11.

67. 1964 General Dynamics Annual Report (New York: General Dynamics Corp., 1965), 6.

68. Personnel records, Electric Boat Division.

69. 1964 General Dynamics

70. Ibid.

71. 1965 General Dynamics Annual Report (New York: General Dynamics Corp., 1966), 13.

72. 1966 General Dynamics Annual Report (New York: General Dynamics Corp., 1967), 10-11.

73. 1965 General Dynamics Annual Report, 13.

74. Kenneth D. Brown, former vice president of operations, Electric Boat Division, in an interview with Steven Marks, Aug. 26, 1994.

75. *From Holland to Ohio*, 8

76. 1968 General Dynamics Annual Report (New York: General Dynamics Corp., 1968), 10.

77. Ibid.

78. Brown interview with S. Marks, Aug. 26 1994.

Chapter IX

1. Patrick Tyler, *Running Critical: The Silent War, Admiral Rickover, and General Dynamics* (New York: Harper & Row, 1986), 51-95.

2. Ibid.

3. 1970 General Dynamics Annual Report (New York: General Dynamics Corp., 1971), 11.

4. Adm. Robert Y. Kaufman, USN (Ret.) in an interview with the author, May 26, 1994.

5. 1971 General Dynamics Annual Report (New York: General Dynamics Corp., 1972), 9.

6. 1972 General Dynamics Annual Report (New York: General Dynamics Corp., 1973), 9.

7. U.S. Department of Defense *Fact File, Fleet Ballistic Missile Submarines*, April 1993.

8. *From Holland to Ohio* (Groton, CT: General Dynamics/Electric Boat Division), 10.

9. Henry J. Nardone, former program director, Electric Boat Division of General Dynamics Corp., in an interview with Steven Marks, Aug. 30, 1994.

10. 1973 General Dynamics Annual Report (New York: General Dynamics Corp., 1974), 8.

11. Tyler, *Running Critical*, 127.

12. 1973 General Dynamics Annual Report, 8.

13. Nardone interview, Aug. 30, 1994.

14. 1974 General Dynamics Annual Report (New York: General Dynamics Corp., 1975), 9.

15. Tyler, *Running Critical*, 148.

16. 1975 General Dynamics

Annual Report (New York: General Dynamics Corp., 1976), 13.

17. Nardone interview, Aug. 30, 1994.
18. Ibid., 152.
19. 1977 General Dynamics Annual Report (New York: General Dynamics Corp., 1978), 4.
20. Ibid., 5.
21. Tyler, Running Critical, 246.
22. Ibid., 169.
23. Ibid., 179.
24. From Holland to Ohio, 11.
25. Nardone interview, Aug. 30, 1994.
26. Tyler, Running Critical, 260.
27. 1980 General Dynamics Annual Report (New York: General Dynamics Corp., 1981), 21.
28. Tyler, Running Critical, 286.
29. Report of the Special Committee to John F. Lehman Jr., Secretary of the Navy, p. 3, April 20, 1981.
30. 1981 General Dynamics Annual Report (New York: General Dynamics Corp., 1982), 17.
31. Ibid., 18.
32. 1982 General Dynamics Annual Report (New York: General Dynamics Corp., 1983), 14.
33. Nardone interview, Aug. 30, 1994.
34. Ibid.
35. 1984 General Dynamics Annual Report (New York: General Dynamics Corp., 1985), 15-16.
36. Tyler, Running Critical, 92.
37. Chuck Lawliss, The Submarine Book (New York, London: Thames and Hudson, 1991), 121.
38. Submarine Acquisition: Design Phases (Groton, CT: Electric Boat, 1971).
39. Ibid.
40. Kenneth D. Brown, retired vice president of operations, Electric Boat Division, General Dynamics Corp., in an interview with Steven Marks, Aug. 24, 1994.
41. Ibid.
42. The "last to slide" slogan was proudly displayed on Electric Boat's invitations to its launch of the USS Columbia.
43. Lt. Dave Wells, CHINFO (U.S. Navy Media Information Division), on the gold team.
44. Kaufman in an interview with the author, 1994.
45. Vice Admiral B.M. Kauderer, USN (Ret.), in an interview with the author on May 26, 1994.
46. Brown interview, Aug. 26, 1994.
47. Lawliss, The Submarine Book, 126-127.

48. Andy Lightbody and Joe Pover, Submarines: Hunter/ Killers & Boomers (New York: Beekman House, 1990).
49. Adm. Robert Y. "Yogi" Kaufman, USN (Ret.), in an interview with the author, May 26, 1994.
50. Brown interview, Aug. 24, 1994.
51. Kauderer interview with author, 1994.
52. Ibid.
53. Lawliss, The Submarine Book, 127.
54. E. R. Hooton (Ed.), Jane's Naval Weapons Systems (Surrey, UK: Jane's Information Group Ltd., 1989).
55. Ibid.
56. Lawliss, The Submarine Book, 127-131.
57. Lightbody and Poyer, Submarines: Hunter/Killers & Boomers, 36.
58. U.S. Department of Defense Fact File, Torpedoes, April 1993.
59. Ibid.
60. Capt. Richard Sharpe, OBE RN (Ed.), Jane's Fighting Ships (Surrey, UK: Jane's Information Group Ltd., 1994), 774.
61. Lightbody and Poyer, Submarines: Hunter/Killers & Boomers, 117.
62. U.S. Department of Defense Fact File, Fleet Ballistic Missile Submarines, April 1993.
63. From Holland to Ohio, 10.
64. Lightbody and Poyer, Submarines: Hunter/Killers & Boomers, 75.
65. From Holland to Ohio, 12-13.

Chapter X

1. Michael J. Sniffen, "Russian Crime Groups Seen As Threat," The Day (New London, CT, May 26, 1994), p. A-3.
2. Sen. Christopher Dodd in an interview with the author, May 23, 1994.
3. James E. Turner Jr., president of Electric Boat Division of General Dynamics Corp., in an interview with the author, May 27, 1994.
4. Turner interview, May 27, 1994.
5. 1990 General Dynamics Annual Report (New York: General Dynamics, 1991), 13.
6. Barbara Nagy, "Navy Sets Forth Timetable for Funding Centurion, Ending Seawolf Program," The Day (New London, CT), Aug. 26, 1991, p. A-1.
7. Barbara Nagy, "Navy Moving Quickly on Key Decisions For Next Subma-

rine," The Day (New London, CT), Oct. 30, 1991 p. A-1.
8. Ibid., p. A-3.
9. 1989 General Dynamics Annual Report (New York: General Dynamics, 1990), 19.
10. Nagy, "Navy Moving Quickly on Key Decisions," p. A-3.
11. Barbara Nagy, "Proposed Sub Class to be Scaled-Down Version of Seawolf," The Day (New London, CT), Aug. 26, 1991, p. A3.
12. 1989 General Dynamics Annual Report, 19.
13. Turner interview, May 27, 1994.
14. 1989 General Dynamics Annual Report, 19.
15. Ibid.
16. From Holland to Ohio (Groton, CT: General Dynamics/Electric Boat Division), 13.
17. 1989 General Dynamics Annual Report, 19.
18. Nagy, "Proposed Sub Class," p. A-3.
19. Barbara Nagy, "Future Prospects Seem Dim for EB," The Day (New London, CT), Jan. 30, 1992, p. A-1.
20. Ibid.
21. Dodd interview, May 23, 1994.
22. 1992 General Dynamics Annual Report (New York: General Dynamics, 1993), 9.
23. Ibid.
24. Ibid.
25. James E. Turner, "Diversification Is Not Enough To Save EB," Electric Boat News (Groton, CT, June 1993), p. 1.
26. Barbara Nagy, "Pentagon Official: Diversification Is Not Enough To Save EB," The Day (New London, CT), May 28, 1993 p. A-1.
27. Ibid., page A-12.
28. Melissa B. Robinson, "Defense Conversion Criticized," The Day (New London, CT), May 25, 1994, p. E-1
29. James E. Turner, "Diversification at Electric Boat," Electric Boat News (Groton, CT, June 1993), p. 3.
30. Barbara Nagy, "EB, Emphasizing Submarines, Lets Diversification Slide," The Day (New London, CT), Sept. 21, 1993, p. A-11.
31. Rep. Ron Machtley in an interview with the author, May 25, 1994.
32. Vice Admiral B.M. Kauderer, USN (Ret.), in an interview with the author, May 26, 1994.
33. John H. Dalton, secretary of the Navy under President Bill Clinton, in re-

marks on Aug. 28, 1993.
34. President Bill Clinton, in remarks at the U.S. Naval Academy graduation ceremony, Annapolis, MD, May 25, 1994.
35. Kenneth D. Brown, former vice president of operations, Electric Boat, in an interview with Steven Marks, Aug. 26, 1994.
36. Barbara Nagy, "Turner Says EB Must Alter Course," The Day (New London, CT), January 20, 1994, p. A-8.
37. Ibid.
38. John K. Welch, division vice president-programs, Electric Boat Division, in an interview with the author, May 27, 1994.
39. Leslie A. Morse, deputy program manager-new attack submarine, Electric Boat Division of General Dynamics Corp., in an interview with Steven Marks, Sept. 2, 1994.
40. "Turner Sketches EB's Future," Electric Boat News (Groton, CT), March/April 1994, p. 1.
41. Ibid., p. 6.
42. John H. Dalton, secretary of the Navy, in remarks made on Sept. 22, 1993.
43. John H. Dalton, secretary of the Navy, in remarks made on June 16, 1994.
44. Lisa Hayden, "Defense Panel Member Tours EB Shipyard," The Day (New London, CT), March 30, 1994, p. D-1.
45. Lisa Hayden, "Murtha to Back New Subs," The Day (New London, CT), p. C-1.
46. Lisa Hayden, "Navy Vice Chief Says Clinton Backs Industrial Base for Subs," The Day (New London, CT), April 28, 1994, p. B-1.
47. Lisa Hayden, "Congress Gets Proposal To Cut Third Seawolf," The Day (New London, CT), April 11, 1994, p. A-1.
48. Lisa Hayden, "Sub Fund Cut Dies In Committee," The Day (New London, CT), May 20, 1994, p. B-2.
49. "Turner Unveils New Structure For Top Management," EB: Employee Bulletin (Groton, CT), April 6, 1994, p. 1.
50. Lisa Hayden, "EB Workers Living With Uncertainty," The Day (New London, CT), April 6, 1994, p. A-1.
51. Electric Boat Division press release dated Aug. 2, 1994.
52. Hayden, "EB Workers Living with Uncertainty," p. A-1.
53. Turner interview, May 27, 1994.